Changing Roles - Women After the Great War

Dedication

This book is for my husband, Ivan. The title may not be the one he hoped for, but I believe the content is. Like all my other books, it could not have been completed without his love, encouragement and probing questions.

Changing Roles - Women After the Great War

Dr Vivien Newman

PEN & SWORD
HISTORY

AN IMPRINT OF PEN & SWORD BOOKS LTD.
YORKSHIRE - PHILADELPHIA

First published in Great Britain in 2021 by
Pen & Sword History
An imprint of
Pen & Sword Books Ltd
Yorkshire - Philadelphia

ISBN 978 1 52677 426 2

A CIP catalogue record for this book is available from the British Library.

Printed and bound in England
By CPI Group (UK) Ltd, Croydon, CR0 4YY

Pen & Sword Books Ltd incorporates the Imprints of Pen & Sword Books
Archaeology, Atlas, Aviation, Battleground, Discovery, Family History,
History, Maritime, Military, Naval, Politics, Railways, Select, Transport,
True Crime, Fiction, Frontline Books, Leo Cooper, Praetorian Press,
Seaforth Publishing, Wharncliffe and White Owl.

For a complete list of Pen & Sword titles please contact

PEN & SWORD BOOKS LIMITED
47 Church Street, Barnsley, South Yorkshire, S70 2AS, England
E-mail: enquiries@pen-and-sword.co.uk
Website: www.pen-and-sword.co.uk

or

PEN AND SWORD BOOKS
1950 Lawrence Rd, Havertown, PA 19083, USA
E-mail: uspen-and-sword@casematepublishers.com
Website: www.penandswordbooks.com

Contents

Acknowledgements

Once again, my thanks to my editor Karyn Burnham. Her eagle eye spots inconsistencies and 'finger fumble'. Any errors that remain are, of course, my own.

My grateful thanks also to Julie Parfitt, who came to the rescue when she was most needed – and to Debbie de Boltz for putting us in touch.

Introduction

In November 1918, British Prime Minister Lloyd George acknowledged, 'It would have been utterly impossible for us to have waged a successful war, had it not been for the skill and ardour, enthusiasm and industry, which the women of the country have thrown into the work of the war.'[1] During the war, the female workforce rose from 4.93 to 6.19 million. Women proved their abilities across all trades, even auxiliary roles within the armed services. Many women hoped that Lloyd George's accolade, along with their gender's February 1918 partial enfranchisement, would usher in a new dawn, or at least herald significant improvements in women's lives. This optimism appeared ill-founded. In his 1919 Annual Report, the Chief Inspector of Factories and Workshops recognised that with 'interesting work taken out of [women's] hands ... they are being forced back into the routine of their hitherto normal occupations'.[2] With misogyny increasingly prevalent, by 1921 a principal female factory inspector wryly remarked that it was 'hard to recall the full measure of pride expressed by the nation in what the women did for it in time of need'.[3]

That women were expected to vacate their jobs and resume their former existence has become integral to the story of the Great War. While inevitably there is truth in this, it is not the whole truth. There were women, be they born to wealth and privilege or hailing from the lowliest backgrounds, who did not creep back and accept their supposedly pre-ordained station in life. Instead they sought to confront bias, question male authority, even alter the course of history. Some intentionally, others unintentionally, became trailblazers, forging different identities, challenging expectations and pre-conceptions, showing that 'tempered by war', women's roles and position could and would be changed.[4]

CHAPTER 1

Team Spirit

Foul Play

'It was like being part of a family, they were good days.'[1]

During the 2020 Covid-19 pandemic, a sports commentator wrote, 'both male and female sport were equally affected' by lockdown restrictions. However, 'that is no longer the case. ... The situation in football is particularly stark.' His explanation was that, unlike men's football with the financial power of the Premier League behind it, the Women's Super [Football] League cannot afford the mandatory 'systematic twice-a-week corona-virus testing programme', making the women's game another 'casualty of the crisis'.[2] While in global terms the delayed return of British women's football is of minimal importance, its lack of status and 'financial power' may stem from a day in early December 1921 when leaders of the Football Association (FA) gathered for a specially convened meeting in London's Russell Square. They held the fate of the women's game in their hands.

The story of women's football is intricately linked to the Great War and its immediate aftermath. Following the so-called (May 1915) Shell Scandal when shortages of ammunition led to it being rationed, working-class women had flocked into rapidly established munitions factories. By July 1918, these employed over a million women. Middle- and upper-class angst about female workers' behaviour was so acute that, operating under the title 'Welfare Supervisor', middle-class women were employed to oversee workers' physical well-being and ensure that off-duty hours were appropriately filled. Such concerns did not, of course, apply to males. Many Welfare Inspectors believed involvement in a physical outdoor sport would help keep the female workforce out of trouble. From the supervisors' point of view, football, which had enjoyed some popularity in the 1880s and 1890s (the first so-called 'international', England v. Scotland being

1

played in Edinburgh in 1881), seemed to fit the bill. Some middle-class girls' schools had even embraced the sport, although others questioned its appropriateness for the developing female frame. Crucial for its subsequent acceptance by working-class factory women, and notwithstanding middle-class women's early, short-lived enthusiasm, football was considered the working-man's game.

Also acting in favour of women's football was the 1915 suspension of the men's game 'For the Duration', leaving fans with no matches to watch. Reports of matches between female teams started appearing in local newspapers from mid-1916, although generally these were 'diverting items', played as part of a plethora of 'entertainments in aid of 'Wounded Heroes'.[3] This association with war charities would be fundamental to the game's initial crowd appeal. For factory owners, managers and welfare supervisors, the team spirit that football fostered between workers, and rivalry with other establishments – potentially even leading to greater productivity in the sheds, was also important. Sometimes it was a challenge from another factory which resulted in the creation of a team. This happened when Messrs. Beardmore's women challenged the Scottish Filling Factory to a match in May 1918, thereby leading to the inception of the Georgetown Girls.[4] What is striking in some reports of inter-factory fundraising matches is that while the 'Ladies of the Committee' who helped organise the match are individually named, those whose endeavours raised in this particular instance 'the splendid sum of £57 (£3,756)' for the 'Crewe Cottage Hospital and the Red Cross funds', are unidentified, merely thanked for the 'splendid effort they made [training] in their spare time'.[5] Such player anonymity anchors women's football as a game played by lower-class women, sanctioned by their social superiors.

Wartime charities' need of funds lay behind the creation, success and ultimate demise of the most successful of all women's teams, Dick, Kerr's Ladies (DKL). In 1916, Private Jimmie Sibbert (Loyal North Lancashire Regiment), was captured and transported to Germany. His wife, Grace, worked at Dick, Kerr's in Preston, now churning out munitions at the rate of 30,000 shells a week. Aware of Jimmie's and the thousands of other prisoners' plight, she soon became an adept fundraiser for POW charities. In autumn 1917, the matron of the local Moor Park Voluntary Aid Detachment Hospital for Wounded Soldiers asked her to galvanise munitions workers into raising money for the hospital via a series of concerts. She agreed on one condition, rather than a concert, the fundraiser would be a Christmas Day football match. She could never have guessed how this would turn the factory's nascent team into a household name, assign celebrity status to a few of England's poorest women, turn one of them into women's football's greatest legend – and contribute to the women's game being banned.

Initially, football enthusiasts at Dick, Kerr's simply spent their lunch break practising kicks, passes and 'shooting at the little square window at the back of the cloakroom', covertly watched by an office worker, Albert Frankland.[6] In autumn 1917, he had suggested to Sibbert that a factory team should be formed in order to play charity matches; the Moor Park request thus came at the ideal time. Frankland had vision, a range of contacts and an ability to network. In late November, a notice appeared across Preston: the DKL football team had challenged another Lancashire factory, Arundel Coulthard Foundry, women's team to a 'Great Christmas Day Attraction' in aid of Moor Park at Preston North Football Club's home ground, Deepdale. Using Deepdale was a bold move; its pitch fee was £20 (£1,318). For a later rescinded £5 (£329) fee, Preston North FC shouldered the responsibility of advertising this first match to be played at Deepdale since football's suspension. This reaped significant rewards. Less confident characters than Sibbert or Frankland may have wondered how the 10,000 spectators and journalists who flocked through the gates on Christmas Day 1917 might react to the match. Initially not quite sure what they were expecting, the crowd began enjoying the players' prowess. Inevitably in a match involving women, clothes featured. Told 'not to wear corsets', DKL's black and white striped shirts, black shorts and matching 'natty, close fitting hats, which were kept on throughout the match', itself a 'distinctive wartime novelty', were commented on as were the Arundel team's 'red and white stripes'.[7] Unusually, however, for these early matches the *Lancashire Daily Post*'s report focuses primarily on the actual football. The journalist concedes that after some initial giggling, the teams 'settled down in earnest', the home team's forward work was 'surprisingly good', while Coulthard were 'strongest in defence'. It is as though, like the spectators, once it was obvious that the teams 'meant business and were "playing the game"', the journalist was prepared to report accordingly and extend the top players the courtesy of naming them as worthy sportswomen, not an amorphous entertaining working-class mass. When the final whistle blew, the home team had won a resounding 4-0 victory and women's football would take a whole new direction. After settling the not inconsiderable costs, about which there were some adverse comments, DKL donated £600 (£49,500) to Moor Park and other charities. They were poised to make sporting history for, long after the guns fell silent and most factory teams disbanded, they continued their fundraising endeavours, initially in aid of veterans' charities, and initiated the first truly international football match. A century later, on 22 December 2017, a massive memorial was unveiled at the home of Preston North End. A 6m by 4m wide granite memorial weighing 3.5 tonnes pays tribute to these footballers who for three years put Preston on the map, raised unimaginable amounts of money for war and other charities and, for a short while, were the face of football.[8]

If Moor Park were delighted with the takings, the crowd entertained and the players eager to capitalise on their success (which had required them to sacrifice their own Christmas Day), the odd whisper of discontent about women players was audible. Whispers that eventually turned into a clamour muttered that 'the female frame wasn't built for such a rough game, and playing football could damage [women's] health'; Molly Walker's boyfriend's family ostracised her for wearing shorts that showed her legs.[9] Nevertheless, Deepdale and Dick, Kerr's Boards pronounced themselves satisfied and agreed to two further charity matches on 23 February and Easter Monday, 1 April 1918. Deepdale would take charge of the gate, 80 per cent 'going to Dick, Kerr to distribute, that is after all expenses incidental to the match are paid'.[10] The team could train on the ground three times a week at a fee of £3 (£200).

By mid-1918, with fewer munitions needed, factories shed workers and football teams disbanded. But not DKL. How exactly he managed this is unclear, but Frankland successfully persuaded the senior management that not only should DKL continue, but it should expand and actively seek talent across the North West. He may have stressed, both to the Board and to the local aldermen who were consulted, local charities' spiralling need of funds and reminded them of the women's well-proven abilities to draw crowds, not to mention that the team's name kept the company in the public's mind. (In 1919 Dick, Kerr's was taken over by English Electric Ltd and re-tooled to revert to its pre-war production of railway carriages but, locally at least, it was still referred to as Dick, Kerr's.) Armed with the company cheque-book, Frankland began his mission. An unexpected defeat on 21 December 1918 strengthened his resolve and he eyed members of the winning Lancaster Ladies' team covetously, and successfully. By the time DKL took to the pitch on 10 January 1919, four of the Lancastrians were both playing and working for Dick, Kerr. Frankland's vision soon paid off. At the start of 1920, DKL drew 35,000 spectators at an 'away' fixture and were considered the country's premier team.[11]

Despite factory closures, there were still some opposing teams to play. The idea of football as a game which fostered team spirit among a female workforce had caught on. Enterprises other than factories continued to nurture, even form, teams. The famous Lyons Corner Houses tea-rooms with their waitresses (initially known as 'Gladys' before acquiring the better-known 'nippy' sobriquet) entered the pitch and inter-Corner House rivalry led to what was seen as a healthy competition between tea-rooms; a League was established between the four 'Corner Houses': Strand (despite lacking a Corner site), Oxford Circus, Marble Arch and Trafalgar Square. The company invested heavily in the teams, Lyons' training ground and facilities at Sudbury (North London) were far superior to those that many male clubs enjoyed. Football was beginning to be seen by women – and not exclusively the working-class women of the wartime factory teams – as a worthwhile and fun occupation.

DKL players, rougher diamonds than the Corner House 'Gladyses', would soon include Lily Parr (b.1905) the youngest of eleven (living) children. Destined to become a legend in her own lifetime, she hailed from St Helens, a poor area of Merseyside; her future seemingly lay in factory or rough domestic work.[12] Rather than play with other girls, Lily kicked a ball around in nearby Queen's Park; by the age of 13, she could hold her own against her older brothers in both rugby and football – and also smoke a packet of Woodbine cigarettes a day. Having joined the recently formed St Helen's Ladies, she could score from any place on the pitch with her left-footed kick. Her second match was against DKL. The watchful Frankland spotted her and her teammate, miner's daughter Alice Woods (b.1895), who had recently lost her job in the huge Sutton Glass Works munitions factory. Better-educated than many workers, Alice had escaped the back-breaking foundry work and, rather than filling shells, had been assigned the more sophisticated work of numbering completed ones. Tall and athletic, she had been involved in factory football and athletics, particularly running, winning in 1918 the first women's 80 yards race at Blackpool F.C ground, believed to be the first women's race under A.A.A. rules.[13]

This DKL v. St Helen's match was played against an increasingly hard economic climate, even tougher for women than for men thanks to the 1919 Restoration of Pre-War Practices Act which stipulated 'that all pre-war customs which were given up during the War, and in connection with the purposes of the War, shall be restored by every employer throughout the country within two months of the passing of the Act.'[14] Women war workers were now expected (or forced) to surrender their jobs to returning men. Potentially facing a long period of unemployment, Woods was relieved when Frankland approached her, offering a job with Dick, Kerr's, 10 shillings (£27) out-of-pocket expenses including loss of time per match played, and lodgings in Preston.[15] She later termed herself as 'one of the first major football transfers'. Alice's widowed mother refused to allow her to move but the rest of the deal was agreed. Frankland also approached Parr making an identical offer, an additional sweetener was negotiated: a daily supply of Woodbines. She would lodge with another player, Alice Norris.

As Frankland began thinking beyond the confines of Lancashire, the Northwest, even England, the players' own skills and hard work were opening up an unimaginably different world, one normally tightly locked against women of their lowly roots. Although on Christmas Eve 1917 an intrepid group of women footballers had crossed the submarine-infested Irish Sea and played 'the first women's international' in front of 20,000 spectators in Belfast, Frankland's thoughts extended far wider.[16] But to stage a truly international match, he needed a like-minded traveller. He found one in Parisienne Alice Milliat, well-known in French sporting circles for daring to challenge the revered Founding Father of the modern Olympics, Baron de Courbetin, who had publicly endorsed the ancient Greeks' view that women's only part in sport should be placing wreaths upon the [male] victors' heads. In 1915, she had assumed the presidency of the Parisian multi-sports club Fémina Sport, and in 1919 had founded and become president of the Fédération des Sociétés Féminines de France (FSFF). Milliat, manager of the Fémina Sports women's football club, was determined to nurture the increasing popularity of the women's game. Frankland must have read her much-quoted statement, 'I do not think it is unwomanly to play football.'[17] In March 1920, he invited her and the team to England; Dick, Kerr's would host a series of four DKL versus France matches in support of British ex-servicemen's charities. She accepted and set about selecting a team drawn from the wider Paris region.

TEAM SPIRIT

John Bell, *Daily News'* Paris correspondent, began drip-feeding details to tantalise a British readership, including the colour of the French strip: horizon blue shirts with a red white and blue cockade on the breast, navy shorts, black socks completed by a stereotypical black beret. The French team finally arrived at Victoria Station on 27 April to a rapturous press welcome. Milliat proved more competent at handling journalists than Frankland, who struggled to push his way through the reporters to welcome DKL's guests who arrived in Lancashire at 6pm. Working-class Preston was about to encounter the chic petite bourgeoisie of suburban Paris. Reporters as well as football fans had a field day. Wearing dainty high heels, cloche caps over fashionably bobbed hair, their captain Madeleine Bracquemonde confessed to her team feeling daunted by the sight of the 'big, strong', Lancashire Amazons who greeted them at the station. Covering the 'French Team's Rousing Welcome in Preston', the Lancashire press reported every detail, including Bracquemonde's cap flying overboard during the Channel crossing. That this was above all a Dick, Kerr's event was underlined by the factory's band playing the 'Marseillaise' as the tourists, followed by their opponents, were driven in style through cheering crowds to the Bull and Royal Hotel. A dinner attended by local dignitaries was followed by a dance after which the French side collapsed into bed before the next day's round of sightseeing which ended with a visit to the factory and presentation of a loving cup made on the premises. The local women who would be playing in the four matches (only just) arranged at Deepdale, Stockport, Manchester and Stamford Bridge must have felt that they were living in some fairy tale to which they had gained entry not through the privilege of birth, but through their own talents and dedicated training. It is easy to overlook how hard the team trained. During their arduous working day, few concessions were made to their sporting commitments. Dick, Kerr players were however, luckier than many teams; the company had invested in an athletic ground, Ashton Park, complete with a football pitch nick-named 'Lively Polly' because of a nearby giant advertisement for Lively Polly washing powder. Equally surprising to these factory hands may have been their opponents' range of employment (football in France was much less closely linked to working-class women), including short-hand typists, bookkeepers, university students and a dental student.

On 30 April 1920, accompanied by Preston's Military Band, the French team's charabanc proceeded to Deepdale ground to play the first ever truly international women's football match. The 25,000-strong crowd greeted them ecstatically. Reporting in detail on the match with its first division referee, *Lancashire Daily Post* (which to its credit made no mention of either side's strip, hats or even lack of corsets) admitted that the home team had not 'been able to record their superiority with more than two goals', and while the French team were not of the same calibre as their opponents, they had played with 'fine zest and pluck'. However, a cartoon published in the paper's 3 May edition, while superficially entertaining, might have appeared to some as subversive, the 'brawny' DKL players and the 'chic' French ones are 'terrorising' the male officials. Interviewed after the match and giving due credit to the home team who had 'played beautifully', Milliat confessed that her side may have been overwhelmed by the size of the crowd which exceeded that of men's games in France. In fact this size crowd had rarely, if ever, been seen before at Deepdale, even for a men's match. The gate takings of £1,295 (£63,584) were earmarked for the building fund 'of a new club for servicemen'.

The next day's 5-2 win at Stockport underlined DKL's superiority; there appears to be less archival newspaper coverage of either this or the subsequent 5 May encounter at Hyde Road, Manchester, which resulted in a 1-1 draw; the Frenchwomen had undoubtedly benefited from three rest days and a 'breezy visit' to Blackpool. The reporter for *Manchester Evening News* commented on the home team having a more 'robust physique' than their 'lithe' opponents, but congratulated both sides' 'dash and alacrity' as they attempted to reach the ball. One French player's 'complete somersault' was enthusiastically greeted by the crowd who undoubtedly felt they had got their money's worth from this 'splendid game'. The gratitude with which the proceeds would be received by the distressed servicemen was emphasised. The three northern matches yielded £2,766 (£135,835).

The players' sternest test was Stamford Bridge (Chelsea's Home ground) on 6 May, the Discharged Soldiers and Soldiers Association (London Division) being the beneficiaries. The fifty-four seconds of recorded film coverage of both teams' entry onto the pitch underscore the developing relationship between newsreel and football.[18] In this Pathé footage, shown nationwide, the players 'spread the gospel of women's football across the land' not as figures of fun, but as athletes in their own right who were daring to tread on men's hallowed ground.[19] Arguably, these fifty-four seconds sowed the seeds of the destruction of women's football. Cheered on by 10,000 spectators, the Parisians achieved their first victory (2-1). While some press reports were trivialising, such as the Frenchwomen wearing, 'Shorts very short', others were more positive. *The Times*' Special Correspondent delivered several backhanded compliments such as 'Both [teams] looked to enjoy it, and exhibited quite enough skill to disappoint those who had come to laugh.'[20]

Before the teams parted company, the Lord Mayor of London honoured them with a Mansion House reception. Football had changed the DKL players' lives, thousands had cheered them on, many thousands more would see them on the Pathé newsreel, not as working-class stereotypes but as serious sportswomen. A close-knit team of female factory workers from Preston had penetrated the capital of the British Empire, achieved near celebrity-status and for them, and indeed women's football, things would never be quite the same again. New teams, some with lofty ideals, were formed, male trainers recruited including former Army PE instructors, and what had previously been seen as a game for 'rough girls', began spreading to more genteel parts of the country, even Bath, and among those whose occupations more closely mirrored the French players than their brawny DKL opponents. In Huddersfield, the Atalanta Sports Club football team was founded with the aim of fostering 'a sporting spirit and a love of honour among its members', who mainly comprised white- rather than blue-collar workers. Working-class Ada Beaumont was unimpressed, accusing them of having 'a very high opinion of their own capacity and that sort of thing'. Showing class-loyalty, Ada felt that it was the working-class women who really 'played football, you see, because we were used to hard knocks in life. What you might call the rough 'eads.'[21]

With the French on their way home to an ecstatic welcome, as the Prestonians left London, they were reminded that working-class women were on the march. In this case, quite literally. They ran into the John Lewis shop girls striking against the company's requirement that they, unlike their male counterparts, live in the shop's own hostels. Undoubtedly intentionally timed for maximum effect, shop girls came out on the opening day of the Silk Department sale. Although the strikers were ultimately defeated, women were coming together to flex their muscles. The sight of the (at that early stage) exuberant strikers must have made an impression on these factory workers who would, in exactly nineteen months' time, also find themselves fighting sexism from an entrenched hierarchy.

The team could not relax its charity commitments. As 1920 advanced so too did charities' need of funds. The 1911 National Insurance Act provided no protection for agricultural, forestry, railway, domestic service workers, teachers, nurses, policemen, even the military – increasing numbers of whom were unemployed. Thanks to their crowd-drawing power, DKL played thirty matches in 1920 (scoring 133 of the 148 goals). A return visit to France, already mooted in May 1920, and supported by Jules Rimet, head of the French Football Association 'soon to become President of FIFA', would once again have a charitable purpose.[22] Frankland drew attention to the FA having yet to arrange a men's 'International' in Europe; astutely claiming international sporting events were a big help to the League of Nations by enabling people to better understand each other, this superlative networker sought support from the British Ambassador to France, the 17th Earl of Derby, honorary President of the Rugby Football League. The recently founded League of Nations was seen as being able to deliver on the hopes of a war-weary world that there could be an end to war. Good-natured rivalry on the pitch and friendship off it would, Frankland argued, further cement the British-French wartime alliance and, with so many Lancashire men – including players' immediate kin – 'sleeping' in France, visits to cemeteries and the laying of wreaths would provide additional press opportunities. And once again servicemen's charities would benefit. In a piece entitled 'Should Girls Play Football?', team Captain Alice Kell also emphasised the forthcoming trip's diplomatic value: 'If the matches with the French ladies serve no other purpose, I feel that they will have done more to cement the good feeling between the two nations than anything which has occurred during the last 50 years, except of course the Great War.' She added that 'football broadens [a girl's] mind as well as develops the physique'.[23] Might broadening working-class women's minds lead them to develop subversive ideas about their lowly status?

On 28 October 1920, following an official reception when DKL's donations of £8,600 (£422,240) to predominantly local war charities were loudly applauded, the team set off for France.[24] Newspaper accounts of their departure underlined the 'Remembrance' theme; they would tour some of the battlefields, the Ypres Salient, place wreaths on the graves of fallen men, including footballers. Visiting cemeteries and wreath laying was already being portrayed as a very female act, women were being constructed as the visible reminder and symbol of the nation's grief;

additionally, these female footballers could be portrayed as honouring the male footballers into whose boots they had stepped during the war – and whose boots they would shortly be forced to remove.

Having left Preston on the 11.20am train, 15-year-old Lily Parr and her roommate got little sleep. After a show at the Palladium, doubtless another 'first' for many, they spent the rest of the night 'broadening their minds' by turning the light switches on and off in their Bonnington Hotel room; they had apparently never before slept in a room with electricity. One can only hope that Parr refrained from stubbing out her Woodbines on the arms of the furniture as she was wont to do in her Preston lodgings to the despair of her landlady, teammate Alice Norris' mother. Parr's powerful kick, allegedly like a First Division man's, meant that some of her less savoury habits, which included 'the regular appropriation of match day footballs which she then sold for 6d a time' were overlooked.[25] Was this merely teenage exuberance or was football rescuing her from a life of loutish behaviour? Met in Calais by Mme Trotman, whose daughter was playing for France, the team proceeded to Paris where, to their delight, they discovered Frankland had pulled off his greatest coup, Lord Derby would attend the inaugural match at the Pershing Stadium, to be kicked off by the French Minister for Aviation on Sunday 2 November.

Alice Woods (who would eventually have played on almost every football ground in England), faithfully recorded her impressions in a specially purchased notebook. While the names of so many of the towns and villages they passed through, such as Etaples where they 'Saw soldiers' graves', were seared on the nation's collective consciousness, seeing these themselves was not something the team would ever have imagined doing. For Alice Kell and Lily Lee seeing the cemeteries must have been particularly poignant, their bothers, Privates Thomas and Gilbert 1st/4th Battalion, the Loyal North Lancashire Regiment, having been posted 'Missing' on 15 June 1915.[26] Similarly, Jessie Walmsley whose 20-year-old brother Joseph had been killed when the war was barely five weeks old; she had been one of the rescuers at the devastating October 1917 White Lund National Projectile Factory explosion, one of the biggest disasters ever to happen in north Lancashire, when she was commended for her bravery.[27] For some players, this was a pilgrimage as well as a football tournament, although none allowed their grief to override their prowess on the pitch.

Greeted by their rivals at Paris' Gare du Nord, the trip involved sightseeing and a visit to the French Military Training School, where Frankland inscribed the visitors' book on his team's behalf, wishing 'to place on record [Dick, Kerr Ladies' Football Club's] grateful appreciation of the splendid manner in which they have been received by the Officers of our Brave French Allies'.[28] Out in force, the French sporting press hoped this 'most prestigious English team', would receive as warm a welcome as was extended to the French team during their 'triumphal tour'.[29] Fortunately both sides were now well-used to crowds; 22,000 spectators had flocked to what many thought would be a novelty match. It was now the British team's turn to be nervous and the French scored first; a DKL goal resulted in a draw. The match ended in a controversy headlined 'First Match Fiasco', noted by the powers that be of English Football who were monitoring the tour: five minutes before the final whistle, a large section of the crowd invaded the pitch after disputing the French referee's decision to award a corner-kick to the English side. The match was deemed to have ended in a draw. Neither team took this 'fiasco' to heart and, as far as the competitors were concerned, an atmosphere of friendliness prevailed, although DKL were disappointed by their result. Kell felt that the French women had made significant progress. Frankland filed the first of his reports which newspapers at home snapped up; the DKL, with its sizeable fan base, was newsworthy.

While football was the main focus, the tour's Remembrance aspect was not overlooked. With 'Pilgrimages' still in their infancy, particularly for the working-classes, the players were trailblazers. Many battlefields were still raw and deeply sobering. Kells remarked on 'barbed wire entanglements, trenches full of water … woods demolished'. Sadly, their hope of placing a wreath tied with the colours of Blackburn Rovers on Eddie Latherton (KIA Passchendaele 14 October 1917), did not materialise. They were however able to place this and other wreaths on the memorials of the four towns they visited including Roubaix which drew 16,000 spectators, swelled, according to 3 November *Le Rappel*, by a noisy British contingent. Some '250 English soldiers and Lancashire workmen' cheered DKL 'with whistles, trumpets, bells and screams' as the team won 2-0. They were 'chaired off the pitch.[30] Roubaix had particular significance. Occupied in August 1914, it had finally been liberated in October 1918 with a significant contingent of Lancashire troops. Some had remained to assist with the rebuilding while cotton workers from the north of England were helping to get the mills on which much of Roubaix's prosperity depended, functioning again. Little wonder that these men were thrilled to hear the women's distinctive Lancashire accents and see their prowess on the field.

The *Le Rappel* reporter felt that 'le football féminin' was increasingly popular; Frankland, whose daily reports back to Dick, Kerr's management, were widely fed to newspapers, commented, 'In the whole of my experience of football, I have never seen a team get a better reception than ours did.' Class boundaries were tumbling, momentarily, 'Even English officers went frantic with delight'.[31] These factory hands, 'the Pride of Preston', were doing their county and their country proud. Roubaix had its poignant as well as its triumphal moments; Kell placed the team's wreath, 12ft in diameter, at the foot of the Great War memorial, a tangible reminder that the war that had started these women on their football odyssey had now taken them as far from their homes as the working-class Lancashire soldiers who had fought (and died) in France and Belgium's foreign fields.

From Roubaix, Kell noted how the team travelled 'in ammunition wagons past Tourcoing cemetery, then through Armentières where every house was demolished', to Le Havre, the Number 1 British wartime port through which nearly 2 million British soldiers had passed during the war. It had also had three general and two stationary hospitals which, with the team's origins in raising money for a war hospital, may have been of interest. Their smallest crowd, a mere 10,000, witnessed DKL's most resounding victory: 6-0. The tour ended at Rouen, a huge wartime logistics centre and home to ten hospitals; the 14,000 spectators were treated to a 2-0 English victory. The football was over, but the solemn duties (laying a wreath at the Paris cenotaph) and the sightseeing were not. The visit to the Hall of Mirrors at the Palace of Versailles left Kell deeply moved, 'I have stood where Peace was signed.'[32]

The team returned home on 9 November. Their 2,000-mile trip had entertained some 56,000 spectators, established DKL's reputation as unsurpassable, established a friendship with the French team (which lasted into the 1950s), which Frankland 'spun' as helping cement the Entente Cordiale. Most of the town turned out to cheer as their charabanc entered Preston, appropriately, the DK band played 'See, the Conquering Hero Comes'. The crowd's adoration resembled twenty-first-century sports heroes' homecomings. The factory works' management hosted a dinner with special entertainment for them and their guests, but for the triumphant players, the next day was a working day and they were expected to clock on as normal. Frankland had been up to his poaching tricks. Goalkeeper Louise Ourry, Lily Parr's exact contemporary, and dental student Carmen Pomies (also a renowned javelin thrower), soon donned DKL's distinctive black and white strip and began working in Preston.[33]

Life in England was growing steadily harsher. The local Unemployed Ex-Servicemen's charity, concerned about providing needy ex-personnel with Christmas food, approached Frankland. All fundraisers acknowledge the need to keep developing new gimmicks. He proposed a Searchlight Match, pitching DKL against 'the rest of England', to be played at Deepdale – which did not boast floodlights. Winston Churchill sanctioned the loan of two anti-aircraft searchlights, placed at either end of the ground with forty carbide lights distributed around the pitch. As white footballs did not exist, lateral thinking was required. Wielding a whitewash brush, Preston player Bob Holmes kept whitewashing and throwing a newly painted ball on to the field at regular intervals.[34]

With this latest football novelty appropriately promoted, Pathé newsmen, hoards of press and 12,000 spectators poured into Deepdale on 16 December 1920. Despite a slightly late kick-off due to a temporary failure of one of the searchlights which resulted in one player, 'little' Jennie Harris (a 1918 poach from Bolton), not being found until a cameraman obligingly set off one of his flash lights. The Rest of England was powerless against the mighty DKL who won 4-0; the Christmas food fund was boosted by some £600 (£30,419). The match went down in Prestonian annals of oral history, closely followed by the match played on Boxing Day ('the best day of the football calendar') when 53,000 people gained entry and 14,000 were turned away. A Police escort was needed to see the women safely to the changing rooms in the match against Woods' and Parr's old team St Helen's; £3,115 (£153,000) was raised for the Ex-Servicemen's Association.

As 1920 turned to 1921, with games booked across the British Isles which now boasted some 150 teams, discussions about a return visit from the Frenchwomen and a possible tour in Canada, DKL were riding high. But although they were changing the face of women's football, arguably of women's sport, and raising hundreds of thousands of pounds for charity, two things had not changed. They were working women who had to clock on and off every day; they were playing and training in their spare time and in their holidays. The 10 shillings they received per match (£25) was for out of pocket expenses and compensation for loss of work time. Alice Norris remembered,

> It was sometimes hard work when we played a match during the week because we would have to work in the morning, travel to play the match, then travel home again and be up for work the next day. But I was proud to be a Dick, Kerr girl; it was worth all the effort we put in.[35]

Although not all players worked for the factory, or even lived in Preston, most did and the remaining few were considered honorary members of the Dick, Kerr family.

It was becoming widely apparent that despite the Representation of the People Act (1918) and the Sex Disqualification (Removal) Act (1919), misogyny remained close to the surface of the British Establishment. Furthermore, women, especially working-class women, were considered to have a responsibility towards the future of the nation which emphatically did not involve playing football. Their pre-ordained role was to produce the next generation of workers (and should needs be, soldiers) on which the future of the Empire depended. It was time they settled down and became wives and mothers. These whispers would soon reach Preston.

Nevertheless, 1921 opened well; it seemed as though every football team in the country wanted to take on the iconic DKL. Mayors and MPs, aware that their local charities needed an injection of cash, begged for a match. Some 120 invitations had to be refused, there were not enough days in the football year for them to meet demand. By the end of 1920, almost all servicemen were demobilised and men's football was getting back into its stride. But, to the fury of the FA, it was the women who continued to draw the crowds. A whisper began circulating that accountancy in women's football, particularly that of DKL, was not all it should be. Rumour breeds rumour and a smear campaign got under way. Some clubs started saying that DKL players were 'too expensive' and that they could not afford to stage matches against them. Frankland pointed out that women's teams carried larger reserves than men's and players needed cabs home from the railway station if they returned late at night.[36] But the whispers refused to be silenced – although the charities which had benefited to such a phenomenal extent were well satisfied.

15

1921 was also a year of industrial unrest. A 'Land fit for Heroes' was proving a vacuous soundbite. Labour began flexing its muscles in terms of industrial action, inevitably affecting England's industrial heartland. The price of coal slumped and, arguing an urgent need to protect assets, coal owners slashed wages by up to 50 per cent. The Miners' Federation of Great Britain refused to accept this draconian cut and on 1 April 1921 the miners were locked out of the pits. The Government reacted by enforcing the Emergency Powers Act and moved soldiers in.

The desperate plight of miners and their families pulled at the Lancashire footballers' hearts, some of whom, including Alice Woods, were miners' daughters. Lancashire women had a long and proud tradition of supporting their menfolk; requests for funds to help feed miners' children fell on fertile ground. Female footballers were now crossing the boundary between charity and politics, further grist to the mill of those determined to stamp out the women's game. Supporting Britain's wounded heroes was politically acceptable, supporting defiant trade unionists was not. These players were directly threatening the social order, already seen to be poised on a knife edge. The press, which had been largely in favour of 'Plucky lasses who had done so much to assist the war effort', began to shove public opinion in the opposite direction.[37] On 4 April 1921, *Nottingham Evening Post* ran an interview denouncing women's football by a star of amateur running, Walter George Goodall,

> As for women's Soccer football, I hardly think that it conforms to the average woman's ideal of modesty, especially when staged as a public exhibition. We have to keep in mind the motherhood of the future … [is] this forcing process in women's sport beneficial or detrimental? This point, I am inclined to believe, calls for an official investigation under Government auspices by medical authorities of the highest repute.

The idea of 'modesty' joined with motherhood now came to the fore. Opinion in newspaper correspondence pages was divided but the 'anti' voices were given plenty of column inches. A correspondent in *Western Morning News* (20 April 1921) asked, 'Is there not great physical danger for ladies playing a game of this kind. From a moral standpoint, it is time to cry halt too.' On the same date, 'A Royal Navy Serviceman' alleged that a friend of his 'would not care to marry among this class of [football playing] women'. Among the most unforgivable attacks was one made by Brigadier General Arthur Lloyd at the AGM of the Royal Salop Infirmary. Responding to the 'indebtedness' expressed by the Infirmary's Treasurer 'for the £500 (£22,000) from a match between St Helens and Chorley', the Brigadier claimed he was 'not a kill-joy ... but do not let women degrade themselves by playing football which was not a game for women and which made fools of them.'[38] This was the Establishment speaking, its voice would get ever louder. Little matter that between 1917 and 1921, female footballers had raised vast sums of money, alleviated significant distress and given huge amounts of pleasure when this was in short supply to the hundreds of thousands of working men and women who had flocked to see them play.

Industrial tension was fuelling the Establishment's fear of 'Bolshevism'. If the working classes were not shown their place, the British aristocracy and bourgeoisie might share the fate of those in Tsarist Russia. And to increase fears, if football were the working [wo]man's game, the mass of spectators were working-class, including locked-out miners. Crowds 20,000 or 30,000 strong might, so the thinking went, incite industrial unrest and if games were being played to alleviate working-class distress, such matches could prove potential breeding grounds for left-wing propaganda. Football played by emancipated women who seemed unwilling 'to know their place' as subservient mothers of the race, threatened the old order. On 18 October 1921, under the prescient headline 'Are Female Football Exhibitions Doomed?' *Dundee Evening Telegraph* reported, 'The women's football match on Bradford City ground tomorrow may be the last of the female football exhibitions because the pundits of the English Football Association do not approve.' Having carefully amassed 'evidence', the FA would soon be ready to pounce.

In Preston, DKL continued with their punishing match schedule. Alice Woods' diary records sixty-six matches played from 1 January to 29 December 1921 and the twenty-five gate receipts which she details totalled £22,525 (£957,312). One of these matches, on 17 May, was against the French Fémina team whose engagements were now with a variety of teams, maybe to the tourists' relief as having gone down 5-1 against Dick, Kerr Ladies, all five goals scored by the increasingly indomitable Parr, they won their remaining four matches.

The wheels of the FA, under the chairmanship of Charles Clegg, dubbed 'the Napoleon of Football' due to his belief that all legislation could be

17

overridden in the interests of football, were turning. On 18 October 1921, at a full FA council meeting in London, a new instruction was issued to professional clubs, headed *Ladies Football Matches,*

> Clubs must not permit matches between ladies' teams to be played on their grounds unless sanction for such matters is first obtained from the Football Association. It will be a condition of application that the Club on whose ground the match is played shall be responsible for the receipts and payments and a Statement of Account must be sent to the Association showing how the receipts were applied.

The closing statement about receipts indicates that this was one of two fronts on which the FA intended to fight the women's game. A 15 October 1921 report in *Western Daily News* implied that Plymouth Ladies' accounting left much to be desired. In their recent match, rather than the totality of the gate receipts an unemployment charity had received a 'donation'. Further underlining the FA's displeasure, Winchester FC was fined for allowing a women's match to go ahead without prior FA permission.

The accusation of financial mismanagement against DKL, almost the public face of women's football, is worth examining. Football historian Tim Tate explores this in considerable detail and concludes that Frankland deducted between £28 (£1,347) and £38 (£1,865) from each match's receipts to pay the 10*s* per head (£25) match fee for each player plus reserves, not to mention Lily Parr's Woodbines, laundry costs, and each team member's transport to her own, sometimes distant, front door. It is not impossible that he was 'diverting some of the profits to enable him to create a serious women's team which was professional or at least semi-professional in all but name'.[39] There is no evidence that he himself profited from any of the matches, but for the FA, which had itself been accused of financial mismanagement, 'the whiff of scandal was enough to hasten … drastic action'.[40] However, if they had really been concerned about the financial aspects, a thorough investigation could have been initiated. The obvious conclusion is that the Association was determined to deal women's football a death blow; they would use expert and pseudo-expert opinion, and accusations of flawed accountancy to impose drastic penalties and enforce its will.

The other front, close to the authorities' hearts was linked to a woman's primary purpose in life: childbearing. 'Expert' medical opinion had been sought and not just from male doctors. Harley Street gynaecologist Dr Mary Scharlieb who, as we shall subsequently see was also vehemently opposed to contraception, conveyed her belief to the all-male committee of the FA, 'I consider it is a most unsuitable game, too much for a woman's physical frame.' This was unsurprising. No doubt those who sought her opinion knew that in 1911 she had pontificated about 'excessive devotion to athletics and gymnastics which tends to produce what may be called ... the neuter type of girl ... flat chested with a badly developed bust, her hips are narrow and in too many instances there is a corresponding failure in function'.[41] The adjective 'neuter' may have prompted an additional shudder, rumours of lesbianism among all classes were outraging the Establishment; might women's sport be a breeding ground for 'abnormal' practices? Medical journalist, doctor and paediatrician Dr Elizabeth Sloan Chesser, who incidentally believed that poverty was largely the fault of the poor, concurred, 'There are physical reasons why the game is harmful to women. It is a rough game at any time, but it is much more harmful to women than men. They may receive injuries from which they may never recover.' Sportsmen joined in the chorus of disproval as Eustace Miles' 'The Game is Bad for Future Mothers' makes cringingly plain. 'Their duties as future mothers could be impaired' warned Miles, whose claim to knowledge – other than being a respected 'real tennis' player – rested upon his eclectic output as an author; considering 'football quite an inappropriate game for most women, especially if they have not been medically tested first'; he bewails, 'the woman who wants to play football won't be medically examined first.' In his expert opinion, 'just as a woman's frame is more rounded than a man's, so her movements should be more rounded'![42] No one seated round the FA table at 42 Russell Square on 5 December 1921, seems to have questioned such wisdom. A (foregone) damning conclusion was handed down:

Complaints have been made as to football being played by women, the Council feel impelled to express their strong opinion that the game of football is quite unsuitable for females and ought not be encouraged.

Being 'further of the opinion that an excessive proportion of the receipts are absorbed in expenses and an inadequate percentage devoted to charitable objects. For these reasons the Council request clubs belonging to the Association to refuse the use of their grounds for such matches.'[43]

The Lyons Corner House teams immediately fought back. On 13 December Lyons Ladies FC staged an exhibition match between the Strand Corner House and the Regent Palace Hotel. Invitations were issued to thirty representatives of the press to attend 'and form an opinion of the desirability of ladies playing the game'. Although reports were less than complimentary about the standard of play, most declared that football was no more strenuous to women than their more traditional sports. An unmoved FA tightened its grip. The Association's Secretary informed clubs and referees' organisations, 'no official referee should take charge of a game not recognised by us.'[44] Without FA pitches or officials, the direction of travel was clear. Women's football was about to be 'sent off'.

Up in Preston, DKL and Alfred Frankland who doubted the FA's ability to judge the women's game – and no doubt wondered on what the medical experts were basing their opinions other than prejudice, were equally determined to offer their own evidence. They would match medical evidence with medical evidence. Luckier than many teams, they could organise a match on 'Lively Polly'. On 28 December 1921, Fleetwood and DKL met in what might be termed an exhibition game, albeit one that was a life and death struggle for women's football itself. Twenty medical practitioners were invited to comment on the game's suitability. They were kicked off by Dr Mary Lowery who helpfully commented, 'Football is no more likely to cause injuries to women than a heavy day's washing.' The following day's *Lancashire Daily Post* reported the medical conclusions: 'football was no more physically harmful for women than tennis or hockey'. This game, in aid of the Poor Children's Fund, attracted 3,000 spectators – few in comparison to the regular attendances for former DKL matches played on FA grounds.

With the ban in place, the DKL nevertheless embarked for Canada; they were scheduled to play twenty-four spaced-out matches. Arriving in Quebec on 22 September 1922, it seemed that they could not escape bad news. Believed to have been subjected to pressure by their British counterpart, the Dominion Football Association had withdrawn permission for the women to play Canadian women's teams; they had hastily arranged for them to play men under the auspices of the Unites

States Football Association. US women's colleges which boasted women's teams had been approached, but declined; they did not wish their 'nice' girls to play working-class Lancashire women. With little choice, the women reluctantly accepted the new terms. Of their nine matches, they won four, drew two and lost three; they attracted big crowds, including women who did not usually attend 'soccer' matches. The last match, held in Philadelphia on 4 November, was played at the city's best ground with a seating capacity of 45,000. The welcome extended across the country was warm. As well as memories to last a life time and for Alice Woods a fiancé, Herbert Stanley team coach and secretary, DKL brought home a remarkable trophy. Fortunately, 17-year-old Lily Parr, hailed by the American press as the 'most brilliant female player in the world', despite the power behind her kick having broken the Philadelphia goalie's arm, had left her football pilfering days behind her. At the 'Welcome Home' party hosted by English Electric Ltd management (the company was now increasingly using this name), they proudly showed off the football signed by US President Harding who had kicked off their match in Washington.[45] At the reception, the former Mayor of Burnley expressed sorrow at the FA ban and 'hoped they would soon see the error of their ways'. They did not.

The renamed company began distancing itself from the illustrious team, banned the use of the name Dick, Kerr and eventually prevented the now 'Preston Ladies' from training at Ashton Park. With ever stricter conditions imposed on Frankland's management of the team, he left the company. DKL's glorious reign was over. Jobs were in increasingly short supply as the difficult post-war years continued. Still determined to look after his players as English Electric made them redundant, Frankland successfully lobbied the matron at Whittingham Hospital Lunatic Asylum (the largest institution of its type in England) to find jobs for those who wanted them, including Lily Parr. The team had raised considerable funds for Whittingham and its shell-shocked inmates, now he called in the favour. It was here that Parr met the love of her life, Mary, with whom she lived until her death. She became a Ward Sister, continuing to play football until the age of 45. Out of the 643 games played since 1917, Frankland calculated that DKL had lost only nine and Parr had scored more than 900 goals. The team folded in 1965, five years before the FA finally lifted the ban on women's football that DKL's phenomenal success both as players and fund-raisers, had done much to initiate. Sadly, she died of breast cancer in 1978. In 2002, Lily Parr, England's best ever woman player, was inducted into the Football Hall of Fame at the National Football Museum.

The December 1921 ban had devastating, ongoing and far-reaching, consequences, spiralling down the century to the Covid-19 crisis. Many can be traced back to the Establishment's fear of women in the early post-war years. Flappers with their short skirts and bobbed hair, women in shorts (albeit less short than the French ones) immodestly playing football, sportswomen enjoying each other's company both on and off the pitch, factory hands reluctant to vacate jobs for returning heroes and working-class women raising money for striking miners rather than raising the nation's future 'jewels', needed to be reminded of their subservience. This, the triumphant FA had done. Working-class female footballers had borne the brunt of the pent-up anger and misogyny simmering beneath the surface of England's green and rather unpleasant land. By 1923, the Pandora's Box of women's football had been tightly shut. Players had proved both a product and a victim of the times. The lights had gone out for women's football. They were not lit again either in their, nor in subsequent generations of players' life times.

Forty Elephants: 'A girl gang like no other the world has seen'[46]
Born in June 1896 in the uncongenial surroundings of Lambeth Workhouse, Alice Diamond's birth was legitimate by a matter of weeks. Her father, Thomas, boasted three criminal convictions, the most dramatic being for pushing the Lord Mayor of London's son's head through a pane of glass. This milieu of violence and crime, servitude, prostitution or poverty was the eight Diamond siblings' birth right. The nearby Elephant and Castle was notorious for its gangs who terrorised the local, and indeed wider, area and attracted new members with their lively parties and lavish spending of their ill-gotten gains in local pubs. The 1911 census lists 14-year-old Alice as fulfilling her destiny as a 'Servant'. Demanding more from life, in 1914 she made her début court appearance, charged with stealing a hat from an Oxford Street store. Nearly 5ft 9in tall, with razors and blackjacks secreted about her person and a handful of diamond rings which she was not averse to using as knuckle dusters on whomever stood in her way, she joined the notorious 'Forty Elephants' girl gang, soon becoming one of the West End's most notorious shoplifters, adept at both disguise and, with multiple aliases, at evading capture.

By late 1918, the teenage Diamond was Commander of the Forty Elephants, having wrested power from 'Queen Thief' Mary Carr. Her cunning and ruthless control propelled the gang to still greater success and notoriety. Gang 'minder' Dan Johnston commented on the intricate preparations which preceded Diamond's often large-scale operations run 'with military precision', employing 'battlefield tactics'.[47] Fundamental to the gang's success was the sense of team spirit she fostered and strict code of honour to which all adhered. Rules included never drinking before a raid, going to bed early, bail money being paid from the Elephants' coffers, proceeds from a job being shared equally between participants, families looked after while a member was in prison. Stealing from another member, including her boyfriend, many of whom were 'minders', was forbidden. Diamond left little to chance. While not always obeyed, these rules fostered group harmony and the sense of honour and mutual trust essential to any group undertaking. Gang loyalty and support included those in the massive distribution organisation including the 'fences' upon which all shoplifting networks depend. Among the most accomplished fences, Ada Macdonald's home was an 'Aladdin's cave of loot'. Frequently raided, she always convinced the police that her emporium of possessions had been legitimately acquired and no charge could be brought against her.[48]

As old as shopping itself, by the early twentieth century shoplifting was considered a quintessentially feminine crime in which both working- and middle-class women engaged. The former, judged deviant, received custodial sentences; the latter, supposedly suffering from 'feminine conditions', were treated sympathetically.[49] Despite shop owners and police begging for prison sentences, magistrates, disbelieving that members of their own middle-class could commit larceny, accepted pleas which included 'kleptomania' (coined to cover well-to-do thieves), having a war-wounded [officer] husband at home, and the culprit's own 'neurasthenia'. A kindly warning followed. When such cases were mentioned in the press, the reporting was relatively sympathetic.[50] Working-class women could anticipate imprisonment [three months for first offenders], sometimes with 'hard labour', which, it was hoped, would act as a deterrent.

The advent of stores such as Selfridges' (1909) had hastened shopping's transformation into a leisure experience – at least for those who indulged in it as opposed to the assistants who worked in this backbreaking industry, often for little more than sweated wages and, in department stores, under the beady eye of the 'shopwalker'. By the early 1920s, with some young single women enjoying increased disposable income, girls shopping in groups were a common sight. For lonely young middle-class wives forced to leave their jobs either because of the marriage bar which banned married women from some occupations, or because their husband saw a working wife as a slur on his earning capacity, visiting the shops could be the major event of the day, dressing appropriately part of the pleasure.[51]

Dress was fundamental to shoplifters' success. Outfits in which loot could quickly be stored were commissioned. Slits in coats were strategically placed so that pilfered items could be dropped into the capacious concealed pockets of the skirt or dress, 'big knickers' took on a whole new meaning. Some gang members joked that rather than referring to their home turf, the Elephant and Castle pub, the Elephants' name related to their size when they exited a shop with their concealed booty, even, on occasion, fur coats. Trainee Shirley Pitts remembered the women, wearing, 'big, expensive fur coats and elastic bags under their skirts.'[52] Indeed many newspaper column inches were devoted to their appearance. Comments abound on their bobbed hair and clothes, 'These women, who are notorious for their good looks, fine stature, and smart clothing, are some of the cleverest shop thieves and receivers of stolen property in London.'[53]

Unlike many shoplifters who stole for their own consumption, Elephants were banned from wearing stolen goods, but there was a ready, ever increasing market for their loot, some purchased by those unwilling to take the risk of lifting for themselves. With dress both a creator of identity and a marker of independence, smart clothes and make-up offered a route into supposed female autonomy. For women born into a life of domestic service, adopting the dress of those who were constructed as their social 'betters' was an act of defiance, 'a performance of social mobility and enhanced status', in an age when even the materials out of which garments were made, clearly defined social status.[54] One young Elephant remembered gazing in awe at the fur coats worn by experienced gang members, equating these with the clothes worn by her idols of the silver screen.

The stores women frequented reflected their class. By shoplifting from fashionable West End department stores, Elephants were crossing social boundaries which, at least for apprentice thieves, added glamour and excitement to their actions. Even what was stolen tended to be class-defined. Middle-class thieves favoured clothes, jewellery (costume and real) and accessories, all easy to conceal. Working-class women concentrated on unfinished fabrics and silk, the latter was popular among thieving servants who, forced into the rough serge and lisle stockings of their hated uniforms, relished the feel of the softest of all fabrics against their skin. The *Ministry of Reconstruction Report on Domestic Service* acknowledged, 'the distinctive dress they are required to wear marks them out as a class apart'. [55] Transgressing class boundaries, servants also frequently operated in groups in upmarket shops close to their place of employment. Temporarily discarding their hated uniform and cap (the loathed 'badge of servitude'), some would wear what they or others had stolen.[56] Reporting on a recent shoplifting case, the 27 March 1919 *Times* noted, 'the girl [a servant] was extremely fond of wearing fine clothes'. Diamond would sometimes instruct 'Elephants' to seek jobs as servants. False references were used to gain positions – although with the much-bewailed post-war dearth of servants, maybe all employers did not check these too carefully. Once employed, items would be pilfered, or even the house ransacked. Seducing male household members was recommended, money earned through the ensuing blackmail nicely swelled the gang's coffers.

One Elephant shoplifting tactic was to operate in frequently noisy groups. While distracted shop assistants brought more and more goods to be examined, a single operator would move in behind and gather up a collection of the items that the group had discarded and make a quiet exit. Alternatively Diamond, recognised and dreaded by shop owners and assistants, would herself act as the decoy. With her every step monitored, another woman would sedately follow, swiping items unobserved. Getaways were equally carefully planned. Members of the gang would cause a diversion while another, still covered by her associates, would exit the shop unnoticed.

Diamond and her lieutenant, 'Baby-face' Maggie Hughes, master-minded the getaway. High-powered cars, often more powerful than those belonging to the police, would await the Elephants' exit and spirit thieves and goods away. Large-scale raids necessitated a team of cars with the loot being distributed around or transferred between vehicles, making detection easier to avoid. Goods were generally driven straight to the Elephant and Castle depot. While male accomplices were often the drivers, both Diamond and Hughes owned their own vehicles, Hughes' allegedly fitted with a periscope through which she could apparently spot police cars.

To ensure a successful getaway, other cars packed with 'heavies' were on standby to take care of anyone who impeded the departure of loot-laden vehicles. Empty suitcases could also be deposited in Left Luggage premises with booty subsequently distributed around these. The police frequently bewailed how, even if an alleged thief were caught in a vehicle, she was usually clean and no arrest could be made. Fast cars also enabled women to descend in groups on provincial stores and be back in London with stolen items stowed in a lockup by midnight. Countless local papers report department stores' losses and frequently unsuccessful attempts to bring wrongdoers to court. The police, conscious that this continuous press coverage of the gang's actions was providing them with the oxygen of publicity, begged newspaper proprietors to desist, to little avail. Even newspaper readers in America and Australia developed an obsession with the 'Forty Elephants'.

Elephants could also arrive for a thieving spree in chauffeur-driven cars; these would draw up outside upmarket premises such as Harrods or Selfridges, car doors graciously opened by commissionaires. One thief remembered, 'They arrived for me in a Chrysler car, and I thought I was going to heaven, not out thieving.'[57] This young woman may never before have stepped inside a private car, going 'on the hoist' was enabling her to enter an unimaginable world and enact a dream of belonging to a different class. While tightly organised groups of four would fan out around the store, chauffeurs remained on the spot ready to spirit the women away when they exited with their carefully concealed booty.[58]

By the early 1920s, stores' security was increasing. As no male detective could search a woman, stores fought back by employing females who appear to have been shared between several premises. In response, cells would descend on various stores at the same time. Shared detectives were so busy rushing from one shop to another that few if any thieves were apprehended. Those confronting the Elephants needed nerves of steel. One of the first, Gertrude Hunter, believed that by 1927, she had detained some 800 shoplifters who had threatened violence on multiple occasions. Crediting herself with 'an uncanny instinct' when it came to thieves, in a much syndicated piece, she explained, 'the woman shop detective was always on the alert, her wits ready to battle against the daring and cunning, the light fingers and the well-laid schemes of the underworld – and [further confirmation that shoplifting crossed class boundaries], the haute monde, too.'[59] Corroborating police statistics, she calculated that women committed 90 per cent of shoplifting crimes.

Surprising hints of admiration for the gang and particularly for 'Annie Diamond' as the police occasionally called her, emerge in reports of some court cases where she and/or other Elephants appear. There is a recognition that Elephants were mistresses of their nefarious art and that Diamond and 'Baby-face' Hughes, almost 12 inches shorter and three years older who had acquired her first criminal record at the age of 14, ruled their Empire with iron fists. They guarded their 'turf', which included the most prestigious stores, with ferocity. Shoplifters who dared to trespass were forced to surrender a percentage of their takings. Elephants' boyfriends or minders ensured that the money was quickly paid over; if it were not forthcoming, a spot of kidnapping would do the trick. Like all such gangs, they were vicious, belying their presentation, even in today's accounts, as glamorous Flappers of the Roaring Twenties, not the thugs they were. They considered themselves a cut above other hoisters, akin with the movie stars and cinema idols who were ushering in the cult of the celebrity.

In line with this sense of themselves as exotic, Diamond, surrounded by her acolytes, would host lavish parties and spend exorbitant sums of ill-gotten money at many of London's most scandalous clubs, hotels and restaurants. Their arrival could strike fear into club owners as noted by Kate Meyrick, owner of the so-called "the 43" nightclub. Britain's first female police officer, Lilian Wyles, reflecting on her multiple interactions with them recollected, 'They do well out of their activities, live under the most comfortable circumstances, rub shoulders with the wealthy in the best hotels and restaurants, and have a thoroughly good time while it lasts.'[60] This 'thoroughly good time' included post-raid celebrations. High on adrenalin, the Elephants would flock to a West End hotel, 'start carousing', knock back the alcohol they had abstained from before the raid, and flirt with staff and clients alike.[61] The venue and its customers might subsequently find that they had been 'swept' when the women departed. Although Diamond is not known ever to have done so, some Elephants were becoming heavy cocaine users. Following significant concerns about troops' use of cocaine during the war, this had been prohibited under the Defence of the Realm Act (DORA). Now outlawed by the 1920 Dangerous Drugs Act, it was becoming part of the dark hidden underbelly of High Society life.[62] That Elephants could afford cocaine at about '£10 [£659] for a sniff or two' is proof of their success; *The Tatler's* 'Eve' points out the cost is well beyond the 'middle classes'.[63]

Shoplifting is sometimes seen as a victimless crime, thus less reprehensible.[64] Mr Charles Davis, furrier, Grosvenor Square, would disagree. In March 1919, Mrs Beatrice Mitchell had engaged him to transform her seventy marten skins into an elegant coat. While awaiting her tardy collection of the finished product, the coat was enticingly displayed in the shop window during the day, being placed in the safe at closing time. Disaster struck when two stylishly dressed young women, 'Diana Black' (alias Alice Diamond) and Maggie Hughes entered his premises in late November.[65] In true Elephant style, they were wearing 'voluminous' fur coats and requested estimates for items in the showroom.[66] The shop assistant summoned Davis who, after satisfying their enquiries which only lasted a matter of minutes, graciously 'bowed them out' of his premises. About thirty minutes later, a horrified Davis contacted the police, although the assistant had been absent for under two minutes, the coat had disappeared from its display cabinet. In a tightly planned operation, the women had made their escape in a Vauxhall Velux car. Despite the police's considerable efforts, it was several weeks before they caught up with the pair; an intense raid across Southwark failed to reveal the coat. On 8 January 1920, the 'world's cleverest shoplifters' were charged with stealing around £2,000 (£98,200) worth of goods in a ten-week shoplifting orgy.[67] The charge sheet included the Davis theft, other fur coats, capes, 363 gowns and 2,006 blouses. The speed at which the women operated was noted. Despite the prisoners being able to lay hands on substantial securities, bail was refused. The case came to trial in February, providing newspapers with many column inches of eagerly awaited copy. Along with the enormity of their haul, many insalubrious details emerged about both women whom the Common Serjeant dubbed 'Pests to Society'.[68] Their previous bad characters were also brought to the court's attention: Hughes' drunkenness and 'obscene language', her string of previous convictions, and that she had always been a source of despair to her 'parents who were poor but respectable'. Also to be taken into consideration was that in 1916 Diamond had used another girl's Labour card to gain work in a munitions factory, an indictable offence although she appears to have escaped with a warning. She apparently hoped to acquire explosives to detonate safes. Although no records of the marriage have been positively identified, it was claimed that her husband had deserted her six months after their 1914 marriage for her 'bad conduct'. Hoping 'to protect society' from their ilk, a sentence of twelve months hard labour was passed on Hughes, reputed to be able to pilfer even under shop assistants' noses, Diamond, whom newspapers called the 'Elephant Queen', was imprisoned for eighteen months hard labour.[69]

The robbed Mr Davis was facing his own tribulations. With her coat not among the recovered items, Mrs Mitchell brought a 'Negligence' case against him. Her Counsel successfully argued that 'he had not taken due care to protect the coat'. The jury agreed and the unfortunate furrier was ordered to pay the value of the skins £500 (£24,500). He was given leave to appeal.'[70] Shoplifting is far from victimless. A Sussex magistrate summed up the Elephants' philosophy: 'You take what you will, without regard to the livelihood of others; you put aside all decency and show no shame at all'.[71]

On 4 May 1921, Diamond was released; wardresses, fearful she was sharing her shoplifting techniques with inmates, were relieved. Holloway may also have proved an excellent recruiting ground for women prepared to work as crooked shop assistants who would turn a blind eye to those pilfering under their noses. More honest assistants would sometimes ignore an Elephant spree out of terror. Following the January 1920 arrests, one assistant was quoted as saying she was afraid of the pair and if there had not been other witnesses, may not have risked identifying them. Despite her incarceration, Diamond remained the undisputed queen.

Many members were deflecting attention away from their evil activities by renting comfortable properties in solidly middle-class areas, far from the squalor of their native Elephant and Castle. The rent and the modern fixtures and fittings they were acquiring would be looked after by others should the owner do time. With forty gang members, there were always enough outside prison to ensure that such protection, and raids continued. Diamond's code of honour remained firmly in place. One crucial rule was that as a clan, Elephants stood by their own. Like modern gangs, they married or cohabited with members of a local (Elephant and Castle) clan. Outsiders were the enemy. A family tree of the Forty Elephants resembles the intermarriages among Europe's nineteenth-century royalty. The breaking of this rule almost broke the gang and ended Diamond's reign. In 1925, Elephant Maria (née Britten), who had done six months hard labour for stealing from Debenhams and Freebody in 1923, became pregnant and, defying Alice's orders, married Redmond Sandys; she claimed that she now intended to 'go straight'. (Whether she did so is unclear, at the trial Hughes alleged that she 'thieves with her husband'.) On the night of 20 December 1925, a Saturday, hence no need to abide by the no drink/early to bed rule, most of the outraged gang gathered at a Social Club in Lambeth's New Cut market. Having drunk themselves into fighting mood, armed with bottles, stones, lumps of concrete and razors, they marched to the Brittens' nearby lodgings where Maria was staying, smashed their way in and held her at gunpoint; her father, William, was beaten senseless, some accounts state he was, 'slashed by razors', needing twenty stitches.[72] Summoned by terrified neighbours, the police broke up the riot and arrested the thugs. The widely reported Old Bailey trial 'lasted the greater part of a week'. *Illustrated Police News* (25 March 1926) excitedly commented on the 'electric atmosphere' and the half-hidden revelations of London's underworld. Most newspapers refer to how, 'Alice Diamond took upon her shoulders the burden of leadership of the 'Forty Elephants. ... She had the perfect right to do so.' The plea that the women had 'not inflicted the injuries' was accepted; they were instead sentenced for being 'the fomenters of the disturbance'.

Diamond received eighteen months hard labour; Hughes, deemed to have incited the riot, twenty-one months. *Illustrated Police News'* presciently predicted this would result in the downfall of Alice Diamond, 'Queen of the "Forty Thieves"'. Replaced by Lilian Kendall, 'the Bobbed-Haired Bandit', while not the force they were during Diamond's five-year reign, the 'Elephants' continued to act as a team and to strike fear into Londoners' hearts.

Recent statistics indicate that some 34 per cent of children and young adults involved in gangs are female.[73] Many are trapped. Like Marie Britten, 'When they try to leave the group, gang members threaten the victim's family with kidnapping and violence.'[74] While the types of crimes these gangsters commit may be drug-related and more violent than 100 years ago, what is striking is how, often from impoverished families and with few prospects, today's girls join because they live in a 'gang' area, consider membership to be empowering, need to belong, and yearn for the sense of protection the gang offers.[75] The same motivations that drove, Diamond, Hughes, Britten, and their ilk into the underworld of crime based around London's Elephant and Castle.

CHAPTER 2

Remembering Them

'Authority has a limit'[1]

Modern visitors to the Commonwealth War Graves Commission (CWGC) cemeteries agree that the tranquillity, the architectural and the floral design represent a fitting tribute to 'The Fallen'. Few realise they were sites of dispute as, even before the war ended, battle for ownership of the dead erupted.

In November 1917, Lieutenant Colonel Sir Frederick Kenyon KCB, Director of the British Museum, travelled to France for the Imperial War Graves Commission (IWGC), incorporated by Royal Charter in May 1917, to gather information on 'How the Cemeteries Abroad Will Be Designed'. Deaf to the National Council of Women's requests for female representation, Commissioners were exclusively male. Fearful of pre-war suffrage activists, considering women 'inefficient', and dismissing 'the thought that bereaved mothers and wives had a right to help formulate policy', women were excluded.[2] Kenyon's report, published in January 1918, acknowledged that the question of 'how the Cemeteries abroad should be laid out, and what form of permanent memorial should be erected in them, contained the seeds for potential controversy'. Hopes that this 'could be avoided' proved ill-founded.[3] A headline in *The Times* of 29 November 1918 proclaimed: 'Comradeship in Death, Soldiers' Bodies Not to Be Brought Home'. Exhumation would not be allowed; the bereaved were assured that, 'the dead themselves in whom the sense of comradeship was so strong, would have preferred to lie with their comrades'. While the dead could not express an opinion, the bereaved could, and indeed would, long after the headline was yesterday's news.

Local newspapers were a popular vehicle for stating opinions and initiating debate. Opinions about the Commission and its plans as revealed in the Report, the prohibition against exhumations and reinterment, the lay-out of the cemeteries, headstones as opposed to the Christian symbol of the Cross, and the accusation that the Commission had been

31

motivated by 'parsimony' (which it vehemently denied), soon featured in correspondence pages. Some were proud, 'however we mourn the loss', that such extensive plans were underway, others distinctly unimpressed.[4] Echoing 'Desolate Mother', many bereaved felt they were 'being robbed' of their rights and the state was retaining 'ownership' of what had been 'freely given in their country's honour', Commissioners thinking 'that nothing matters except their schemes and plans'.[5] Some bereaved mothers would take their complaints to the heart of the British Establishment. Nor did the debate centre solely upon British troops. A hint of arguments and discussions to come relating to the Dominions first appears on 20 February 1919 in the *Sheffield Daily Telegraph,* 'it would be quite impracticable to exhume the British dead for the purpose of reinterment in various parts of the Empire.'

To help understand the Commission's stance, we should turn the clock back to 13 April 1915; a German sniper killed Lieutenant William Gladstone, MP, grandson of the former British Prime Minister. *The Sketch* (28 April) featured a half-page photograph under the headline 'MP Fallen on the Field of Honour', and included detailed information about his elaborate burial. Following intervention at the highest level, he had been repatriated and buried in 'the Gladstone family vault in Hawarden, Chester'; local people lined the streets and subsequently 'visited the memorial'.[6] Major Fabian Ware, leading the British Army Graves Registration Commission (BAGRC), was furious at this case of blatant class privilege. Like soldiers of all ranks, Gladstone should have lain where he fell. His would be the last repatriation. The public were informed that the BAGRC, subsequently the IWGC, would create cemeteries, design grave markers and tend graves in perpetuity, and, as would become apparent over the ensuing decade, this decision was final. One piece of information the IWGC did not dare share and which may have underpinned their insistence on bodies remaining in situ was that many battlefield graves (unlike ones near medical facilities) only contained bits of the soldier, the rest of him may have been scattered across the field or indeed mixed in with another soldier's remains. How the bereaved might react should they discover this was too painful to contemplate.

In Leeds, Sarah Smith may not have noted Gladstone's 1915 repatriation. Her 16-year-old son, Frederick was beyond the Army's reach. However, on 28 August 1918, Private Smith died of wounds and was buried in Grevillers, France. With the war over, Smith, mother of 'one of our heroes', requested the authorities return her 19-year-old son's body. Her request was declined. Her response, printed in the 15 April 1919 *Yorkshire Evening Post*, captioned 'Our Heroic Dead', was the opening salvo in a long campaign. She urged mothers and widows of soldiers to:

Protest against the attitude of the Government robbing us of our beloved dead. They were taken from us, and have sacrificed their lives, and still [we] are [not allowed] to have their remains brought home. They are to be left in foreign lands, and they are only worthy of a paltry concrete cross. Exhumation would not appeal to everyone, but to the majority, where possible, it would; and what a comfort it would be to our aching hearts to have our dear ones placed in the family vault, and be enabled to tend their graves ourselves.

Hearteningly for the Commission, not everyone agreed. 'Mother of Two of Them' argued that the 'proper and right and humane thing is to let them rest where they have had to meet their grave. I for one forbid anyone to lay his hand on either of my two fallen sons to desecrate their remains.'[7]

The 1917 Report had emphasised the IWGC's mantra, 'equality of treatment'; the next point of increasingly vociferous contention was the uniformity of headstones.[8] Fuelling further anger, those who had at least cherished hopes of designing their own memorial or tributes discovered that the state's ownership of the dead extended to how (s)he was remembered. What was done for one should be done for all; whatever their military rank or position in civil life, all would have equal treatment in their graves. A brief possible ray of light appeared, at least according to a snippet in *Halifax Evening Courier* (10 April 1919): 'The War Graves Commission do not wish to set up a hard and fast rule but they consider it undesirable to allow the removal of bodies or the erection of special tombstones because very few relatives of those who have fallen are in a position to bear the cost.' This was 'false news'.

It was soon apparent that the Government was as inflexible as the Commission. In the House of Lords, Lord Selborne, probably at the behest of his wife, veteran women's rights campaigner Beatrix Maud, declared it, 'tyranny and bureaucracy run mad', for the Government to prevent English families from bringing their dead back to their own country.[9] Countering Lord Peel's argument that there 'should be equality of treatment' and that few could afford the costs, Selborne did 'not believe for one single moment that there is a family in this land, however humble, which would resent it'.[10] Having read of the Lords' discussion, 'Desolate Mother' agreed; the premise that the 'removal of remains to this country cannot be allowed because it would differentiate in favour of the well-to do' was disingenuous, 'Would anyone be so mean as to resent it?'[11] This being a question to which the Government did not wish to discover the answer, the interdiction stood. The dead would remain overseas.

In 1920, reluctantly acceding to popular demands, France, Belgium and Germany now tolerated repatriation.[12] In 1919, the US Secretary of State for War had confirmed that the commitment to repatriating the dead would be honoured, despite a July 1918 Presidential statement. Referring to their dead son, 'Mrs Roosevelt and I ... have always felt that where the tree falls, there it lay.'[13] Seventy per cent of American bereaved disagreed and these bodies were returned.[14] If American boys could be transported across the Atlantic, why not British ones across the Channel? Still the British Government stood firm despite some disquiet in Parliament; Colonel Sir James Remnant, for example, while recognising that this was a 'painful and fateful subject', believed 'where it is possible the body itself might be brought home to rest in England.'[15] Sarah Smith re-entered the lists. *Yorkshire Evening Post* (22 May 1919) announced a 'petition [is] being got up to the Prince of Wales, [IWGC President] to allow those relatives who so wish, to have the bodies brought over to this country. Anyone having suffered loss is invited to sign.' Some 2,500 rapidly responded, requesting the prince intervene on behalf of 'his broken-hearted subjects'. He did not. Unsuccessful with the prince, Smith now lobbied Queen Mary, 'Many thousands of mothers and wives are slowly dying for the want of the grave of their loved ones, to visit and tend themselves, and we feel deeply hurt that the right granted by other countries is denied us.'[16]

It was soon common knowledge that the Government intended to 'remove the remains of the fallen from the scattered cemeteries in France and Belgium to new cemeteries'; Smith was not alone in arguing these exhumed remains could easily be repatriated. Adding insult to injury, these exhumations and reburials were being undertaken 'without in any way communicating with the relatives'.[17] Judging by newspaper correspondence these amalgamations whatever the practical reasons, particularly outraged mothers. These mass cemeteries raised among poorer women the spectre of the dreaded pauper's funeral. Churchill's explanation to the Commons, that the numbers involved, some '231,000, were in isolated or other graves and in view of the magnitude of the task, it has not been possible to communicate with the relatives individually before concentration took place', provided little consolation to those who felt that their loved-one's body was being shifted around in order to conform to the Commission's vision of perfect cemeteries which, it was obvious, did not comply with their own.

If defeat over repatriation would finally, albeit reluctantly, be accepted, anger at the shape and 'uniformity of headstones' ['four feet in height, two feet in breadth, and six inches in thickness'] gained ground.[18] For Commissioners, this represented 'equality of treatment'.[19] To the mantra that just as men of all ranks and classes were equal in sacrifice, so they were equal in death, many bereaved begged to differ. If they could not have their beloved back, then the least they could do was choose how to honour him with their own memorial stone overseas. Many joined Smith in being outraged that these 'heroes' were only deemed worthy of 'a paltry concrete cross'. She was slightly wrong in one respect, the 'concrete' would (and continues to) be made of Portland stone. Even those who were prepared for their loved one to remain overseas balked at the impersonal military precision of what many referred to as a 'slab of concrete like milestones', atop the loved one's grave. Attempting to mollify the public, artists' impressions of the cemeteries started appearing, *The Sphere* (19 April 1919) devoted a whole page to three 'drawings' of a 'Cemetery for British soldiers as it will appear'. The first three, Le Tréport, Forceville, with its garden designed by Gertrude Jekyll, and Louvencourt would be complete within three months, no mean feat.

One artist's impression image represents the 'Cross of Sacrifice' to be installed in (nearly) all cemeteries. To the devout, this cross replacing a cruciform gravestone offered scant comfort. The Bishop of Exeter's wife, Florence Cecil, voiced a heartfelt opinion. Bereaved of three sons, it was only deep religious faith that enabled the parents to shoulder their unimaginable loss with outward calm and resignation. An individual cross would connect their sons' sacrifice to Christ's, for, as Florence explained in her petition to the Prince of Wales which garnered 8,000 signatures and covered 244 pages, 'It is only through the hope of the cross that most of us are able to carry on the life from which all the sunshine seems to have gone and to deny us the emblem of that strength and hope adds heavily to the burden of our sorrows.' [20] Ensuring HRH was left in no doubt, the first page of the petition explains these 'deep' wounds and the dismay that 'no crosses are to be erected over the individual graves of those who gave their lives to protect the life and liberty of others.' The litany of loss: 'four dear sons out of five', 'Widow, only son killed, my husband died of grief six weeks later', 'sister of three dead brothers', remains searing; behind every name beats the heart of a distraught woman who felt that, in the interests of uniformity, the state was intent on denying the symbol of Christian comfort to those who had given their all.[21] 'That the cemeteries would in some way remind of the ranked battalions of men who had marched away to their death may, a few conceded, be visually pleasing but offered no consolation to those who mourned them, indeed the opposite. Rather than career soldiers, these men were civilians who had done their duty; they should be remembered the way their families, not the state, required. 'Died of wounds', 'Killed in Action', 'Not Buried in a Cemetery'; privates, NCOs, all officer ranks, these 8,000 petitioners give insight into the nation's grief over which the Commissioners were seemingly riding roughshod. They remained unmoved, on each uniform headstone a Cross (unless specifically requested otherwise) would be carved; Cecil feared this would be 'defaced by time and weather'.

This women-led clamour was deafening. A parliamentary debate on 4 May 1920 inevitably confirmed the official line. Winston Churchill, Secretary of State for War and by default Chair of the Commission, resoundingly supported the IWGC's stated ideal:

> the community of sacrifice, the service of a common cause, the comradeship of arms which has brought together men of all ranks and grades – these are greater ideas, which should be commemorated in those cemeteries where they lie together, the representatives of their country in the lands in which they served.[22]

The bereaved could pay for a brief inscription (3½d a letter or c.79p today), as long as this was deemed 'appropriate' and, hopefully, uplifting; three lines was the maximum. The charge, but not the 'appropriateness', was eventually withdrawn but too late for some who declined an inscription. Aware there could be dissatisfaction with the impersonal, albeit 'individual headstone ... [and] disappoint[ment] that they are not allowed to erect their own monument over their own dead', Kenyon believed that 'the individual grave, will serve as centre and focus of the emotions of the relatives who visit it.'[23] He should have added, 'who could afford to' before the word 'visit'.

In July 1920, Selborne published her damning 'Review of the IWGC, National Socialism in War Cemeteries.' She concluded, 'The rights of the individual swept away by a stroke of a pen'. Such 'unreasonably autocratic behaviour [as] ... the conscription of bodies', was 'worthy of Lenin'. Referring to the maximum 'sixty-three letters' permitted on the tombstone, she felt that 'the common conditions of state action are obvious'. She also advised 'those who wish to obtain leave to bring home the remains of soldiers' to contact their MPs as Mr Churchill had confirmed that the IWGC "carries out the policy approved by the Government."'[24] The Commissioners may have issued a collective sigh of relief and hoped that MPs rather than they themselves would receive the flood of angry letters (peaking at 3,000 a day) addressed to the Commission. Kenyon's stated desire in the Report (p.3) that 'the subject of war graves should not become the subject of controversy, if it could be avoided', was proving unfounded.

Ruth Jervis whose only child had been 'dragged from her and butchered' in 1917 had lived in hope of being able to visit his finally repatriated remains. Now, 'it seems even that hope is gone. It is cruelty in the extreme.' Her outrage at the IWGC's 'autocracy' is palpable in the letter she sent. As a railway signalman's wife, she felt she would never be able to visit Harry's grave. But, in the unlikely event of this happening, 'May I ask how long we are to remain at the graveside?' Beneath the sarcasm lurks the fury of a mother whose son 'destroyed by militarism' now has to beg the Government for what she considers her right, ownership of his grave. In a cowardly action, the IWGC placed a memo on the Jervis file, 'I don't think it is any use attempting an answer ... it will only irate her further.'[25]

With the dead not coming home, then the living would visit them in situ. This was within the means of some; companies like Thomas Cook, not to mention enterprising individuals, began organising 'pilgrimages' to the battlefields and cemeteries. In the spring of 1920, for £8 11 6*d* (£420), about half the average annual wage of a male factory worker, a pilgrim could visit France and Flanders. South Eastern and Chatham Railway offered a day trip – although this must have been long and exhausting. The following year, travel companies reported demand outstripping supply. It was patently obvious that the ambition for equality in death with an officer lying next to a private under an identical headstone, did not extend to who could visit the graves.

In May 1920, with the repatriation debate still raging, Sarah Smith had founded the British War Graves Association (BWGA) believing that the greater the number of voices, the greater the lobbying power, and Lady Florence Cecil became Vice-President. On Remembrance Day 1920, the second of the nation's two officially sanctioned repatriations took place: the Unknown Warrior was buried with all the pomp and ceremony that a nation which excels at such trappings could muster.[26] In Leeds, BWGA members assembled for a service in Victoria Square, followed later by a mass meeting.[27] Rather than adopting the platitude that it may just be their loved one being interred in the Abbey, they were angered by this repatriation. A year later, a local paper reminded readers that as the Association (whose membership was steadily rising) 'exists not only to comfort the bereaved, but also to remember those heroes who returned from the war and are maimed or workless', it would be throwing its weight behind the new Poppy Appeal.[28] Accompanied by the Boy Scouts' band, BWGA members 'walked in procession to the Town Hall'. After the service, a number of the ladies fanned out across Leeds selling poppies, including three who, 'cloaked and hooded in crimson robes, with eyes masked, toured the city in a motor-car, invading all hotels, restaurants, and places of business, where they held up shoppers and diners with imitation revolvers, and did good business.'[29] If the Association's main purpose remained repatriation, arguably more in hope than expectation, it was now committed to supporting ex-Servicemen.

Six months later, the BWGA boasted more than 3,000 members, an additional Vice-President, (Lady Margaret Horlick), branches in Leeds, Sheffield and Wakefield, Smith remained Honorary Treasurer, still lobbying the Government, explaining that as the number of graves in the rapidly created cemeteries could lead to squashing, more space between burials should be permitted. She also requested continued Government funding for families to visit graves. Grants had been made available to those bereaved who wished to visit graveyards, according to 13 March 1923 *Yorkshire Post and Leeds Intelligencer*, 'in light of the financial climate [these would] end with the 1922–1923 financial year'. Smith was undaunted that this, like all her demands, was refused. She now launched her most audacious venture. Forging links with Savings Clubs that allowed people to save for a holiday, the BWGA began organising pilgrimages to take place every Whitsun weekend (the Bank Holiday enabled more pilgrims to travel). 'Lantern Lectures' with titles such as 'The Graves of the Fallen in France and Belgium' proved popular fundraisers.

An announcement at the September 1923 Leeds BWGA meeting gave solace to many. Although the boys would never come home, the 'temporary wooden crosses removed from the graves of British soldiers when they were replaced with more permanent memorials', including a 'number of crosses from the graves of Leeds men' were ready for distribution following a special service of dedication to be held on 16 September. 'Many wooden crosses have been obtained direct from Flanders, and some clergymen are setting aside small portions of churchyards for the re-erection of the crosses of local men. Other crosses could be reverently placed around war memorials.'[30] The first of these services was held at the Church of the Annunciation, Marble Arch, the second in Leeds. Smith's BWGA was heavily involved in the distribution for which the IWGC had to grant permission, this at least was forthcoming. This service may have provided some closure; the funeral, the final leave-taking of the deceased, lies at the heart of the Christian tradition, but denied this essential ritual, grief had had no focus.

The BWGA pilgrimages started in 1923. Figures are hard to find, however, a 9 January 1928 report confirms that the previous year 'about 130 [BWGA] members travelled to France at Whitsuntide, and a small party went in August'.[31] Smith herself was a frequent pilgrim, becoming a knowledgeable and empathetic guide. With the cost even of a 'no frills' pilgrimage being about £4 (£216) per head, that so many were organised is a tribute to the committee's fundraising skills and potentially the two titled ladies' leverage. Each pilgrim would have returned comforted, found peace by touching their beloved's grave and maybe even recognised the beauty of the cemetery in which (s)he lay. *Sheffield Independent* noted, 'Sir Frederick Kenyon spoke with warmest admiration' of the BWGA parties. He 'hoped they would encourage others to visit the Silent Cities' which, a point lost in all the controversy, had been intended to comfort the living as much as honour the dead.[32] To the IWGC's satisfaction, the bereaved could not 'speak too highly of the way our sons' graves are looked after in France. To see them was very heartening.'[33] The hatchet was finally buried.

Smith lost the repatriation battle but, as the CWGC acknowledges, this very ordinary woman, just one in the vast army of the bereaved, helped 'shape the work of the Commission, which manages military cemeteries today'. News of her death (June 1936) travelled far beyond her native Yorkshire. She had come to be widely respected not only by those who had lost loved ones and who shared her views, but also by those with whom she had clashed swords. Writing on Sir Fabian Ware's instructions, the Commission paid tribute to her 'most valuable services' on behalf of the bereaved.[34] A fitting eulogy.

'An abiding and supreme memorial': Creating the Cemeteries' Gardens[35]

What sets British cemeteries apart from those of all other combatant nations are their gardens. In his 1918 report Kenyon stated, 'much of the general effect of the cemeteries will depend on the planting, and it is essential that the architectural designers of the cemeteries should work in the closest cooperation with the horticultural experts.'[36] Although overlooked in the IWGC story, one such 'expert' was Gertrude Jekyll (b.1843); the cemetery gardens that continue to delight and comfort visitors owe much to her vision and her determination to reproduce the best of the 'English country garden' for those who lay in foreign fields.

In June 1917, Ware had invited Sir Edwin Lutyens, one of the country's leading architects, to come to France to view the battlefields and develop ideas for designing the cemeteries. Lutyens was adamant that the cemeteries should be neither gloomy nor sad-looking. With Ware convinced of the need for attractive gardens and with the Royal Botanic Gardens (Kew)'s horticulturalists already involved, Lutyens turned to his elderly friend, garden designer, Gertrude Jekyll, whom he affectionately called 'Bumps' and to whom he owed a significant amount of his success.[37]

By mid-1917, Ware had accepted two architectural proposals that are a central feature of most CWGC cemeteries. Lutyens' erstwhile friend Sir Reginald Blomfield had proposed that each cemetery should contain a Cross of Sacrifice; Lutyens favoured some type of Great Stone 'creating the illusion of memorial chapels whose vault is the sky'.[38] In August, Lutyens visited Jekyll's Surrey home, telling his wife Emily, 'Bumps has written out a Great War Stone idea so well. Now she is taking up the monument idea.'[39] While Jekyll and Lutyens had previously collaborated on several projects where clients required enclosed gardens, cemetery gardens were for both uncharted territory. Despite her advancing years, Jekyll approached the idea with her usual enthusiasm, dedication and skill. She agreed to design the planting of a number of these proposed 'walled cemetery' gardens.[40] No wall was to be so high as to obscure the headstones; flower borders would be 45cm to 60cm wide, graves must be visible from the road. Every gravestone should have three herbaceous plants, 'forming patterns of 12 to 20 plants which repeat every five graves. ... Floribunda roses are planted every couple of gravestones, usually in rows of the same colour.' When seeking a colour palette, she was fond of reminding Commissioners that green was also a colour.[41]

Lutyens would send Jekyll the draft cemetery design and she furnished his drawings with her planting proposal. With trees already on the plans, she made suggestions such as cypress and yew, iris, magnolia, clematis and lavender. Where there was space, she added garden features, such as the pond in Auchonvillers or a pergola to provide shelter. Apprised of the different soil types, she would indicate appropriate trees, shrubs and evergreens and in cemeteries where there would be numbers of men from the Dominions, plants from 'home' that might flourish. In time, she was involved with the great South African cemetery at Delville Wood, still among the most shining jewels in the CWGC crown.

Jekyll's contribution stretched beyond her inspired vision, one 1917 December day saw her supervising the lifting from her own Surrey garden of 1,800 of her beloved white thrift to be packed and dispatched to the Commission offices for transit to France, 'The war has brought me an altered life', she told her family.[42] But the flowers also needed to serve a practical purpose. As rain can lash Northern France and Flanders (meaning 'Wet Lands'), she advised plantings to mitigate the effects of mud that would be splashed on the white headstones, advocating simple English cottage garden plants such as columbine, pansies and white thrift, which, in the Victorian language of flowers, means 'sympathy'. Above all, she wanted to include England's symbolic flower, the rose.[43] 'The shadow of an English rose [should] fall at some point each day on every headstone.'[44] But the planting in front of each headstone must not obscure the inscription; she instinctively understood that reading and touching his beloved name would help assuage the grief of the pilgrim who finally stood at his graveside. Inevitably, in the charged atmosphere of the time, once plans for gardens became widely known there were protests that the gardens would obscure what had been slaughter on an industrial level.

Nevertheless, like the cemeteries themselves, once the bitterest wounds healed, the gardens were recognised for both their beauty and the tribute they paid to those who were interred.

Jekyll also paid attention to the vista surrounding the cemetery, suggesting a holly or yew hedge with native trees providing both shelter and focus; cemetery borders and spare pieces of land should include shrubs of England's country lanes, blackthorn, whitethorn, hazel, guelder rose and honeysuckle. She advocated using (ideally Kew-) trained English gardeners who would instinctively understand her vision and see their task as keeping faith with the dead. By March 1921, the Commission employed 1,362 gardeners – some settled in France, even having descendants working for the CWGC today. While the chief horticultural advisor was Arthur Hill from the Royal Botanic Gardens at Kew, Jekyll's input via her collaboration with Lutyens has been long, undeservedly, overlooked.

Jekyll's final war-related commission came from Winchester College. Schools across the land were eager to commemorate their Old Boys who had not returned. While more modest schools had to settle for a name-engraved plaque, elite ones sought elaborate commemoration. Reputedly the largest private war memorial in Europe, Winchester School's Cloisters outdid them all. Jekyll was retained to advise on the Garden of Remembrance: planted with roses and white lilies, four grass lawns separated by paths lead to a central memorial cross. Since re-designed, the Cloisters provides a permanent reminder of the 513 Wykehamists who perished between 1914 and 1918.[45]

For Jekyll, 'the first purpose of a garden is to be a place of quiet beauty such as will give delight to the eye and repose and refreshment to the mind'.[46] Visitors to the garden cemeteries both then and now would conclude that this elderly, largely self-taught, horticulturalist had designed gardens that provide a fitting tribute to the dead and comfort the living. In the words of the Imperial War Museum's website Lives of the First World War, 'although her designs were not followed to the letter', her influence cannot be overestimated and 'it was her sense of the Englishness of the country garden that determined and still determines the appearance of the cemeteries today.'[47]

'That France which holds thee here enclasped in earth'[48]

From the outset, men from the Dominion of Canada joined the Canadian Expeditionary Force. [William] Arthur Durie (b.1881) was among their number. His widowed mother Anna followed her only son overseas, basing herself in London. Arthur was seriously wounded near Ypres in May 1916, whereupon, against official orders, she travelled to Belgium; when he was evacuated to Brighton, she went too. With his Medical Board considering him still unfit for Active Service, he was sent to Menton (South of France) where she joined him. That, she hoped, was that. To her dismay, having volunteered for active duty, in March 1917 Arthur was gassed at Vimy. He survived and, to his mother's fury, refused the 'desk job' she had wrangled for him and returned to his regiment (Central Ontario). His luck gave out and he was killed near Lens on 29 December 1917. Buried in Corkscrew Cemetery, just one among the 67,000 Canadians who would never return home.[49]

Initially, Durie's grief took a traditional form, writing letters to newspapers extolling her son's bravery, having memorial tablets erected in his school and in their local church. No matter that his school reports stated that he 'was not very bright', to his grieving mother and seemingly to his men, he was a brave and compassionate officer who had nobly returned to the trenches, and that was how he should be remembered. A minor author, Durie joined her voice to those of the army of bereaved women and took up her pen. *Our Absent Heroes* is a series of elegiac poems to a beloved son. This text would earn her a mention in Canada's Great War literature. However, Durie was poised for a different form of fame.

Bereaved Canadian women also longed to bring their boys home; eventually, like their British counterparts, they accepted that this would never happen. Anna Durie was less compliant. Her opening salvo was mild, she contacted the IWGC seeking reassurance that it really was her son's body in Corkscrew Cemetery and simply stated she desired he be repatriated at her expense. With permission refused, she visited Corkscrew where she met a Captain Chanter. Claiming to be from the IWGC, he was placing flowers for families on graves; she was distraught by what she discovered. Situated in the midst of mines and proposed railway tracks, even the IWGC admitted, 'it was in a "most desolate area"'. Chanter 'let slip' that Corkscrew burials would be incorporated into Loos Cemetery as the land was being reclaimed by the French and that some families were organising exhumations and repatriations; perhaps this planted an idea in her mind.[50] A letter queried the Commission's right to soldiers' bodies and requested she might 'buy a zinc coffin for him'; she wanted 'to remove Captain Durie's body from the blanket it had been buried in and place it into a coffin so that he would not lie in the cold earth.'[51] Refused, this was the last pleasant communication the two sides exchanged.

Durie would not let the matter rest. Seeking a groundswell of public opinion, she mobilised Canadian bereaved via the press. Increasingly antagonistic letters were dispatched to the IWGC, Canadian MPs, even Prime Minister Arthur Meighen, whom she seemingly waylaid in a Toronto hotel, arguing that as American soldiers were being repatriated, Canadians should be too. In her grief, she felt that Canada should shoulder the cost (approximately) C$150million (£1,043,804,870). Meighen listened sympathetically and instructed the Canadian High Commissioner in the UK to contact the IWGC on behalf of this 'very estimable' individual.[52] The Commission remained intractable.

It was not only Canadians whom she lobbied. By 1921, she was a familiar figure on the old Western Front, mingling among pilgrims, voicing her beliefs, 'trying to raise [them] out of their complacency'; even the kindly Reverend Molyneux, himself closely connected with the Battlefield Pilgrimages, begged her, unsuccessfully, to desist.[53] Now almost under surveillance whenever she was sighted in Corkscrew, when a sign stating 'No Bodies To Be Removed' appeared, she tore it into pieces. Major W.S. Brown, the area superintendent informed the Commission, 'I regret I found her to be most unreasonable and one of the most difficult women I have ever had to deal with while engaged in this work.'[54] Almost demented by grief, she had told Brown that should Arthur's body be moved when the cemetery amalgamation occurred, she 'would shoot' whoever removed him.

Things would get worse. On 1 August 1921, Brown learned that the grave had been disturbed. Working by night, two Frenchmen had exhumed Arthur's body, placing it in the coffin she had purchased. By a macabre twist, the horse waiting outside the cemetery had bolted, broken its cart and, badly injured, had subsequently been destroyed. With no means of transporting the body, it was reinterred.[55] However, she pinned a note to Arthur's (still then a) cross, saying she would return.

Undeterred, by mid-1924 she stepped up the pressure, writing to all and sundry, including Commissioner Rudyard Kipling, himself a bereaved father. The IWGC were increasingly worried about what might happen when Corkscrew was finally amalgamated, about which 'the French insist'.[56] Her actions may have been behind the delay. As promised, in January 1925, the IWGC communicated their intentions to her. Her reply astounded them; her level of knowledge about the plans and the cemetery led them to conclude, 'this lady must have an agent in this country who is watching our movements.'[57] Was the mysterious Captain Chanter a mole? Aware of the power of the press, she launched a public relations campaign in Toronto newspapers generating the adverse publicity the IWGC so dreaded and had finally quashed in England. She claimed that the Commission had broken their 'vow' not to disturb the bodies; economising with the truth she stated Corkscrew contained '215 Canadian bodies', when only thirty-six were Canadian.[58] Although some politicians objected to the amalgamation, and questions were asked in the Canadian Parliament, the storm subsided and in the summer the move went ahead.

With Arthur now interred in Grave 19, Row 20, Durie was ready. The new cemetery being denuded of turf and flowers, and the ground well turned, the exhumation would be easier to conceal. She arrived in France in July, meeting up again with Chanter who had made the necessary arrangements.[59] However, he now apparently informed her that contrary to her expectations, and blaming the 1921 debacle, they could not use a coffin to transport Arthur's body, a significant blow.

At dawn on 26 July 1925, she seemingly questioned her actions. Using two hired grave-robbers, Arthur's remains would be removed and placed in a valise for his return journey to Canada. To provide Arthur with what she deemed a Christian resting place, she had done the very thing she had sought to avoid, desecrated his remains. Whatever her inner reservations, she organised the elaborate interment of which she had long dreamed. Unaware of the robbery, it was an article in the *Toronto Daily Star* on 22 August 1925 describing Captain Arthur Durie's 'reverent' funeral service at St James' Cemetery, Toronto, which alerted the Commission. 'After eight years of effort,' she had 'succeeded in obtaining custody of his remains.'[60] His 10ft tall memorial bears two striking resemblances to IWGC cemeteries. Shaped uncannily like the Blomfield Cross of Sacrifice, one of the two inscriptions reads, 'His Name Liveth For Evermore'. Perhaps, like so many of the bereaved, Durie had come to admire what the Commission had created – as long as her son's remains were elsewhere.

The IWGC began an investigation. The 5 September 1925 findings were macabre. Rather than being opened to its whole length, the coffin had been forced open, the contents 'scraped out'; some bones and fragments of uniform remained inside the coffin which had been reburied.[61] Aware of the potential for body-snatchers and a black market, even of bodies being 'kidnapped', the French police were called in. 'Goodness knows the dreadful things that might happen once it became known that this could be done', one memo notes. The outraged French authorities wanted to cross the Atlantic and interview Durie, the obvious suspect. Aware that this could be interpreted as hounding a distraught, bereaved mother and that additional publicity may potentially lead to copycat actions, the Commission restrained them.

The inscribing of gravestones continued. In 1928, 'Mrs A Durie, Toronto', received communication D21078 signed by Fabian Ware. This requested she forward the sum of 13s 8d as payment for her chosen epitaph for her son Captain W.A.P. Durie buried in Loos Cemetery, 'He took the only way / And followed it / Unto the glorious end'. The payment was subsequently returned, the gravestone never materialised, Arthur's name was removed from the Loos cemetery register. The eloquent space between Graves 18 and 20, stands as visible testimony to Durie's tenacity – and grief.

To the Commission, Durie was a 'most unpleasant and unreasonable woman'.[62] What they failed to understand – and may have done had there been at least one bereaved woman among their ranks, was she had become demented by anger, the second stage of the grieving process.[63] The epitaph she chose for her son summarises her own actions, she had followed through her plan unto what she perceived as its 'glorious end'. The Canadian Dictionary of Biography recognises she had 'almost lost her senses in this one regard'. With her goal achieved she returned to semi-obscurity, although until her 1933 death she frequently broadcast her long poem 'Vimy Ridge' on local radio, commemorating the intense sacrifices of Canadian troops and remembering the beloved son who had played his part in this most devastating battle. She had answered the question posed across the British Empire,' to whom do the dead belong?'

A Tale of Two (Warring) Ladies

A YouGov survey conducted between May 2019 and May 2020 indicated that the Royal British Legion (RBL) was the UK's 15th most popular charity, 95 per cent of those surveyed had heard of it, of these, only 3 per cent had a 'negative' and 15 per cent a 'neutral' opinion.[64] It did not reveal how many of the 82 per cent 'positive' interviewees knew that the RBL's symbolic Poppy owed its origins to two, at times warring, ladies, French-born Anna Guérin and American Moina Michael.

Guérin had appeared on the anglophone lecture circuit in the years before war broke out. Speaking for the Alliance Française, in 1914 she was commissioned to lecture in America. For as long as America remained neutral, she avoided war-related topics although she would do a little discreet fundraising for French war causes. Once American soldiers were fighting on French soil, her war talks earned her the reputation of 'the most compelling wartime speaker'.[65] She was returning to Europe for further engagements when the Armistice was signed. Optimism that her fundraising days were behind her was dashed when she witnessed the full impact of war on French women and children, especially those in the formerly Occupied Areas. Touring her devastated homeland, she noticed children near the (then makeshift) American cemetery at Romagne making 'wreaths of brilliant red poppies for the graves of overseas soldiers'.[66] Hoping to use the new Victory Loan to rally American support, in early 1919 she founded the 'Ligue des enfants de France et d'Amérique'. She anticipated boosting fundraising at the talks she proposed to give in America about French children's pitiful plight by selling a symbolic poppy (or tag) made by those for whom the donations were intended. Her poppy-selling mission was underway; harnessing the local press to promote her talks, when proclaimed the '"Poppy Lady of France" … my joy was so deep tears filled my eyes and I could hardly contain my emotion.'[67]

Publicists with whom she worked frequently blurred the line between advertisement and article, references to Guérin and her 'Poppy Days' for the Children of France, abound. On 23 October 1919, *The Baltimore Sun* alerted readers that 'A national campaign to aid the destitute children of devastated France will be started in this city on Saturday with a tag day for the Franco-American Children's League', headed by Mme Guérin, 'three times decorated by the French Government for her war work, who has been in this city for several days'. Variously described as a 'delegate from France' and 'Mme Guérin of Paris', the first anniversary of the Armistice 'will be celebrated today, when the public will be tagged with red, white and blue poppies'. A 'number of girls prominent in society' had mustered to help the 'drive for funds to be used for the orphans of devastated France'. To forestall any potential scepticism, the beneficiaries were 'under the auspices of the French Government'.[68] Sellers wore their own poppy badge apparently inscribed with poet John McRae's words, 'In Flanders Fields the Poppies Blow.'

Building up to America's 1920 'Memorial Day', with the 'needs of French children in the devastated sections' remaining overwhelming, Guérin's name constantly appeared in newspapers.[69] Readers learned that 'women and children are living in cellars and caves and mines, in fact any hole that will provide a little shelter; 450,000 of these are children', over half of whom were orphaned by the Germans.[70] Citizens, often with state governors' endorsement, were encouraged to dig deep. Guérin criss-crossed America, speaking, rallying support for the 'Ligue', being imaginative – when a 'Poppy Day Ball' risked being rained off, it was rebranded a 'Poppy Day Cyclone!' – raising $2,000 ($25,639).[71] Guérin was intent on linking Americans' sacrifice in France to both French children and the poppy, telling an audience in Salt Lake City, 'Our Yankee boys are now sleeping in Flanders' fields where the poppies will ever bloom in springtime. The poppy day we shall never forget. We must not forget.'[72] Donors often like to hear how their gifts have been spent, on this occasion 'a dairy to give milk to the wasted children of Verdun. The dairy is called Utah.'[73]

Sensing the tide turning away from direct fundraising for the French children, she knew she must start nurturing the manufacturing arm which provided work for so many in France. With increasing demand for silk poppies, disabled French soldiers had started producing them in hospitals, this idea gained traction. In 1921, the poppy was widely promoted as the tag for America's 'Memorial Day', held on 30 May until 1970. The enterprise had grown so large that an Isobel Mack was in France overseeing production and the logistics of shipping the symbolic flower overseas. The 13 April *Indianapolis Star* announced '2,000,000 Poppies Arrive in America'. The American Legion and its female ancillary organisations now actively supported the Ligue appealing for every American citizen to wear the symbol on 30 May. Despite the undoubted success of the Memorial Day poppy sales, Guérin was concerned that the Legion was reneging on its promise that the poppy would be its representative emblem. Attending the November 1921 American Legion Convention in Missouri, for once her powers of persuasion failed and, incongruously, the daisy was the chosen symbol (although the American Legion's Women's Auxiliary kept faith with the poppy). For the next two years, Memorial Day saw Daisy not Poppy Drives. Then in January 1922, the Legion, including the Women's Auxiliary, withdrew its support from the Ligue, wishing to focus on American veterans' needs. That there were two competing Leagues for French children, a high-profile court case and mounting ill-feeling between them did not help Guérin's cause. Nevertheless, for a short while, poppies would continue to be sourced, at least in part, from France. But there was another issue for her to confront; American academic Moina Michael, with a similar vision to Guérin, also wanted to adopt the poppy symbol, but an American-manufactured one. Conflict between the two poppy champions became rancorous. In 1922, French-manufactured poppies made their last appearance, making up the deficit in the American supply.[74] By 1924, the Veterans of Foreign Wars, who until 1923 had supported the French initiative, had patented its own "Buddy Poppy", made by veterans. It guaranteed that all poppies were, and remain, the work of bona fide disabled and needy veterans.[75] Guérin had lost the American battle.

Guérin's vision was not restricted to America. In early July 1921, she visited Canada to enlist the support of the Canadian Great War Veterans' Association. Her idea appealed; Canadians enthusiastically adopted the poppy as their Remembrance symbol. Once again, the focus would shift from French to Canadian manufacture, assumed by Canadian veterans by 1923. South Africa, Australia and New Zealand became and remained enthusiastic supporters, the New Zealand story taking an unexpected turn.[76] In September 1921, the New Zealand Returned Soldiers' Association had agreed to launch an inaugural Poppy Appeal which, like the one planned for Great Britain, would mark Armistice Day. An order for 350,000 small and 16,000 large silk poppies was placed. However, delayed by five months the post ship, *Westmoreland* arrived too late. Determined not to waste the emblems, Poppy Day was postponed until 'ANZAC Day', 25 April, already a national holiday commemorating the Gallipoli Landings. The success was overwhelming, 'Sold Out' by midday, a total £13,166 (£669,732) was raised of which roughly 25 per cent went to France, the remainder earmarked for New Zealand's own needy veterans.[77] Guérin's poppy symbol, if not her French manufacturers, had taken root on four continents.

The 2018 Royal British Legion Poppy Appeal 'raised more than £50,000,000 from the British public' with its sale of poppies and poppy-related goods, a far cry from the first British Poppy Day when Guérin subsidised the British Legion's purchases (subsequently refunded from sales) because, despite her August 1921 meeting with Sir Douglas Haig, the Legion was sceptical.[78] This reluctance to invest in poppies may have stemmed from the national mood, captured in *The Times* (19 October 1921). This reported an unwillingness to promote what was seen as 'another flag day', notwithstanding the belief that 'Poppy Day' would be a much more important function than the ordinary flag day.[79] Weariness with flag days is hardly surprising; the first wartime one (supporting Belgian refugees) had occurred on 1 September 1914 with no respite throughout the war. Although the 1921 appeal gained significant coverage, no contemporary British newspaper appears to credit Guérin with initiating the effort, and even 'widows and children of French soldiers' are more usually referred to as 'French peasants'. Officers' and soldiers' 'widows, wives and daughters' were requested to offer to sell the tokens in aid of the British Legion; the French merely profiting by supplying the 'red poppies'.[80] That women were predominantly involved in poppy selling mirrored what had happened in America and indeed wartime flag-days, where men were often the enthusiastic purchasers and leisured women the sellers.[81] 1921 was the only year that British poppies were sourced in France, wounded British veterans subsequently undertook their manufacture at The Poppy Factory, Richmond, and from 1926 at Lady Haig's Poppy Factory, Edinburgh.

At much the same time that Guérin was watching the youngsters in Romagne, teacher Moina Michael's thoughts were also turning to poppies. Having been holidaying in Germany when war broke out and assisting Americans to return, like herself, to their homeland, she had been desperate to serve in France with the YMCA. Rejected due to her age, she worked stateside under the auspices of the YMCA, her tasks included escorting the bereaved to a New York hospital morgue. This had familiarised her to a sense of the 'loss and the sacrifice', and the need for this not to be seen as having been made in vain. It may have accentuated her own feeling that as a spinster with no kin at the Front, she was excluded from this great sorority of suffering.[82] Only those in the direct bloodline could wear a mourning armband or the soldier's mother's Gold Star.

On 8 November 1918, Michael was in the YMCA offices awaiting the appearance of conference delegates. Reaching for *The Ladies' Home Journal,* the page fell open on John McRae's poem 'In Flanders Field' and she experienced an epiphany. She subsequently explained, 'I pledged my soul to that crimson cup flower of Flanders, the red poppy which caught the sacrificial blood of ten million men dying for the Peace of the World.'[83] Determination was one of her many talents, compassion among her virtues. These would combine and further propel the poppy onto the world remembrance stage. Penning her 'Response', she poetically vowed: 'We shall keep faith [with] you who sleep in Flanders Fields'. One of the so-called surplus women of the war, unmarried, childless, Michael had given birth to her 'spirit child', the poppy. She showed her poem to the delegates and, when they handed her $10 for organising their conference accommodation, she rushed onto the street, determined to invest this money in poppies. She finally found some silk ones in Wannamakers. The 'young assistant whose brother had recently been killed and was sleeping behind the battle lines in France' shared her enthusiasm.[84] She sensed she was reading the national mood. With the delegates now wearing a poppy, the first exchange of poppies and cash for a war cause had occurred. As she explained in a 7 December 1918 letter to her Congressman, the poppy symbol's additional benefit was that all could wear it in support of the Boys.

Despite this initial enthusiasm, the idea seemed to stall; Michael lobbied unsuccessfully at the YMCA December 1918 conference for the YMCA to adopt the poppy as its symbol. By February 1919, she was back teaching in Georgia and it was only in June 1919 that she was reminded that poppies chimed with people's sentiments. In Milwaukee, a rapturous crowd was welcoming returning Doughboys. Coffee booths, supported by the American Legion, had been bedecked with poppies but, in return for donations amounting to several hundred dollars, crowds had stripped these, each wanting to wear the symbol now associated with Flanders Fields. Legion member Mary Henecy suggested to colleagues that they distribute poppies in the run up to Memorial Day.[85] With Michael lobbying hard for the American Legion to adopt the symbol, Georgian delegates promised their support at the forthcoming American Legion National Conference in Ohio which Michael attended. Guérin, with her wider vision that the poppy would extend to all Allied nations and her desire to assist French children through the Ligue, was also present. Both women now claimed that the 'Poppy' idea was hers and a deep antagonism ensued. In her 1941 autobiography, Michael does not even name her French counterpart, simply referring to her as '"the French visitor" or Madame _____.' Other sources suggest that Guérin withheld permission to be named.[86] What is apparent is that being so caught up in the struggle for ownership of the poppy symbol, the women overlooked how their initial aims were very different: Guérin's energies were focused on French widows and children, Michael's on veterans and keeping faith with the dead. Michael would lobby government and organisations on veterans' behalf but considered that French-made poppies competed with the American ones and that funds raised in America should go to American veterans.

While Guérin had sought publicity via talks and, up to a point, stunts such as the Poppy Cyclone, Michael promoted her vision differently, lobbying the press and sending 'letters by the thousands ... to every possible educating group'.[87] Once the American Legion adopted the American-made poppy, Michael may have felt that the final triumph was hers. Both women invested significant amounts of physical and emotional energy in the Flanders poppy; by the mid-1920s, thanks largely to Guérin's more international efforts, it had flowered across all anglophone nations. Michael's 'spirit child' had almost 'consumed her', and she experienced some bitterness that, irrespective of her efforts, which had 'indirectly raised $70 million dollars', she herself 'had barely enough to buy actual necessities.'[88]

Public honours were showered upon her. In 1940, the American Legion cited her 'most distinguished and humanitarian service to our sick and disabled comrades and their dependents'.[89] At her 1944 military funeral, soldiers from the University of Georgia and the American Legion stood guard, red poppies fastened to their bayonets. A blanket of 3,000 poppies designed by veterans in the shape of a cross covered her coffin. A carved poppy and entwined torch adorn her tombstone. Months later, the US government christened a 'liberty ship' the *Moina Michael* and on 9 November 1948, exactly thirty years after her vision of the Remembrance Poppy, a three-cent postage stamp was issued to honour her efforts – which, as she complained she had had to pay for a stamp on every letter she ever posted, even for Legion correspondence, she may have considered ironic. Yet despite these accolades, the poppy being America's official Remembrance flower, and the huge sums of money that were raised, it is not widely recognised as a symbol among Americans today.

Guérin's poppy remained but her name faded. Although it was she who lobbied the British, Canadian, Australian and New Zealand Legions for the poppy which over the last century has come to symbolise the sacrifices of the Great War, her name remains almost unknown. Even in her native

France, the official symbol (adopted 1925) was the bleuet or cornflower, first proposed in 1916 by two women who have faded from history, nurse and war widow Suzanne Lenhardt and Charlotte Malleterre.[90] This once ubiquitous wildflower symbolising delicacy and innocence, manufactured by veterans, remains France's token of Remembrance and a fundraising vehicle for those referred to as 'les mutilés de guerre'.

Irrespective of their antagonism, Guérin and Michael's legacy is greater than their feud. Thanks to their vision, the homely poppy that determinedly flourished across France and Flanders' blood-swept lands still provides an income for war-injured personnel and support for dependents of those who gave all they could give. When we purchase a poppy in the Poppy Appeal during the fortnight preceding Remembrance Sunday, we too are 'Keep[ing] the faith', with the symbol and all that it has come to represent. And it is an RBL poppy which accompanies many pilgrims when they visit a CWGC cemetery. Having gazed around in awe, they reverently place their token, be it elaborate wreath or simple 'In Remembrance' wooden cross with its glued poppy on the grave marker of their long dead family member, reassured that he or she will continue to sleep peacefully in this Jekyll-inspired English country garden created, initially with such resentment, in these foreign fields.

CHAPTER 3

Changing Others' Lives

To Russia (and the Central Powers) with Love

By November 1918, Central Europe was starving. The Armistice made little material difference to millions of 'enemy' mothers and children, largely because, to the outrage of many, Great Britain's naval blockade that restricted the entry of goods into German ports continued for a further eight months. The tactic aimed to weaken German morale thus leading to acceptance of the harsh Treaty of Versailles. Groups of predominantly female activists including many Quakers (Friends) decided to challenge what they considered a barbaric strategy which harmed the most vulnerable and innocent citizens.

On 4 January 1919, *Westminster Gazette* reported that the Women's International League (WIL) had applied 'for permission to send 1,000,000 rubber teats' to Germany to feed 'starving babies' ... unable to suckle on 'the bone teats, now the only thing available.' Funds were desperately required to cover the £5,000 to £6,000 (£270,000 to £324,000) cost.[1] The teats were the forerunner of what Quaker Ruth Fry termed the stream of Liebensgaben [gifts of love] from a so-called victorious population to a defeated one; notes were often included assuring German mothers that British women condemned the Blockade. While some newspapers criticised this charitable endeavour, most were favourable.[2] A 25 January 1919 London meeting held to raise awareness of famine and sufferings engendered in Europe and beyond resulted in the formation of a Fight the Famine Council (FFC). Perhaps intentionally, both 'Germany' and the Blockade were unmentioned.

In Cologne, British soldiers forming part of the Army of Occupation shared their rations with starving children; in Vienna children were without milk or any fats. Even MPs expressed disquiet. By March 1919, some women who considered their Government's actions a national scandal opted for Deeds Not Words, calling a 'Lift the Hunger Blockade' rally at Trafalgar Square on 6 April 1919. Speakers to the 10,000-strong crowd included veteran suffragette, Emmeline Pethick-Lawrence. Flanked by soldiers marching four abreast (incited by a national newspaper to 'break up' the demonstration they instead joined it), she led a deputation to Downing Street to hand in their resolution, which may not have resulted in the demands being met but garnered significant publicity.[3] Another accomplished rally speaker was FFC committee member and *Manchester Guardian* journalist Evelyn Sharp. Her next day's report outspokenly condemned the blockade's disastrous effects on Germany's young. Although not a Quaker, Sharp was soon immersed in their relief work; inside information from her German-speaking journalist lover Henry Nevinson's despatches from Germany, added veracity to her heart-rending accounts of deprivation and want. Having struggled to get a passport (she was considered 'potentially subversive' partly thanks to her brandishing placards in Parliament Square), she finally arrived in Germany in May 1920.

A small number of British and American Friends had been working in Germany since early 1919. Following the signing of the Peace Treaty, the blockade was lifted in July; by the time Sharp arrived, some child-feeding programmes were functioning, but nevertheless, visible signs of deprivation abounded.[4] The Treaty of Versailles having forced the surrender of 140,000 'milch' cows, 555,000 children were deprived of this essential nutrient while postpartum mothers were too undernourished to lactate.[5] When Sharp commented on 'how few babies there were', she was told 'many had died for want of milk'.[6] The basic necessities of life were non-existent, soap was composed of 'grit and grease', clothes, even bicycle tyres, were made of paper. With the draconian reparations being far greater than Germany's ability to pay, the situation could only deteriorate. Seemingly every child in Berlin was 'malnourished'; cats and dogs had long since disappeared from the streets having all been eaten.[7] Outraged by the extent of German children's deprivation, Sharp was nevertheless moved by British people's extensive generosity; in the first eighteen months of peace, they donated today's equivalent of £6,904,170 in money and gifts to support the FFC mission.[8] Many letters accompanying the gifts averred, 'We did not fight for 5 years in order to watch German children dying of hunger after the war was over.'[9]

Several British women were involved with the various Quaker relief efforts working across Central Europe including Vienna. Born into one of the most prestigious Quaker families, Dr Hilda Clark had worked in northern France with the Friends War Victims Relief Committee (FWVRC) of which Fry was general secretary from November 1914. The Clark/Fry relationship could be prickly as Clark's vision, autonomy and self-determination could lead her to act on her own initiative rather than through the Committee, although her total dedication to the programme was never questioned.[10] According to co-worker Francesca Wilson, she was quick to grasp a problem as a whole, and had the kind of constructive imagination that saw a way of tackling it, as well as a faith that overcame the numerous, seemingly insurmountable obstacles which abounded when the Quakers arrived in Vienna to 'find out the truth of the sad stories of suffering which were filtering through the few open channels of communication'.[11] Among Clark's qualities was her ability to delegate responsibility to those she considered able and, having done so, allowing the individual to develop their own ideas resulting in her being surrounded by a strong and loyal team; 'Talents were used, not stifled by autocracy or entangled in a bureaucratic machine.'[12]

Clark arrived in Vienna in May 1919, where life for aid workers was unremittingly hard. Through the Peace Treaty, Austria had lost 44 million of its 50 million inhabitants and crucially 90 per cent of her fertile land. Former coal supplies were in Czechoslovakia, grain in Hungary, and Austria had no money to buy these. Vienna was like a pathetic head whose body had been cut away with 'not a drop of milk' for Vienna's babies.[13] Fearful of taking even one crumb from the starving population, aid-workers lived on rations supplied by the British Army, complete with 'maggots in the ship biscuits', and messed in the freezing rooms of a former palace whose 'only glory was their size'.[14] The task facing Clark would have daunted a lesser woman: feed and clothe 64,000 starving infants, set up Welfare Clinics to attempt to stem the waves of TB and rickets, and somehow help the Viennese to stand again on their own feet. Working alongside the Save the Children Fund that soon had a presence in Vienna, one quickly devised scheme was to create a milk supply. A cow being more use than a tin of condensed milk, and with Austria having lost nearly 315,000 cattle while those remaining were of poor stock, urgent action was needed. Two hundred and fifty-five Swiss (subsequently augmented by Dutch) cows and four bulls were imported. On arrival in Austria these had been boosted by the birth of four calves. In return for the gift of a cow, farmers were bound to give 6,500 annual litres of milk per cow. As farmers could keep any calves that were born, the bulls, two of whom were named Quaker and Leo Freund, must have been in demand. This initiative turned into a highly structured agricultural relief programme; by 1921, Vienna was being supplied with 1,429,298 litres of milk, and children who had never previously tasted fresh milk received a daily pint.[15] Some young Viennese were sent to Switzerland for recuperation, jointly funded by the Friends and the Swiss authorities, occasionally with tragic consequences. Unable to face returning to the horrors of Vienna, one boy took his own life.[16]

Feeding children under the age of 6 (older ones profited from the Herbert Hoover Programme) was neither the Friends' nor Clark's only remit. Initially aided by Dr Hector Monro and subsequently joined by her partner, midwife Edith Pye, Clark turned her attention to Vienna's now non-existent hospital services – and supplies. Not one of Vienna's 60,000 hospital beds was fit for purpose. Clark reported to the Committee that there was no linen, bandages, towels or any kind of medical supply, just 'endless vegetable soup' with precious few vegetables; 50 per cent of infants of 6 months had rickets and 100 per cent of those aged 9 months.[17] Initially only 3 per cent of the children examined were not 'under-nourished, with 47 per cent of them severely under-nourished'. To many it seemed as though it was largely thanks to Clark's indomitable will and Pye's experience in infant welfare (her clinics examined 206,807 children and devised feeding programmes for many of them) that by 1922, hospitals were once again functioning. Wilson considered both women 'pure in heart and quite incorruptible'.[18]

Children and adults needed clothes, to which the Mission turned its attention. Some 76,000 garments and 100,000 yards of material (which also provided employment) were 'sold' to hundreds of needy families at the Hofburg Palace where once the bejewelled cream of Viennese society had fawned upon their Hapsburg rulers. With supplies rationed to ensure equitable distribution, stories of ragged children and their families receiving a new, warm garment thanks to generous British families who had donated money, which sometimes they themselves could ill afford, to the Clothing Depot of the Friends' Relief Mission remain heart-warming. Many children had never before seen 'clothes made of wool instead of vegetable fibre or nettles and shoes of leather instead of paper'.[19] For Friends, messages of love were stronger than the hatred still filling the newspapers.

The ongoing suffering across Central Europe soon paled into insignificance in relation to those in Russia; in the grip of civil war, the situation was close to catastrophic. In January 1920, the British Foreign Office had agreed to permit 'the export of goods for the use in children's hospitals in Russia despite the fact that the policy of the government was still one of blockade of the Russian ports'.[20] Quaker women volunteered to assist with this aid. Passports to travel to Russia, granted willingly by neither the British nor the Russian governments, were sought and finally issued. Those who were averse to assisting 'enemy' countries argued that any aid would be stolen by the demonised Red Army. Fry countered that she had seen more goods 'pilfered' from British trains than she ever encountered in Russia.[21]

Due to a drought of monumental proportions, 1921 became the Year of the Famine, increasing Russian's sufferings. Millions perished in the Volga region (among Russia's richest) and Ukraine. With near total crop failure, over 25 million people were without sustenance. Desperately needed food aid was a political hot potato exercising the minds of both the British Government and Anglican bishops, aware of ongoing persecution of Christians.[22] There were fears that aid would prop up the Bolsheviks, prolong the civil war, and place a still greater fiscal burden upon British tax-payers; withholding aid raised the real prospect of 10 million deaths. The League of Nations rejected an appeal for an international effort lest it bolster the Bolsheviks.

With its apolitical agenda, FFC entered the fray. A fundraising press campaign boosted by graphic descriptions of conditions in the famine area from respected news agencies such as Reuters, was initiated. Determined to 'prove to the [inevitable] sceptics here' that Friends actually are feeding starving Russians, journalist Sharp volunteered for the relief effort.[23] Female Friends were the only women Russia permitted to work in one of the worst hit areas, Buzuluk province (about the size of Belgium). Doubtful she would be awarded a passport, Sharp commented, 'Only the Quakers could have convinced them [the British authorities] that I was going to Russia on an unpolitical mission and not to plot the downfall of the British Constitution'.[24] She and Fry (whose chronic respiratory illness meant she had once been considered too frail to leave home), set off on 1 January 1922, reaching Buzuluk, 2,780 miles away, on 16 January 1922. Here, 'death seemed more real than life'.[25] Shortly after their arrival, relief worker nurse Violet Tillard succumbed to the inevitably widespread typhus. Despite a former baptism of fire in starving Berlin, nothing had prepared Sharp for the sights that assailed her. One look at her colleagues' faces revealed 'what horrors they had all looked upon'. She continued, 'As we left the house that [first] morning, we saw the body of a man lying face downwards in the snow. Before the day was out, I came to think he was the happiest thing that I had seen that day'.[26] *Manchester Guardian* (24 February 1922), never afraid of hard-hitting reporting, did not spare readers the extent of Russia's agony, mothers even implored strangers to 'take our children from us' to spare them a 'life worse than death'. With bodies left unburied, one Friend lost her wits and had to be evacuated, a significant undertaking because trains, if they arrived at all, could be up to one week late.

Fry's departure to raise more funds left Sharp as the only female worker. Letters to Nevinson suggest someone struggling to hold on to both her wits and her humanity. On 25 January 1922 she wrote: 'I'm not sure that it consoles me to hear that in time you get used to seeing people drop dead: it is that fatal propensity to "get used to things" ... that causes most of the cruelty in the world to go on.' There is no evidence that she did 'get used' to it and her accounts in both *Manchester Guardian* and *Daily Herald* proved shocking eye-openers, and effective fund-raisers. The coming of spring brought signs of significant improvement and the programme was scaled back. Some 30 million people were affected by the famine with 3 million dying of typhus alone. The international Quakers' herculean efforts found little favour with the Soviet government, who saw bread as a propaganda weapon that could be used against them. Offers of relief in subsequent famines were declined.

Sanity had not yet been restored to Europe and a new disaster was about to befall Germans struggling to pay the reparations imposed by the vindictive Peace Treaty. In early 1923, Britain abstained at a meeting of the War Reparations Committee when Germany was declared to be in default over payments of coal to France. On 11 January, acting on President Poincaré's orders, France and Belgium occupied Germany's industrial heartland, the Ruhr, causing significant further suffering and renewed famine, the most vulnerable again paid the heaviest price. Twelve-year-old Käthe Bosse noted, 'The French are doing more bad things ... they have broken the Peace Agreement and it will surely do much harm to our industries ... nobody knows what will happen.'[27] With France proud of her firm stance against her former foes, Frenchwomen's reactions ranged from sending tiny ill-afforded monetary gifts via a charity founded specifically to assist German children affected by the Occupation, stating they were embarrassed by their government, to cheering in cinemas when newsreels of advancing soldiers were shown.[28]

Once again, Sharp was soon on the spot, one of a tiny group of pioneer women foreign correspondents in post-war Germany. She started turning her impressions of life in both 'occupied' and 'unoccupied' Germany into newspaper articles and stories published in *Daily Herald* and *Manchester Guardian*, alerting British readers to the ongoing German suffering – which was being questioned by sections of the Northcliffe press. When sceptics quizzed her about her sources, she replied that she had been on the ground, graphically describing the 'starved and sparsely clad' children and the prevalence of tuberculosis.[29] For both Fry and Sharp, although the horrors of Buzuluk, caused primarily by a failure of the harvest, were materially greater, being a natural catastrophe some light was visible at the end of the tunnel; the man-made situation in Germany could, with compassion and wisdom, have been averted.

Daily Herald's 'Special Correspondent', Sharp was quick to share impressions of the Occupied towns and to point out the 'knock-on' effect of the occupation on 'non-occupied' Germany, on both industrial workers and the small industries, often run by women, such as 'glove-making and stocking-embroidery', upon whom a family's welfare frequently depended.[30] When these collapsed, so too did a family's ability to feed itself, exacerbated by the plunging value of the mark. She felt that to a 'harassed, tormented, apprehensive population ... the shock of the occupation ... seems to have been the last straw.'[31] Hard-hitting short stories, such as 'The Cheap Holiday and What Aunt Johanna Thought About It', sought to debunk the myth proclaimed by one character, 'there's no more distress in Germany than there is in other countries'; they feel Germany was a good choice as a cheap holiday destination. Going to Belgium 'where the mark or whatever it is hasn't slumped at all, would have been *tragic*.'[32] The holidaymakers refuse to realise that the 'shops filled with luxuries' are Berliners' personal possessions, being sold in the hopes of raising enough money (from complacent tourists) to buy a loaf of bread. One of Sharp's colleagues who 'had witnessed the Russian revolution', believed Germany to be suffering a greater economic catastrophe with 'scarcely a ray of light on the horizon'.[33] Pacifist Sharp was aware that the seeds of another war were being sown. Gaining an interview with General Jacquemot at the French [Occupation] HQ, to each probing question he replied, 'the French were there to collect Reparations.'[34] She was horrified by the visible indoctrination of young French squaddies via 'Hate' posters in their barracks. Touring Germany for three weeks for additional copy, in Dresden she noted hotel guests' nervousness when what she called 'Hitler boys' paraded through the streets. Only returning to Germany in 1931, her agonised prophecies of the immediate post-war years seemed to be coming true. The pacifist guitar-strumming youths of 1920 had been 'replaced by those who had undergone severe privation as post-war children'; they held 'revolvers not guitars in their hands.'[35] A retributive peace, hunger, poverty, unemployment and a crippling Occupation had resulted in something sinister in the German air.

Images that Saved the Children

On a cloudy mid-April day in 1919, two respectable women descended on Trafalgar Square. Visitors to the National Gallery, to St Martins-in-the-Fields, or those simply idling were handed a disturbing pamphlet with a photograph of an Austrian girl that retains the power to shock. This 2½-year-old appears barely human. According to the caption, she was one of 'millions of such children starving today'. The police arrived and, still distributing their leaflets, the women were escorted away; one would march into the history books as co-founder of the world's greatest children's charity. On 15 May (the day of Nurse Edith Cavell's state funeral, thereby deflating press interest), crowds flocked to the Mansion House where the two women, Barbara Ayrton Gould, Eglantyne Jebb, and the pamphlet printers were charged under the Defence of the Realm Act (DORA) with procuring publication and distributing printed material that had not been passed by the censor. Conducting her own defence, Jebb argued that it had never occurred to her that humanitarian aid had anything to do with DORA, which, with the war over, was surely redundant. Evelyn Sharp (who had struggled to gain admittance to the court such was the press of people) wrote, 'she swept aside the technical arguments … and spoke on the Christian aspect of what she had done.' Sharp vividly described this woman whose 'gentleness covered a fire of the Spirit'.[36] Following the 'Guilty' verdict both defendants were fined £5 (£270). There was no doubt who had won the moral victory and Director of Public Prosecutions Sir Archibald Bodkin donated a symbolic £5 towards their cause.[37] This, closely followed by the 2s 6d donated by Jebb's housekeeper, were the first donations to the as yet unborn Save the Children Fund (SCF). Seizing a publicity opportunity, in an open letter to the Press, Jebb argued that Cavell's statement, 'We must have no hatred or bitterness in our hearts towards anyone', could be lived out practically by saving Europe's starving children, an action of which the nation's dead martyr would undoubtedly have approved.

Aware that a token £5 2s 6d would do little to alleviate Central European distress, the FFC took the bold step of hiring the Royal Albert Hall (seating capacity 8,000) for a 19 May 1919 fundraising rally. Using cajolery or flattery, FFC begged supporters and their friends to attend. This was not the last time that the putative SCF would risk spending significant sums to raise larger ones. Inevitably, not all the capacity crowd was sympathetic. Sceptical about the veracity of the reported suffering, some arrived with pocketsful of rotten fruit to hurl at speakers who advocated feeding 'enemy' children. The meeting was opened by left-wing journalist Henry Brailsford, supported by Robert Smillie, President of the Miners' Federation, which became one of SCF's most powerful and generous champions. Jebb was next. Unlike her sister Dorothy, MP Charlie Buxton's wife, Jebb was unused to public speaking but her statement, 'it is impossible for us to watch children starve to death without making an effort to save them', was no less powerful for its simplicity. In contrast, Buxton's method was dramatic: waving a tin of condensed milk aloft, she proclaimed: 'There is more practical reality in this tin than in all the creeds.'[38] To tumultuous applause and a spontaneous public collection, SCF was born.

With Jebb already Honorary Secretary to the FFC, Buxton, who in April 1919 had raised the idea with the FFC committee of a child-focused charity, accepted this role. Close since their childhood days, the sisters were excellent collaborators, knowing how to harness Buxton's political know-how and press contacts with Jebb's vision and management skills to benefit this new child-focused charity. Presented as a non-political organisation in order to garner maximum public support, the founder members, many of whom had contacts with, or were members of, other campaigning organisations, realised that a total separation from these was imperative. Many FFC members were Left-leaning activists, privately at least, unimpressed by the new League of Nations, arguing it represented 'the power and wealth of the many concentrated in the hands of the few', condemning the exclusion of Germany, Austria and Russia as fatal flaws.'[39] Others, not believing that the charity with its international humanitarian vision of friendship between nations would appeal to a war-weary, still Germanophobic British public, prophesised its rapid demise.[40] Buxton, who enjoyed the cut and thrust of politics and was a committed campaigner on her husband's behalf, soon found the non-political aspect of her SCF work irksome, although her deep concerns about the starving children in Central Europe and Russia never diminished. To help 'crystallise in the minds of the public the distance between SCF and political movements', Buxton stepped aside in June 1919 leaving Jebb as the charity's public face.[41]

Nevertheless, the political, at least in these early days, was never far from the surface; supporters quietly pressurised MPs and the Lords to revise the peace treaties with Germany. Had such pressure been widely known, it may have been highly detrimental because the idea of feeding German children was anathema to cross-sections of the population. *The Scotsman* (13 November 1919) carried a long letter from war-decorated Red Cross worker Agnes Romanes who, serving in Soissons, had witnessed 'a good deal of the devastation and heart-breaking misery caused by the German occupation'. She was unashamed to have 'no use' for the type of humanitarianism that seemed to favour enemy children over Allied ones. Wanting to focus her efforts on children in recently German-occupied France, she sought 'like-minded people' to join her. From the ensuing lively newspaper correspondence, others agreed. Helen Neaves noted that £17,000 (£918,000) had been spent on 'our malignant enemies' Germany and Austria, while Serbian and Italian children had merely benefited to the sum of £675 (£36,450). Those who supported the new SCF were quick to point out Allied countries were receiving significant amounts of aid while Germany, Austria and Russia were dependent upon charity; furthermore, not having made the war, all children were simply innocent victims. Irrespective of the divided opinions, that SCF was now able to provide aid totalling nearly £1,000,000 today is testimony to fundraisers' skills and public generosity. Further exercising correspondents' minds was that with Britain demonstrably still not a 'land fit for heroes', and with charity supposedly beginning at home, why were donations not being made to 'our poor clergy at home and their children? Are we to neglect our friends to assist our enemies?'[42] But for those familiar with the harrowing realities of Central European starvation, British children's suffering paled in comparison. Unpopular with some Committee members, a motion was eventually passed to change the Constitution to encompass British children.

Whether wariness in further stirring up public opinion lay behind his rebuttal is impossible to know, but in December 1919, Jebb (now SCF's highly visible face), contacted Randall Davidson, Archbishop of Canterbury, requesting him to issue an appeal to Anglican congregations to support SCF's humanitarian work. His refusal, with the added comment that Davidson imagined the Pope, should he receive a similar request, would agree with him, spurred her on to find out for herself. On 23 December 1919, *Westminster Gazette* reported the result of her letter to His Holiness: a meeting (it overran its allocated time by nearly two hours), and an encyclical instructing all Catholic churches throughout the world to collect money for the distressed children of Europe on Holy Innocents' Day. This was the first time that a Pope had openly supported a non-Catholic charity with an immediate donation of £25,000 (£1,162,500). Like so many charismatic individuals, 'when [Jebb] spoke everything else seemed to lose its importance, and one agreed to do whatever she wishes.'[43] The Church of England, non-Conformists, and other faith groups, fell into line; 28 December 1919 was to be 'a day of prayer and alms on behalf of the starving children of Europe and the Near East'. This observance was unique in its united appeal, especially as the collection was ringfenced for the SCF. Told to foreswear amusements for the day and put their hands in their pockets, churchgoers obeyed. Donations flooded in from far and wide, including the Pitcairn Islanders (more than 3,000 miles from any continent) who 'loaded up two boxes and five barrels of supplies and flagged down a passing ship to carry them to Europe, care of the Fund.'[44] The Jebb sisters had placed a girdle of compassion around the earth; starving children were seen simply as innocent victims, not the enemies' offspring.

Never one to sit back on her laurels, building on this momentum, Jebb worked to develop an International Union of the Save the Children Fund in Geneva which, as the proposed home of the League of Nations and the established home of the International Red Cross (ICRC), was becoming the humanitarian centre of the world. On 5 January 1920, the Union was inaugurated in the Palais de l'Athénée which, in 1863, had witnessed the birth of the ICRC. With former Swiss President and now President of the ICRC Gustav Ador on the new International Union's board, the Pope represented on the council, the ICRC having offered its patronage, SCF was on the world's stage coordinating reciprocal child welfare aid between nations. As director of the British and the International Union,

Jebb travelled extensively between England and Switzerland, sapping her rapidly declining health (due to a recurrence of the thyroid issues she had experienced in young adulthood). Just ten months after the image of the starving Austrian baby had shocked the British public and outraged the authorities, the Union's first international conference was held with delegates from former belligerent countries.

The Fund may have become international, so too was children's plight. By September 1920, the estimate of 13 million 'starved and diseased children' in Central Europe may have been conservative. With disease knowing no national boundaries, a speaker at one fundraising event who had travelled to these famine areas, also hinted that if 'nothing were done to halt the spread of infectious diseases, these "might extend even to our own shores"'.[45] With the Spanish 'flu pandemic barely abated, this provided pause for thought and prompted donations. By October 1920, SCF held reserves of £632,945 (£31,000,000) with an additional £38,000 (£1,865,800) worth of clothing and material; £21,000 (£1,000,000) was donated by the Miners' Federation. As the most virulent Germanophobia abated, some supporters believed that Jebb had 'focus[ed] humanity's distracted conscience on what to do first by singling out the youngest generation and concentrating on that' and had channelled negative energy into a different, more positive direction resulting in a softening of attitudes.[46]

Jebb was being assailed by conflicting, strident demands: were Austrian children being helped more than German ones? Were Russian émigré children getting too much milk? Did, the public demanded to know, left-wing committee members support Bolshevism? Should Mrs Lloyd George's name feature on the headed notepaper? Such questions needed tactful handling and above all, 'the cry of the child for bread', heard.[47] Looking much older than her years, taxing herself ever further, Jebb was a prominent speaker on the international conference circuit, dubbed, due to her premature white hair, 'The White Flame'. Oblivious to her appearance, her hallmark brown clothes were often 'dreadfully grubby ... and I fear getting ragged as well'; her clothes seemed unimportant while children went hungry.[48] At times, she confessed to feeling suicidal at the thought of the world's misery, while in-fighting among various relief agencies, not to mention their self-interest, appalled her, writing in November 1920 to her mother, 'Alas for human nature.'[49]

Equally worrying were the sisters' 1920 and 1921 visits to Germany. Despite the FFC, which received extensive grants from SCF's herculean efforts, intense sufferings continued. Buxton feared that, 'the hatred felt by the German people who have to look on helplessly at the suffering of their children and the elderly could have disastrous consequences for the future.[50] The German cause was not helped by the FFC representative refusing to visit England to present the country's case for aid. Fundraising was perforce unremitting and new ideas needed.

During her three years in Vienna with the FFC, Francesca Wilson was introduced to what we would now call an art therapist, Franz Cizek who worked with traumatised Viennese and Serbian youngsters. The idea of fundraising via an Exhibition of Austrian and Serbian Children's Art took root. Prepared to spend money to raise money and capitalising on a growing interest in children's art, SCF hired the British Institute of Industrial Art in Knightsbridge. Postcards and other examples of the children's art work were reproduced to whet the public appetite and to boost funds. *The Times, Burlington Magazine* and the *Daily Sketch* (19 November 1920) covered the opening. 'It is a desperate appeal that is being made to YOU to-day ... again bring back your mind to the awful plight of Europe's starving babies.' With collection boxes strategically placed around the gallery, the exhibition was an immediate hit, visiting over seventy venues in forty British towns, welcoming some 200,000 visitors. The press slavered over schoolchildren asking to walk home so that their fares could be donated to 'starving babies'. In 1923, the Exhibition relocated to the New York Metropolitan Museum and onwards across America; a planned ten-month tour lasted four years – just as Wilson's proposed three weeks overseas had extended into years.[51] Pamphlets explained the psychological interest of the artwork which reflected upon the effect of war and its aftermath on children. Estimates indicate that £3,000 (£147,350) was raised in Great Britain out of which a £600 (£27,900) donation was made to Cizek for maintaining his classes. SCF realised that photographs, children's artwork and subsequently moving images, were powerful ways of encouraging donors to open their purses wide.

With the 1921 Russian famine, SCF felt they too had a part to play – the SCF sometimes criticised Quakers as being so intent on bringing their message of peace and brotherhood that immediate needs were overlooked. Partly fuelled by anti-Bolshevik 'White' Russian émigrés, appeals made by SCF encountered the same hostile reactions as those made by FFC, particularly from the political Right. With 'Bolshevik'

Russia excluded from the League of Nations, some refused to support the projected humanitarian aid mission arguing that Bolshevism was a greater scourge to the world than famine.[52] There is evidence that Buxton was not alone in 'supporting famine relief [as] partly at least a demonstration of solidarity with the Soviet administration.'[53] To try to deflect such damaging criticisms, the widely respected League of Nations' delegate for refugees, Fridtjof Nansen, headed a team of nineteen Russian-speaking English people who arrived in Russia to coordinate the distribution of food supplies on behalf of fourteen different member nations of the SCF's International Union.

Winning over a hostile British press and wider public to Russian children's sufferings remained an uphill struggle; many, not unreasonably, blamed Bolshevik policies for, if not causing, then at least significantly aggravating the famine. Inevitably newspapers entered the fray. 18 November 1921 *Pall Mall Gazette* believed that, 'It is quite evident that the stories [of] the Russian famine, spread abroad for British and American consumption, have been greatly exaggerated'. The British public should 'keep such money as they can spare for the relief of our own distress'. Countering this, *Western Daily Press* of 24 November 1921 considered 'the relief movement well worthy of British support'. Fundraisers became the butt for heated feelings: two women flag-sellers narrowly missed a dip in the Thames; thousands of unemployed men, with hungry children at home, demonstrated vociferously outside the Fund's London office. Somehow, the support of the British public had to be acquired and the trust of the Russian government maintained. Beneath this tightrope were millions of guiltless starving children for whom assistance was simply a statement of humanity – which Jebb and the SCF member organisations were determined to make.

If the British public and/or their press were sceptical about the level of suffering, and if a picture speaks a thousand words, then images would once again be harnessed to counter scepticism and raise money. Aware of the unprecedented impact of the 'Starving Baby' image, Jebb commissioned the *Daily Mirror*'s George Mewes to film famine conditions and the Fund's feeding centres in operation. Shown both privately and in cinemas, widely covered in local newspapers, *Famine* with its heart-rending images (critics claimed these had been 'staged') of starving and dead children huddled together, as well as milk and soup kitchens funded by humanitarian action, shocked. To increase the impact, the evening always closed with eye-witness accounts followed by a 'Silver Collection'. Such was *Famine*'s success, on 7 September 1921, the SCF-chartered SS *Torcello* departed for Riga (Latvia) carrying 600 tons of British-donated aid. Over 157 million rations were issued from the winter of 1921 through most of 1922. According to *The World's Children,* starving children consumed more than 120 million meals via hundreds of SCF feeding centres. Child deaths from starvation in Saratov province eventually dropped from over thirty a day to one or two a week.[54] By 1923, with shoots of recovery visible, the programme was scaled back. The harrowing images now so frequently beamed into our living rooms from the world's disaster zones, and the resulting donations, owe their genesis to Jebb's 1921 vision.

For left-wing committee members and supporters, the Fund's most controversial campaign involved taking a stall at the 1924 year-long Wembley Empire Exhibition; adding insult to injury, this was situated close 'to the Government pavilion'.[55] While SCF (with associations in twenty-four countries in Europe and the Near East), prided itself on being an internationalist humanitarian organisation, the exhibition was a blatant promotion of Empire. Press secretary Edward Fuller, hired by Jebb in 1920, was convinced that the cost of £200 (£11,500), a third of SCF's annual promotion budget, would pale into insignificance in relation to the money raised and the positive impact upon the charity's profile – now also working quite extensively for British children. The committee wisely heeded his advice. Opening on 23 April 1924, the exhibition welcomed 27 million visitors.[56]

Equally controversial, and tied in with the Empire Exhibition decision, was the one to ally SCF with the Conservative-led Imperial War Relief Fund. In her letter to Dorothy Buxton, humanitarian Emily Hobhouse likened such actions to asking a 'murderer to head a public subscription fund for a coffin for his victims'.[57] The more hard-headed Jebb accepted that such moves were astute and could halt the critical right-wing press in its tracks. SCF's annual Empire Day Appeal (24 May 1924) even proclaimed the 1918 victory as a 'Glorious Victory of Empire', which had ensured Britain's continuing primacy on the world stage. Some left-wing supporters wondered whether the charity had now lurched totally to the right; for others this was a pragmatic move. With the fate of the world (or at least Europe and the Near East's) children at stake, all donors needed nurturing, not just those who shared SCF's founding mothers' political ideals.

The International Union was now moving into child protection. Hiking up Mont Salève overlooking Geneva, Jebb's thoughts turned to her next brainchild, a Children's Charter; its five stunningly simple points covered a child's essential needs. The Fifth Assembly of the League of Nations adopted this 'Declaration of the Rights of the Child' on 27 September 1924. Translated into thirty-five languages, it became the basis for national laws for child welfare in many countries. Appointed an assessor, Jebb ran thither and yon across Europe, addressing international conferences and dropping, as she told her mother, into her allocated chair 'like a billiard ball into a socket'.[58] Did any who listened to her with rapt attention guess that as a young History graduate of Lady Margaret Hall, Oxford, she had reluctantly, unsuccessfully, taken up teaching only to discover that she did not really like children, although she felt sorry for a number of them as she witnessed their poverty-stricken lives? Did she herself remember how, as she nervously took the stage at the inaugural meeting at the Royal Albert Hall in May 1919, she had told her sister that she loathed public speaking? The 700 delegates representing thirty-eight governments and fifty-four nations who attended the first General Congress on Child Welfare would have suspected neither secret. In November 1989, with some up-to-date modifications, this charter became the United Nations Convention on the Rights of the Child, making children a central concern of the global community. It is the most universally accepted human rights instrument in history. Only three countries in the world still refuse to ratify it.[59]

Increasingly frail, bed-ridden from her thyroid condition (committee meetings were conducted in her bedroom), Jebb seemed unable to pass on the torch. Diagnosed with multi-nodular goitre, she died aged 52 in a Geneva nursing home in December 1928. Her funeral was held at the English Church in Geneva and she is buried in Cimetière Saint Georges in full view of the Mont Salève where she had first penned children's rights into international law. Appropriately, her coffin was draped not with the Union Jack but with the silk banner of the International Union of the Save the Children Fund. On the same day, children from the SCF choir sang 'humanity's conscience' to her rest at a Memorial Service at St Martin's-in-the Field, within sight of Trafalgar Square where, nine years previously and in contravention of DORA, she had distributed leaflets with the shocking image of a Starving Austrian Baby, forcing nations to acknowledge the child as the helpless, innocent victim of a war-maddened world – and the power of the image as a fundraising tool.[60]

Marie Stopes: 'The book the world has been waiting for'[61]

In 1909, the University of Manchester created the post of lecturer in Palaeobotany for an academic whose recent work on Japanese flora and fossils had solved what Charles Darwin called an 'an abominable mystery', the evolutionary origin of flowers. An eighteen-month study trip to Japan, funded by the Royal Society, granted celebrity status to the young academic. When the horrified university realised that their new appointee was female, unaware of either Dr Marie Stopes' refusal to be cowed or her ability to use influential friends to further her cause, they tried unsuccessfully to rescind their offer.[62] Once appointed, Stopes began crawling down inhospitable Lancashire coal mines collecting 300-million-year-old plant fossils which shed light on the coal which enabled Great Britain to retain its imperial position and fuel its industries. 'The practical importance of her work is evident when anyone flicks on a light switch. Her findings are [still] used to optimise the way coal is burned in power stations and are key to efficient generation of electricity.'[63] A glittering academic career seemed assured.

In 1912, having married Canadian botanist Reginald Ruggles Gates, whom she met when the Canadian Government extended an invitation to study the carboniferous flora of New Brunswick, Stopes (she insisted on retaining her maiden name) accepted a lectureship at her Alma Mater, the 'Godless University on Gower Street' (University College, London). Learned associations soon extended invitations to her as guest speaker on topics not exclusively scientific. An outspoken supporter of women's suffrage and a key speaker for the Women's Tax Resistance League, she gave 'a clear and definite explanation of the curious and anomalous position of the married woman vis-a-vis the tax-collector, pointing out that money paid indirectly or otherwise to the Government helped its tyrannical treatment of women.' Her solution: 'women should transfer their invested property to other countries, informing [Chancellor of the Exchequer] Mr Lloyd George of this step.'[64] She was honing her public speaking skills and learning to handle hecklers; both would stand her in excellent stead. She was also busy bringing newspaper readers' attention to the Government's 'penalising' of women who committed the 'crime of matrimony' by forcing them to resign their employment.[65]

With her public and suffrage star in the ascendant, all was not well with Stopes' marriage. Concerned that she had not become pregnant and with such subjects deeply taboo, she began her own research into her marital problems via the dusty volumes locked away in 'the Cupboard' of the British Museum. Her doctoral thesis may have studied 'the sexual habits of certain primitive plants called cycads', but her knowledge of human reproduction was close to non-existent.[66] In 1916 the marriage, which she claimed was unconsummated, was annulled. She had left the marital home early in 1914 and, quite literally, pitched her tent in Northumberland, returning to London when war broke out. As well as lecturing she was busy writing *Married Love*. In 1916, the British Government commissioned her as a coal expert to research how coal could be used to boost the war effort. Stopes' *Monograph on the Constitution of Coal* (co-authored with R.V. Wheeler), changed the way coal was both classified and burned in power stations.[67]

In July 1915, Stopes had met American birth control campaigner Margaret Sanger, temporarily in England having fled a potential twelve years' prison sentence for her dissemination of contraceptive advice, illegal under America's 'Comstock Laws'.[68] Working among desperately poor women, Sanger, who had witnessed unimagined misery caused by continuous pregnancies, 'had started a monthly magazine *Woman Rebel* which included articles on sex education for girls from fourteen to eighteen, and founded a National Birth Control League'.[69] Impressed by Sanger's pamphlet *Family Limitation*, Stopes, who always advocated going to the top, suggested petitioning the puritanical President Woodrow Wilson. With her ability to network, signatories included H.G. Wells. Enough publicity was generated on both sides of the Atlantic that Sanger's case, (but not Stopes' interest in contraception) was dropped.

Through her growing involvement in the Birth Control Movement, Stopes met and married a wealthy Royal Flying Corps Officer, Humphrey Roe. Son of a Manchester doctor, Roe had witnessed the plight of Manchester's continuously pregnant poor and was committed to providing working-class women with contraceptive advice. Impressed by the now completed *Married Love: A New Contribution to the Solution of Sex Difficulties*, for which Stopes had failed to find a publisher, he offered to

71

put up the £200 (£13,180) which the small publishing house, Fifield & Co., demanded. Neither Stopes, Roe, nor even the publisher could have anticipated its February 1918 success – running through six printings in a matter of weeks. Immediately banned in the USA, it remained banned for over twenty years.[70] To prevent the book being tossed aside as 'smut', Stopes' impressive qualifications: Doctor of Science, London; Doctor of Philosophy, Munich; Fellow of University College, London; Fellow of the Royal Society of Literature, were prominently placed. Her battles with the Catholic Church far in the future, *Married Love* was even endorsed by a Catholic priest. Striking, although rarely commented upon, is that seventy-three years ahead of her time (in English Law), Stopes acknowledges that rape can exist within marriage; 'No means No!' whatever the circumstances. The correspondence the book generated was soon overwhelming and she was quick to quote snippets from her 'adoring' public whenever the occasion demanded.

Married Love only touched upon the subject that would form Stopes' life work – although she never lost interest in palaeobotany. Contraception came to the fore in *Wise Parenthood* (November 1918), by which time Stopes (never Mrs Humphrey Roe) was pregnant. Aware that contraception was only easily available to educated middle- and upper-class couples, the sixteen-page pamphlet, *A Letter to Working Mothers* (1919) was produced for poorer women. Published at Stopes' own expense, her attempts to get this disseminated in the East End were greeted with suspicion, partly because potential recipients assumed distributors were from 'the Welfare'.[71] Working-class women were only too familiar with their lives being snooped upon by middle-class do-gooders, keen to criticise their homes, their families and, during the war, withhold their separation allowances.[72]

Research undertaken between 1918 and 1920 by the National Birth-rate Commission (of which Stopes was a member) resulted in the publication of the *Problems of Population and Parenthood*. Stopes was bemused that although Commissioners declared themselves in favour of limiting the birth-rate, they were against artificial contraception. Her letter demanding clarification of Commissioners' views lay unanswered.[73] However, the carefully engineered ensuing widespread press coverage resulted in a lucrative writing commission for the *Daily Chronicle*. With a semi-invalid sister and a mother to support, as well as a desire to be financially independent of her wealthy husband, Stopes always embraced money-making opportunities.

1919, which began with the runaway success of *Wise Parenthood*, was marred by the stillbirth of her longed-for son; she blamed medical incompetence which deprived her of autonomy over her body at the time she most needed it. The Medical Protection Society threatened legal action for defamatory remarks made against the doctor and nursing home; she did not withdraw, believing she had been 'wantonly tortured', laying the blame for the stillbirth at their door.[74] Overwhelmed by grief, she was in a poor mental state to withstand either the 12 September 1919 *New Witness* attack on *Wise Parenthood* which is 'couched in pseudoscientific terms', or letters which accused *Married Love* of offering 'dirty advice'. Such diatribes were soon, however, as familiar as the adulatory letters which filled her own and her publisher's mail box.

Radiant Motherhood appeared in 1920. With Stopes' and Roe's thoughts turning towards opening their own Birth Control Clinic, contraception needed public endorsement from a high authority. With the Lambeth Palace conference of Anglican bishops forthcoming, Stopes, who now saw herself as something between a prophetess and a priestess, adopted the role of God's emissary. She contacted the 267 episcopal attendees advising them that as sexual union was not solely for the purpose of procreating, they should encourage the widespread use of contraceptives among their flock. The generally unmarried bishops countered by emphasising 'the grave physical, moral and spiritual perils incurred by the use of contraceptives' (Resolution 70, 1920). Nevertheless, thousands of women would have echoed Mrs G.K. who, on 23 October 1920, informed Stopes, 'The bishops don't have to have children. They are not the people to judge whether birth control is right or wrong.'[75] Continuing with her rather bizarre ecclesiastical campaign, following the receipt of a number of 'Agony Aunt' type letters from clergymen's wives, in 1922 2,000 Anglican clergymen taken at random from Cockford's *Directory* received a questionnaire enquiring about their sexual habits.[76] The number of answers she received was disappointing.

Having failed to convert the Anglican bishops, Stopes tried royalty. However, Queens Alexandra and Mary graciously declined copies of her books (subsequently, Princess Elizabeth and her fiancé accepted her 1947 wedding gift of *Married Love*, which she hoped they would read together).[77] She also tilted at Prime Minister Lloyd George using Frances Stevenson, his secretary, mistress, and eventually wife as the conduit. Knowing the premier's private sympathies with the increasingly popular eugenics argument, she hoped he would enjoy *Radiant Motherhood* and acknowledge that she was doing more to promote a healthy race than 'a dozen ministries will ever do'.[78] The many eugenicists among the intelligentsia believed that population 'improvement would be achieved by reducing the birth-rate among poor and working-class people'.[79] Stopes own growing enthusiasm for eugenics is hard to reconcile with her undoubted empathy for the working-class women for whom she established her Mothers' Clinic; her views on racial superiority/inferiority now frequently overshadow her achievements. That her eugenicist views are deeply distasteful yet chimed with the times is undeniable.

By September 1920, Stopes was a household name. Loved or loathed, her opinions counted and through multiple press photographs, her face was widely recognised. Nowadays, it is hard to fully comprehend that she really was a pioneer, even medical graduates had little scientific knowledge or understanding of contraception, which was not included on the medical curriculum. Dr Isabel Emslie (b.1887), who enjoyed an illustrious medical career, remembered that when she qualified, 'The subject was taboo', she could be little more than a 'patient listener' to women who were devastated at once again having conceived, or desperate to ensure that they did not do so.[80] For good or ill, Stopes was now present in the nation's bedrooms.

Contraception advice was banned from Ministry of Health Infant Welfare Clinics but not from private ones – the fee for whose services was far beyond working-class women. Midwife Maud Hebbes believed, 'If it were possible to give information on birth control at infant welfare centres as freely as it is given about baby feeding, we would do away with much of the unnecessary suffering of both mothers and babies.'[81] On 17 March 1921, in an event which *The Times* declined to cover, Stopes and Roe's long cherished dream reached fulfilment. The Mothers' Clinic for Constructive Birth Control (CBC) opened at 61 Marlborough Road, Holloway. Sandwiched between a grocer's and a confectioner's shop the house, bought by Stopes and Roe, was converted into a clinic which she was determined would be friendly and welcoming. With four main aims: help the poor, try to understand working-class attitudes toward birth control, collect data on contraception, and broaden the scope of knowledge about women's sexuality. The female nursing staff were supplemented by Honorary Consultant, Harley Street doctor Jane Lorrimer Hawthorne, who visited weekly and to whom the nurses referred difficult gynaecological cases. As consultant at Islington Maternal and Child Welfare Centre, she was painfully familiar with many working-class women's situation, 'I see so many of [these working mothers] every day. ... It is pathetic to see them struggling along through such hard, monotonous lives as though they were not entitled to anything better'.[82] She believed women needed contraception as 'protection against brutal husbands', giving heart-wrenching examples. One patient 'who had had fifteen babies' explained: 'When I tell him there is another baby coming, he kicks me downstairs.'[83] She was subsequently joined by former suffragist, Dr Maud Kerslake, the first female Medical Officer in Middlesbrough; she reported identical examples of husbands' brutality.[84] Stopes sought the best female practitioners for her clinic, paying salaries out of her own pocket. Not all women doctors were supportive, however; the vehement opposition of Harley Street Consultant Gynaecologist, Roman Catholic Dr Mary Scharlieb (b.1845) was shared by co-religionist Professor of Obstetrics and Gynaecology at the Royal Free, Dr Louise McIlroy (b.1874). Both claimed that contraception would lead to 'unbridled sexual activity and excess'.[85]

As well as offering free contraceptive services, the nurse- rather than doctor-led Mothers' Clinic was innovative. Much-loved chief midwife, Maud Hebbes, had both an illustrious suffrage record (she lent Sylvia Pankhurst her nurse's uniform to help her to evade the police) and intimate knowledge of clients' grinding poverty, having worked with impoverished war-time mothers and babies in the East End 'Mothers' Arms'.[86] Hebbes was joined by Gwendolen Roberts, also no stranger to poverty. Accepting a cut in salary she had worked in a Welfare Clinic in one of Birmingham's poorest areas where, 'Seldom did a day go by when, in the course of visiting, I did not find some poor mother in great distress because she had conceived once again, frequently the last arrival only a few months old.'[87] While Stopes' clinic's primary aim was contraception, it was also willing to offer fertility advice; one subject that midwives were banned under solemn oath from discussing, however, was abortion – the legality of which lay far in the future.

During the gestation of the Mothers' Clinic, Margaret Sanger returned to England. Her October 1916 attempts to open a Brooklyn birth control clinic where, for 'ten cents, any woman who wanted it could get information from a trained nurse that was nearly impossible to find anywhere else, [namely] a medically accurate explanation of how the reproductive system works, and instructions on using contraceptives', had resulted in her arrest and sentence of thirty days in a public workhouse for 'maintaining a public nuisance'.[88] A flyer publicising the clinic had fallen into police hands; ten days after opening, it was raided, being definitively closed on 16 November 1916. With no softening in post-war American attitudes, Sanger crossed the Atlantic. This time Stopes, passionately protective of her proposed clinic and anxious that no one should steal her thunder, was less welcoming. A rift, which never fully healed, opened between the two women.[89] Both advocates of planned pregnancy had overlooked the common ground between them and descended into point scoring – to neither's credit.

Stopes' clinic was comfortably furnished, privacy was ensured, her leaflets were available and consultations were free. Women who could afford to pay the cost price were fitted with Stopes' favoured device of a 'small rubber check pessary' (she would carry one of these around in her handbag for demonstration purposes and thought nothing of passing it round during dinner parties and at fundraising events); the impecunious were not charged. In order to raise much-needed funds, Stopes developed an audacious plan, 'the first public meeting on the subject of Birth Control'.[90] Having spoken successfully at the Minerva Café, a radical feminist centre in Holborn, London, where, building on its suffrage past, eminently well-qualified speakers continued to present lectures relating to 'The Freedom and Progress of Women', she aimed to fill London's giant Queens Hall, preceded by a well-managed advertising campaign, 2,000 tickets were snapped up via the Keith Prowse ticket agency as though for a West End show. While entrance was free to welfare workers, tickets to listen to the priestess of contraception and her supporting cast of prestigious speakers, cost 2s 6d to 5s, With the audience warmed up by the Chapel Royal Organist, Stopes took the platform at 8.30pm; the meeting was an enormous success. Not for nothing had the undergraduate Stopes been nominated President of University College Women's Debating Society; she had honed her skills ever since.[91] *Common Cause* (10 June 1921), in awe of how her 'attempt to fill such a large hall was amply rewarded', reported key snippets of the speeches. Those unable to attend could purchase a 'Verbatim Report of all Speeches' made by the illustrious speakers, 'Together with Impressions of the Meeting'.[92] Despite her stellar performance, Stopes considered the ensuing press coverage disappointing. *The Times* was not alone in withholding the oxygen of publicity. As increasingly heated arguments raged, *Common Cause* (29 July 1921) insisted that correspondence, which was becoming acrimonious and, in one correspondent's view, weighted towards [contraception's] advocates, 'must now cease'.

Following this, Stopes was invited to speak at New York's newly opened Town Hall. Never afraid of controversy, she criticised her host country's 'barbaric laws on obscenity', and volunteered to rewrite the Declaration of Independence to include the right to control their unborn children, which, with more than a nod to eugenics was, 'in the interests of the Race'.[93] The lecture was a huge success, her public speaking gifts on full display. Reporting on the event, Sylvia Pankhurst, editor of the 'British Organ for International Communism', *Worker's Dreadnought* (19 November 1921), was convinced that the reason behind Governments' anti-contraception laws was Capital's desire to ensure that Labour did not 'become a scarce commodity', and that there was sufficient cannon fodder for the next war. Pankhurst reminded readers that the penalty for providing contraceptive advice in America (as in France, following a draconian August 1921 law) was imprisonment.

Stopes' advocacy of contraception touched a moral and ongoing nerve. A horrified nation had recently discovered that during the war, some 416,891 British and Dominion heroes had been admitted to hospital suffering from venereal disease.[94] For some, Stopes' books seemed to point the way forward towards harmonious marital relations and a potential reduction in STDs, others claimed she was feeding a moral degeneracy threatening to submerge the nation. Arguing if condoms were made available, 'moral degeneration and sex excesses would rot the very foundation of society', the Federation of Medical Women weighed in.[95] Dr Mary Scharlieb prophesised in the *British Medical Journal* of 16 July 1921, that contraception 'would lead to degeneracy and effeminacy and called for drill halls and tea gardens to be established to divert the men's minds from drink and women'! More welcome to Stopes was the request of Sir W. Arbuthnot Lane (consultant surgeon to Guy's Hospital) that she write *The Truth about VD.*[96] This was the type of medical recognition that, despite holding two doctorates, she both craved and welcomed.

Stopes' ability to arouse strong feelings was amply demonstrated in her exchanges with the medical profession. Those with strong religious principles seemed the most easily outraged. Dr Mary Kidd, medical officer at the Hampstead antenatal clinic, informed Nurse Hebbes, 'I entirely and utterly disapprove of Dr Marie Stopes' action in setting up this clinic both as a doctor and as woman and as a Christian.'[97] Kidd does not specify her Christian confession, but there is no doubt that the Roman Catholic church now had Stopes in their sights. Critical letters began to feature in the Catholic journal *Universe*, and Stopes developed a persecution mania. The aforementioned Louise McIlroy told a distinguished audience attending the 7 July 1921 meeting of the Medico-Legal Society that 'the consequences of married life should be left in Divine hands', citing as an example, 'the joy of Irish peasants with large families'; in a move calculated to bring the Mothers' Clinic into disrepute, she condemned the small rubber check pessaries used at the clinic which she subsequently condemned as 'dangerous' – despite having no experience of them.[98] Attendees included recent convert to Catholicism Dr Halliday Sutherland, who reported on the meeting for *The Month,* a Jesuit publication. This report was expanded into *Birth Control* (1922). Fiercely anti-eugenicist, he accused Stopes of 'using her work distributing contraceptives among poor women as a eugenic experiment targeting society's most vulnerable'; he went so far as to imply that Nurse Hebbes was only 'dressed as a nurse', which might help explain her spirited performance at the subsequent libel trial.[99] Capitalising on still rampant Germanophobia, he stressed that 'a doctor of German Philosophy (Munich) has opened a birth control clinic', and quoted McIlroy's statement that the clinic advocated 'the most harmful method of which [she] had experience'.[100] The remark about 'German Philosophy' was disingenuous, Stopes' PhD was for her thesis on palaeobotany.

Sutherland having not replied to her challenge to engage in a public debate, and disregarding legal advice, Stopes sued for libel.[101] The complicated case did no one credit. Cardinal Bourne of Westminster volunteered to assist Sutherland with his legal costs, which he could ill afford, 'to the end'.[102] Dubbed by some newspapers as 'sensational', the case opened in the High Court on 21 February 1923, before Lord Chief Justice of England, Lord Hewart, with twelve male jurors. Hewart's prejudice against the plaintiff (Stopes) was obvious. Stopes rejected her defence Counsel Patrick Hastings K.C.'s advice against appearing in the witness box and neither she nor Sutherland's chief witness McIlroy acquitted themselves well under cross-examination. Stopes was visibly furious at Hewart's accusation that her 'teachings about sex and contraception threatened the young, the family, the life and morals of the nation'; McIlroy failed to answer the questions put to her. The case became mired in accusation and counter-accusation. Even the verdict was unclear. While the jury found Sutherland's comments 'defamatory', they also found them 'true in substance and fact'. They were not however, 'fair comment', and the jury awarded '£100 damages'. Both sides asked for judgment in their favour which was deferred. Two days later, despite the press having hailed the jury's verdict as a victory for Stopes, Hewart pronounced in Sutherland's favour. Stopes lodged an appeal. The case rumbled on, the Court of Appeal found in favour of Stopes and then, with the Catholic Church's backing, Sutherland appealed to the House of Lords who, on 4 December 1924, found (4-1) for Sutherland, handing Stopes the hefty bill of all costs, £12,000 (c.£732,000). The case generated significant publicity and sympathy for Stopes; many found the outcome 'terribly unjust' with admirers assuring her she had achieved a breakthrough for womanhood.[103] In some respects, the case marked the apogee of Stopes' career; publications which would not carry her advertisements breathlessly covered the trial and subsequent appeals, while her books flew off the shelves.[104] For George Bernard Shaw, 'The decision is scandalous but I am not surprised at it.'[105]

By the time of the Lords' judgement, Stopes had achieved her maternal ambition, Harry had been born on 27 March 1924; *The Times* which had covered the trial erroneously referring to her as 'Mrs' as opposed to 'Dr' Stopes, declined to print the birth announcement. *The Sketch* was more obliging, featuring a posed photograph of the adoring parents on 30 April with Harry Stopes-Roe's christening awarded a full-page photographic spread on 6 August. Stopes was understandably outraged when letters asking if Harry were planned or 'a failure' of preventative measures arrived.[106] Sadly, Stopes' relationship with her deeply longed-for son became increasingly tempestuous, leading eventually to a barely healed rift when he married a woman she considered unsuitable.

Four years after the Mothers' Clinic opened and although the constant stream of patients never materialised, by 1924 some 5,000 women had received contraceptive services and bigger premises were required, opening at 108 Whitfield Street, Bloomsbury, now 'Marie Stopes Central London Centre'. Its present-day mission to give 'a warm welcome without judgement' where clients 'feel supported' is in line with Stopes' initial objective of ensuring that there was a kind, non-judgemental heart to listen.[107]

In 1926, contraceptive advice and devices were still prohibitively expensive. Only the Mother's Clinic was within their reach. Lord Buckmaster presented a Private Member's Bill which, in suitably verbose language, requested [HM Government] 'to withdraw all instructions given to, or conditions imposed on welfare committees' which prevented them from disseminating contraceptive advice.[108] Buckmaster asked whether Parliament would continue to 'withhold from the poor the knowledge that is possessed and practised by the rich?'[109] Their lordships were firmly in favour of this advice being available in welfare clinics, 'making it the first legislative body in the world to pass such a bill.'[110] Reinforcing Pankhurst's view that Capital was determined to maintain a stream of labour, the Lower House defeated Ernest Thurtle, Labour MP for Shoreditch's similar bill by 167 to 81 in a subsequent Free Vote.

Stopes felt that with no affordable birth control clinics outside London, then it was time to take contraception to the regions. Modifying a proven idea from the Church Army, a caravan providing contraceptive advice would tour the country. Despite the idea, originally promoted by her personal assistant Bertram Talbot, not meeting with her executive committee's unanimous support, she pressed ahead. Having failed to get a caravan donated, the merits of various designs and methods of locomotion were debated, concluding that it would be cheaper for a horse-drawn model because a horse and driver could simply be hired when the van changed location, with longer journeys being taken by train. A fund was established to raise the necessary £1,000 (£57,800) with Stopes personally covering some of the ongoing costs. Mr Selfridge made a substantial anonymous donation but declined her invitation to become a Vice President of the CBC movement.[111]

With the caravan purchased and welcomingly equipped, midwives led by a Nurse Thompson engaged (at a weekly salary of 3 guineas), and a publicity campaign having raised public awareness and interest, on 6 June 1928 it arrived at its first pitch, municipal ground near Bethnal Green Library, subsequently moving to Stratford.[112] In our highly mobile age, these locations seem close to the Mothers' Clinic in Bloomsbury. However for most patients, going 'Up West' would have been akin to entering unknown territory. It was soon obvious that pitch prices varied according to whether town councillors were supportive or otherwise. Pitch locations needed careful selection, stable or factory yards led to clients being jeered with subsequent low attendances; opening hours had to be flexible to accommodate local work patterns. Midwives did not sleep in the van; Stopes, presciently as it turned out, was concerned for their safety; she feared Roman Catholic-led sabotage.

Safety quickly became an issue. Following a first, unsuccessful attempt, on 24 November 1928, many newspapers (including the *Gloucester Journal*) reported that 34-year-old Roman Catholic confectionery employee Elizabeth Ellis had set fire to and destroyed the caravan which had arrived in Bradford on 20 October. She claimed it was being used to encourage young girls into prostitution and that she had 'destroyed a source of immorality and venereal disease', adding she intended no malice but was acting according to God's law which was stronger than common law. To stress their professionalism, Stopes instructed the nurses to appear at the ensuing court case in uniform. When the inevitable question was raised, they were to emphasise that they had sworn an oath not to perform abortions, a point from which Stopes never publicly waivered; any breath of breaking the law would have sounded CBC's death knell.[113] Ellis was sentenced to three months imprisonment. Showing the compassion and generosity that could be part of her character, although emphatically not always as she was often considered authoritarian and hard to work with, Stopes insisted on replacing Nurse Cook's destroyed coat at above its value, and paid for the midwives to have a two-week holiday to enable them to recuperate.[114] Although Cook appeared to experience no outward trauma, a note from a colleague subsequently commented on her heavy drinking.

Bradford was generous in donations towards a replacement caravan and provided a night watchman. Enough publicity was generated for two caravans, one each for the Southern and Northern circuits, staying from a few weeks to several months in each venue. The interdiction banning staff from sleeping in the vans continued; they lodged with local supporters (often members of the Women's Section of the Royal British Legion, the Co-operative Women's Guild and Independent Labour Party). That the nurses tolerated these arrangements, which could prove trying, shows their dedication. It is hard not to feel great sympathy with these women who spent prolonged periods away from their homes, lodging with strangers, sometimes subjected to abuse, their every move scrutinised by both a potentially hostile press and by Stopes, who never trusted anyone to act autonomously; her demand for copious, not always relevant reports, adding strain to an already long working day.[115] Nevertheless, her midwives remained loyal to her cause and the Birth Control Caravans were the forerunners of the mobile NHS centres we are familiar with today.

Stopes' antipathy to Roman Catholicism was further fuelled when Halliday Sutherland, who 'saw the falling birth rate as national suicide', filed a libel case against her, her husband, and the publisher of *Birth Control News*. His Counsel argued that Stopes' remarks about Sutherland had been prompted by the destruction of a caravan 'concerned with the dissemination of propaganda'. Conducting her own defence, Stopes denied the charge. She emphasised that like his co-religionists, Sutherland was anti-birth control per se, adding that Cardinal Bourne (who had paid Sutherland's 1923 legal costs) had preached against contraception.[116] This time the judge found in Stopes' favour. While George Bernard Shaw congratulated her on her victory, he felt that this time she had 'been obviously in the wrong' and the remarks could be construed as libellous.[117]

Stopes' abilities to raise awareness of her achievements continued unabated. She ensured coverage of the great CBC meeting held in Sheffield in November 1929 when a Resolution put to the 2,400 attendees was carried unanimously,

> This public meeting of the Citizens of Sheffield demands that the Ministry of Health shall cease its interference with the medical practitioners and trained nurses in its employment, and shall no longer debar them from using their best professional skill in the interests of their women patients who need on good grounds to control their maternity.

Stopes was angry that *Woman's Leader* (which had merged with *Common Cause*) had not covered what she considered to be her victories 'for womanhood'. Another victory for which Stopes may have claimed more than passing responsibility was that finally, in 1930, official instruction in birth control was included in the medical syllabus. In July 1930, a Ministry of Health circular permitted local health authorities to 'provide birth control advice for married women for whom a further pregnancy would be detrimental to health'.[118]

Stopes' mission had far-reaching consequences. On 31 December 1930, Pope Pius XI published the first papal encyclical on marriage for fifty years and instructed priests to thunder its message from the pulpits.

'Casti Connubzi' stated that contraception was inherently evil: spouses practicing any act of contraception 'violate the law of God and nature', and were 'stained by a great and mortal flaw'.[119] This encyclical, Pope Paul VI's 1968 reiteration, 'Humanae Vitae', and ongoing teachings, have bound millions of Roman Catholic women to the chains of continuous pregnancy from which Stopes was seeking to free them.

Stopes still arouses heated feelings; opinions are split over whether she should continue to be honoured among UCL luminaries.[120] Somewhat ironically, the Marie Stopes' clinics offer an abortion service of which she may have disapproved, although she would have approved of the non-judgemental attitudes of the professional staff who support women as they make what, for many, may be the hardest decision of their lives. In 2008, Stopes was one of 'six formidable women' to be honoured by a Royal Mail stamp; a decision which some organisations, including feminist ones, condemned.[121] Yet her Mothers' Clinics and the Birth Control Caravans offered free contraception advice to those who could not otherwise afford it and working-class women gained control over their own fertility for the first time. The charity to which she gave her name sums her up admirably: 'Controversy she may have courted, but it is difficult not to be astounded by Marie Stopes' achievements.'[122]

CHAPTER 4

Becoming a 'Person'

'Women are not persons'[1]

In 1888 Eliza Orme achieved a female first: a Law degree from University College London. Her gender barring her from professional recognition, she carved out a prestigious career as 'Senior Lady Assistant Commissioner to the Royal Commission in Labour'.[2] While a few other women subsequently studied Law, none succeeded in joining the professional bodies or practising as either barristers or solicitors; there thus seemed little point in women undertaking legal studies at university.

In 1894, 12-year-old fatherless Helena Normanton listened intently to the solicitor giving her mother legal advice relating to a mortgage. Realising that his client was struggling to absorb the information which could be crucial to her own and her two daughters' livelihood, he turned to the attentive child, suggesting she enlighten her parent. His praise at her explanation, 'Quite the little lawyer', would ultimately result in Normanton changing the face of English law. This, however, lay in the future as, needing to earn her living, at the age of 17, Normanton registered as a 'pupil teacher' at Edge Hill College, Liverpool, before achieving First Class Honours in History in 1912 from the University of London. A member of the suffrage-supporting Women's Freedom League, unwilling to modify her lessons to conform to an imperialist, patriarchal syllabus, she abandoned teaching. The Law still fascinated her and the 13 February 1913 *Coventry Evening Telegraph* informed readers that, 'The application of Miss Helena Normanton, B.A., for admission to the Middle Temple as a student is to be considered by the Petitions Committee.' This was not the first attempt by a woman to gain admission to the Bar. In 1903 Bertha Cave's application to join Gray's Inn was rejected, there being 'no precedent' which would allow women to become barristers.[3] And that, as far as the Gray's Inns Benchers (authorities) were concerned, was that. Middle Temple would also use 'lack of precedent' to refuse Normanton's 1913 application. In early March 1918, following women's partial enfranchisement, the outraged suffrage-supporting *Vote* reported Normanton's further rejection by 'the self-governing Benchers who control the rules and regulations of the Bar, and who are outside the jurisdiction of Parliament'. *Illustrated War News* (6 March 1918) felt Middle Temple's latest rejection newsworthy enough to report it at length and include Normanton's photograph. The many MPs with legal backgrounds resisted attempts made through Parliament to open the legal profession to women.[4]

With some women now enfranchised and an election looming, the 6 December 1918 *Vote* published a letter from Normanton advising enfranchised women to quiz parliamentary candidates on their position regarding women entering the Law and vote accordingly. She reminded readers, 'My appeal to the Lord Chancellor against [yet another] refusal of the Benchers of the Middle Temple to admit me as a law student still remains unheard, although it was delivered on July 24 last.' As such matters would have been of concern to *Vote*'s readers, she emphasised the 'multiple areas of domestic and working life where [women] needed the protection of the Law and included an emotional plea to 'mother[s] of a wronged girl child, ... injured wives [to] recollect what the prohibition of women to give them legal advice, or to appear in the Courts for them, has involved'. She pointed out that many countries, including France, Switzerland and Canada, had female lawyers and no catastrophe had befallen their legal systems. She was also courting support from across the political spectrum including Prime Minister Lloyd George. Sympathetic to women's issues, former Lord Chancellor Lord Buckmaster and MP Holford Knight went on record as being unable to understand the Bar's continuing rejection of women applicants.[5]

Press interest continued: *Coventry Evening Telegraph* (20 January 1919) noted Normanton had drawn Sir F.E. Smith, the new Lord Chancellor's attention to Middle Temple Benchers' silence pertaining to her application. A former Solicitor General, his was considered one of the finest (male) legal brains in the land. Having noted Smith's statement made 'during the general election that he would never again oppose the entry of women to the Bar, [she] now [sought] a speedy hearing of her appeal.' The hearing was neither speedy nor positive. On 23 February 1919, the reply arrived. Couched in suitable legalese, it had been,

decided that by the Common Law there is a disability on the part of a woman to be admitted as a student of an Inn of Court with a view to being called to the Bar, which disability has not been removed by statute.

Furthermore, harking back to the old precedent argument,

> I think we are all of the opinion that we cannot make a precedent, or suggest to the Inns of Court that they alter the course of practice which has now lasted for some centuries. ...[W]e do not think it necessary to give any other reasons than there is no precedent for such a proceeding.

That, they may have hoped, was that.

Aware that she needed to keep herself and her request in the public eye, Normanton continued to court press interest. She accepted speaking engagements where she demonstrated that her admission was not simply a 'vanity' project but was driven by the conviction that women needed the opportunity to be represented by women. She would quote from letters received from individuals like Millicent Blewell Stone, whose litany of abuse included: probable marital rape (not then recognised in law) and her husband's refusal to provide her with money to feed her children and herself. Advised by a solicitor that there was no redress except to go to the High Court (which she could not afford) or to divorce him (again too expensive), despite receiving no allowance from her husband, in desperation, she moved out of the matrimonial home with the children. She knew she was not alone, 'the women of England are not catered for at all in the laws man made or become the victims of unprincipled or amoral men'. She begged Normanton to 'continue her fight and stop this kind of "living torture" and "slow murder"'.[6]

The wheels of Government were turning, slowly. The wide-reaching Labour Party's Women's Emancipation Bill had its second reading on 4 April 1919. The Bill said nothing against women entering the legal professions. Even the Law Society passed a resolution: 'in view of the present economic and political position of women, it is the opinion of this meeting expedient that the obstacles to their entry into the legal profession should be removed'.[7] The Inns of Court disagreed, no female could enter their hallowed precincts. Benchers may have taken heart from Lord Chancellor, F.E. Smith, now Lord Birkenhead's opposition to the 'revolutionary' Bill. He expressed fears about women working after marriage and competing in open exams for entry to the civil service. Married women working was 'incompatible with married life'.[8] Additionally, he doubted whether, 'if the legal professions were thrown open by Statute to them it would be necessary expressly to throw open those offices the qualification for which is membership of one or other of the professions.' Despite having passed through the Commons, the Lords dealt this Women's Emancipation Bill which, among other benefits, would have given women the parliamentary franchise on the same terms as men and allowed women to enter all the professions, its death blow. The watered-down Sex Disqualification (Removal) Act now began its journey through Parliament. By November 1919, it was clear that this would become law; on 12 November, the Under Treasurer at Middle Temple took a telephone call in which Normanton requested admission. Denied, her admission 'must stand over until the Act actually become law'.[9]

Women's long struggle to enter the legal profession was nevertheless almost over. With the parliamentary ink hardly dry, Normanton arrived at Middle Temple. Rather than making a new application, she retrieved her former one, thereby ensuring her status as the first of several 1919/1920 women to be admitted to an Inn of Court. Archived at the Women's Library, her library card dated 24 December 1919 has 'Mr' scrubbed out, replaced by 'Miss' and a receipt for £40 7s 6d (£2,160). One strange Bar requirement is the need to eat thirty-six dinners within the student's Inn. In early 1920, she sat down to consume the first of these [still] necessary meals for aspiring barristers. The press had a field day, 'the 'First Woman to Dine With Benchers ... for 300 years', the last being, as she herself reminded colleagues, 'Good Queen Bess' who danced with the Templars having made merry on their fare. Whether Normanton and the three other women who had also been admitted, found their 'pea-soup and plum pudding' to their taste, *The Sketch* (21 January 1920) does not reveal, although it noted that Normanton was wigless. Despite this lack of head covering, the Benchers survived the ordeal of women breaching their hallowed precincts.

Had Normanton not drawn Benchers' attention to her earlier application, the accolade of first woman accepted by an Inn of Court, would have gone to Gwyneth Thomson (née Bebb). She too had been skirmishing with the law for over a decade and as Miss Bebb had discovered that 'a woman is not a person'. With a 1911 [equivalent] First in Jurisprudence (Oxford), she took up an appointment with the Board of Trade. In 1913, she and three other women initiated an unsuccessful legal action claiming that the Law Society should be compelled to admit them to its preliminary examinations. An accident of alphabet meant that her name appeared on the findings. Represented by Lord Buckmaster, Bebb sought to establish that she 'was a person' under the terms of the 1843 Solicitors Act. While not clarifying what a woman was if she were not a person, Lord Justice Swinfen Eady rejected the demand, upheld by the Court of Appeal. *Pall Mall Gazette* (15 December) despairingly explained, 'For hundreds of years there has never been a female attorney, and that is enough for the Lords of Appeal. They are not obliged to discuss or to consider the relative positions or merits of men and women.'

During the war, Bebb (who married in 1917) was an assistant commissioner with the Ministry of Food, gaining an OBE for her work; her legal knowledge had enabled the successful prosecution of black-marketeers. Now Gwyneth Thomson, she applied to Lincoln's Inn, being admitted in December 1919. To the consternation and disapproval of many, this young mother continued to work, only resigning from the Ministry of Food in August 1920 to give herself more time to study and assist her husband with his legal practice. Tragically, in August 1921 and at the age of 31, she and her second daughter to whom she had just given birth died. But for her untimely death, the honour of being the first woman 'called' (having successfully completed the required studies for the Bar examinations following her admission to an Inn of Court) would undoubtedly have been hers.

The accolade went to Ivy Williams, another brilliant Oxford scholar. Five years Normanton's senior, she had studied Law at St Anne's, subsequently achieving an LLD (Doctor of Law degree) from London; she was admitted to Inner Temple in January 1920. Writing in *Woman's World* in 1921, she unequivocally stated that if she were not called, she would petition Parliament.[10] Such drastic action was not needed and, ahead of Normanton, she was called in May 1922, aged 45. Her Certificate of Honour (First class) in her final bar examinations excused her from two terms of dinners and assured her place in women's legal history. The *Law Journal* described her Call to the Bar as 'one of the most memorable days in the long annals of the legal profession', adding in a back-handed compliment that the admission of women 'was never likely to be justified by any success they will achieve in the field of advocacy'.[11] However, unlike either Normanton or Thomson, Williams never intended to practice

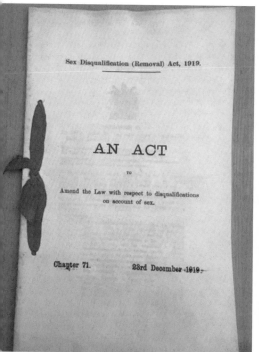

The Act that women hoped would herald quality. *(UK Parliament)*

Allice Miliat, as visionary as Alfred Frankland. *(Changemeakers.com)*

Carmen Pomies (L) and Florrie Redford (R). Pioneers of women's football. *(Wikimedia Commons)*

The iconic Lily Parr. *(Nationalfootballmuseum.com)*

'40 Elephant' Florrie Holmes. *(Pinterest)*

The first Poppy Lady, Anna Guérin.
(www.play.acast.com)

Philatelic homage to the other 'Poppy Lady'.
(Author's collection)

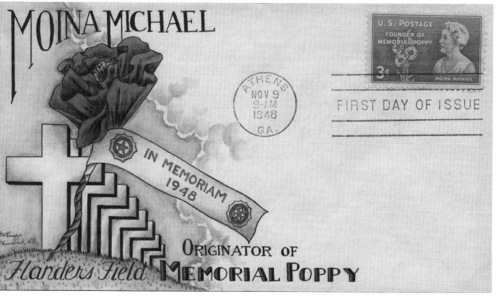

Sarah Smith –
spokeswoman
for the bereaved.
(Dailymirror.co.uk)

Gertrude Jekyll believed cemetery gardens should remind one of home. *(Wikipedia)*

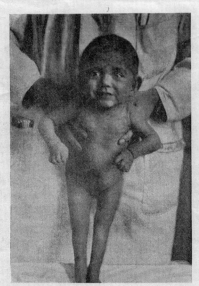

The image that shocked a nation.
(Save the Children Fund)

Quaker Dr Hilda Clark, determined to feed the hungry.
(Whitefeatherdiaries.org)

Marie Stopes, never averse to controversy.
(Wikipedia)

Dame Anne Louise McIlroy, no friend
to female footballers.
(https://history.rcplondon.ac.uk/inspiring-physicians/dame-anne-louise-mcilroy)

A pioneering 'walk-in' health centre, the first birth control caravan. *(Wikipedia)*

Helena Normanton, the foremost legal pioneer. *(Wikipedia)*

Fleet of foot Carrie Morrison. *(Simplylawjobs.com)*

'Ladies and Gentlemen of the Jury'. *(British Newspaper Archive)*

An infamous love triangle: Freddie Bywaters (L) Edith and Percy Thompson. *(Wikipedia)*

Queen Marie, Romania's secret weapon. *(Europecentenary.eu)*

The extraordinary
Gertrude Bell.
(Youtube.com)

Gertrude Bell and Faisal, the man she made
king (foreground right). *(dkfindout.com)*

as a barrister, becoming instead the first woman to teach Law at an English university. A Doctor of Civil Law, she represented Great Britain at the 1930 Conference for the Codification of International Law in The Hague.

Of the first three female entrants, it was thus Normanton (who was called in October 1922 following a rather disappointing Third) who attempted to establish a successful career in the 'field of advocacy'. The path would prove stony with courts, clerks and solicitors barely concealing their disapproval. The Bar's prohibition on self-advertisement or self-publicising proved particularly contentious; this and the press's interest in her dogged her throughout her career. A further significant disadvantage was that rather than coming from either the Establishment or one of England's legal families, she hailed from the ranks of the lower middle-class with no social network of contacts upon which to draw. Finding a pupillage, in itself an expensive prospect as pupils had to fund themselves and pay for the privilege, was the next challenge. Legal Chambers were so reluctant to take women that some cited the lack of female lavatories as the reason places were not offered. One newly called barrister, Hannah Cross, had to undertake to use the unsavoury public lavatories in Lincoln's Inn Fields before she was accepted.[12]

On the day her Continuing Legal Education certificate was issued, Normanton married Gavin Watson Clark. To her fury, the Registrar leaked news of the forthcoming nuptials to the Press – immediately opening her up to the unfair charge of self-publicising (this even prevented her being appointed to the Western Circuit – being a barrister on a circuit was essential for a successful legal career). Normanton and her new husband had to run the gauntlet of press photographers as they headed to the station for their honeymoon. Soon another announcement would take the press and newspaper readers by surprise. England's first female barrister intended to continue to practise under her maiden name while appending the title 'Mrs'. So unusual was this that she had to petition the Benchers of the four Inns of Court, who acquiesced. For Normanton, retaining her name was integral to her identity as a person. She had fought her battles as Helena Normanton, nobody knew her as Mrs Clark and it was as Mrs Normanton that she was determined to practise. As she reminded *Yorkshire Post* readers on 26 March 1954, Henry VIII 'had the decency to leave [Anne Boleyn] with her own name even though he took her head'.

The press continued to take an interest in the progress of this first female lawyer or so-called 'Modern Portia'. However, on the first Call

Night to include women, so momentous in the annals of English Law with eleven women being 'Called to the Bar', the *Evening Standard* (18 November 1922) chose to comment on 'Women Barristers' Hidden Tresses', and also how Normanton had had the temerity to be Called in her maiden rather than her married name. She was again reprimanded for self-publicising – although no one knew how she could prevent a free press from publishing what they wanted. So avid was the press to discuss her name that she paid to insert a statement in *The Times* (22 November 1922): Mrs Helena Normanton was 'her legal and only name in public and private life and that she hereby formally denies all statements to other effect' (she subsequently discovered she should have first discussed this with the Secretary of the Bar Council).

Normanton's hope that briefs would come flocking in proved ill-founded and she was never briefed as regularly as male barristers. Her first case, Searle v. Searle opened in the High Court on 21 December 1922, almost three years to the day since she had finally breached the walls of Middle Temple. A divorce case was not how she had dreamed of opening her legal career in the High Court as matrimonial matters were automatically considered a more 'feminine brief' than a criminal one. She appeared for the Petitioner and her opening words, while in themselves nothing unusual, were nevertheless groundbreaking, being the first uttered by a woman barrister in this hallowed legal space, 'This is a wife's petition, my Lord for dissolution of marriage on the ground of adultery and desertion for two years and upwards.' Referred to as an 'Historic Occasion' in several newspapers, some could not refrain from passing comment on her maiden name, others drew comparisons with Portia. The newness of her wig and her stiff white collar also excited comment. This appearance lasted eleven minutes, with the petitioner awarded 'decree and costs'. While English legal history may have been quietly made, 'Mr Justice Horridge said nothing.'[13] Following significant national and international coverage of the case, begging letters came flooding in from women 'desperate' for legal assistance which she could not offer as barristers had to be briefed by a solicitor. Justice through the courts was still beyond the reach of vulnerable women unable to afford legal costs.

Neither interest in her name nor her determination that women should have the right to retain their maiden name abated. Her feelings were influenced by the continuing legal doctrine of coverture (a married woman was under the protection and authority of her husband); adopting his name seemed to symbolise his dominant position. She now requested that a passport be issued to 'Mrs Helena Normanton'. Initially refused, she then 'went to the chief of the legal department of the Foreign Office who said that as I had won recognition from the Benchers of the Middle Temple to be a barrister-at-law in my maiden name, I was entitled to a passport.'[14] In December 1924, with the *Westminster Gazette* cock-a-hoop that she had succeeded where American women who had been lobbying for a similar outcome had failed, this first married woman to travel on a passport issued in her maiden name, crossed the Atlantic to suitable press interest.[15] At some point during her lecture tour, journalist Ruby Black, eager to challenge the ruling brought in by Woodrow Wilson during the war that a married woman could only be issued with a passport in her husband's name, contacted her. Black 'did not want to travel ... under an assumed name'.[16] A long hearing followed. Although she played down her part, Normanton appeared as a witness for Black; as a barrister familiar with English law who subsequently lodged a 'bulky brief' with the American Secretary of State, her intervention was almost certainly not inconsequential.[17]

The money earned from the speaking tour would have been welcome. Still dogged by accusations of self-publicising, briefs were intermittent, although she was starting to move away from divorce and into criminal cases. Almost every time that a reference was made to her in the press she had to explain to Middle Temple that the words had been written without her consent and she had reprimanded the newspaper in question.[18] She must have found needing to defend herself in this way deeply frustrating, a waste of time as well as career-blocking; she also accepted fewer and fewer lucrative speaking engagements for fear of accusations.

If Searle v. Searle was the first time that a woman barrister had appeared in court, in March 1930, Normanton achieved another 'first': the first woman to appear for the defence in an attempted murder trial. Her archive indicates the copious preparation undertaken for the defence of 23-year-old workman Leslie Aynsley, charged with the attempted murder of his teenage wife Ethel, and his father-in-law John Hume, by 'striking them on the head with a hammer'; Ethel did not wish to press charges. Normanton advised Aynsley to change his plea to 'guilty to unlawful wounding', which the Newcastle Assizes judge accepted, sentencing him to a short term of imprisonment while being watched for insanity.[19] This sad little case attracted extensive press coverage due to Normanton's spirited defence delivered in an incisive 'soft and silvery voice', and the outcome achieved by this 'modern Portia'.[20] She and her female legal colleagues must have become heartily sick of these constant Shakespearean allusions, not to mention the column inches devoted to their appearance. Gaining admittance to Inns of Court and being called to the Bar clearly had led neither the press nor indeed the judiciary to becoming gender blind; 'Portia smiles on male counsel' was undoubtedly not the headline she longed for.[21] Normanton's considerable achievements were being subsumed into those of a character in a sixteenth-century play. Twenty-four years later she achieved another first, being the first woman to prosecute in a murder trial, R. v. Sloan. He was found guilty.

Briefs remained slow and she frequently had to accept 'dock work' (criminal briefs given directly by prisoners in the dock to a barrister selected from a panel of barristers waiting in the courtroom). Her first dock brief occurred on 6 February 1924. Having pleaded for Charles Eyles, charged with fraud, the judge congratulated her deft handling of the case which led to Eyles' acquittal. [22] The papers reported that Eyles had not realised he had selected a woman counsel. However, he may have been more grateful when both his co-defendants went down. Few papers followed the lead of *Portsmouth Evening News* (8 February 1924) in quoting the judge's praise that she had, 'in difficult circumstances conducted the case with considerable skill'. Whether the difficult circumstances related to the case itself or the press attention centred upon her is unclear.

Although not wishing to be pigeon-holed as a divorce lawyer, divorce did interest her, which may be why she accepted the brief for the bizarre case of Benson v. Benson (December 1933). Appearing for the Petitioner, a now more confident Normanton (whose wig was seemingly now less white) explained that the Petitioner's husband was undergoing seven years' penal servitude for the attempted murder of his wife. She requested divorce. The case depended on Normanton proving adultery had been committed prior to his imprisonment. Had Normanton failed to do so, the contemporary law was such that divorce would have been disallowed. As Mr Justice Swift neatly pointed out,

> Cruelty and attempted murder and seven years' penal servitude are, in this country, no ground for the wife to obtain her freedom from her husband. But fortunately in this case she satisfies me that

his activities as a man were not solely confined to wife beating and ill-treating and attempting to murder her but were directed to procreating children by other women.[23]

Both Swift and Normanton also saw the irony of the Defendant requesting custody of his child, wondering if he proposed to bring up his son in his current abode, Dartmoor Prison. The case was, however, a further reminder to Normanton of women's ongoing lack of rights, and she campaigned vigorously for more equitable divorce law. By breaching the walls of the Inns of Court, being called to the Bar, by becoming solicitors, women had successfully demonstrated their personhood, but as far as divorce went, the balance was heavily weighted against them – although reforms were creeping in.

In 1932, Normanton accepted the position of honorary secretary and legal adviser to the newly created National Council for Equal Citizenship. She undertook a survey of the gender inequalities which continued to be enshrined in law and provided an expert legal examination of Bills coming before Parliament, advising the Council accordingly. Eager to make the law more accessible to women, in 1932 she published the 415 page *Everyday Law for Women*, the first legal text written by 'the first English woman barrister'. Its purpose was to summarise all those parts of English law which had a practical bearing on the lives of women. Beginning with her own 'back story', reviewers agreed that the text justified its claim of covering 'every aspect of a woman's life from the cradle to the grave, [and] should become a standard reference work for women'.[24] It contains hidden gems, such as wedding presents form part of the wife's estate irrespective of which 'side' gave them, and that in a broken engagement, the woman should only keep the ring if the man broke the engagement. The female magistrate reviewer in *Vote* (6 January 1933) was fulsome in her praise, emphasising how Normanton was painfully aware that in terms of legal knowledge there is so much information which a man can easily acquire 'at his club', and about which 'a woman is entirely ignorant, while the fear of incurring the displeasure of the law is a terrible bugbear'. Normanton continued to 'incur the displeasure of the law', accusations of self-publicising still hounded her. This had recently occurred when, in a piece for the *Daily Herald*, she voiced concerns relating to the death penalty for women. The paper referred to her as a 'senior barrister', Middle Temple mounted another attack.

Although from 1934 the press speculated about her taking silk, this only occurred in 1949, sharing this, her final 'first', with Rose Heilbron. Now officially recognised as 'one of His Majesty's Counsel learned in the law', it was time to hand the torch to a new generation who would continue the struggle that she and Gwyneth Bebb had individually initiated in 1913, when they had sought to demonstrate that a woman was 'a person', thus establishing the vital precedent which allowed women to enter the legal professions.[25]

Women Jurors: the 'defect of sex'

The 1919 Sex Disqualification (Removal) Act's opening words state, 'A person shall not be disqualified by sex or marriage from the exercise of any public function.' One such function was women joining the ranks of the 'twelve good men and true' who have to decide 'whether, on the facts of the case, a person is guilty or not guilty of the offence for which he or she has been charged.'[26] With women partially enfranchised, that they could be called for jury service seemed to some women to conclude their journey towards full citizenship. Others saw such service as an unimaginable aberration. The arguments included jury service meaning a woman juror might not be available to cook her husband's dinner, fears that her delicate ears might be sullied by listening to 'certain matters which no decent woman would for one moment think of mentioning even to her husband', and, to make matters worse, they would be compelled to discuss these with members of the opposite sex.[27] Writing to *The Times*, Colonel Hawkes disbelieved that such indelicacy could 'have been contemplated even by our enlightened legislators'; to prove that outrage was not reserved for males, a letter from 'Homemaking Woman' explained: 'Women are gifted in many ways, [but] they ... lack knowledge of the law and some are ignorant of sin and crime. These women look to their menfolk to stand between them and the discomforts of such tasks as serving upon a jury.' The Act 'must be amended'.[28] Irrespective of the opinions being expressed in the nation's newspapers, corridors of power, or private houses, women jurors were soon part of the changing post-war landscape; some relished this outward recognition of their personhood, others found it burdensome, worrying, even distressing.

The first potential trial by mixed jury could have occurred on 27 April 1920 at Colchester Quarter Sessions when John Butler was tried for stealing a bicycle worth £7 (£343). This case would have attracted little interest but for three women having been summoned as jurors. For reasons that no newspaper reported, Butler exercised his right to object to their presence. *Dundee Evening Telegraph* (29 April 1920) explained that 'Mr Holford Knight, barrister-at law, says that a prisoner – male or female – can object to any man or woman sitting on a jury. It isn't necessary to give any reason.' While most of the papers contented themselves with reporting that the women immediately withdrew to be replaced by three men, Miss Underwood of the Women's Freedom League wondered why they had departed so meekly, feeling strongly that 'their places ought to have been taken by three other women'. An official of the National Union of Women's Societies for Equal Citizenship, whose opinion was also sought, 'protested that it was unfair to allow the law enabling women to sit on juries to be nullified at the whim of a prisoner' – or his Counsel. Many challenges to women jurors may have been advised by counsels who, privately at least, shared the eighteenth-century view that women should be excluded from jury service *'propter defectum sexus'*.[29]

A detailed recent study has revealed that Butler's was the first of many peremptory challenges used to keep women off the juries, particularly if the charge was either infanticide or rape. For the latter, it was argued that the details of the case might be too shocking for delicate female sensibilities. Sometimes it was the women themselves who, given the option by the judge, chose to stand down. One rape victim was appalled when two women jurors, hearing that 'the evidence may be unpleasant', chose to retire. The unfortunate victim felt, 'that they might have thought what I would have to go through all alone with men, in that court. I did wish there was just *one* woman there – I did think they might have stayed.'[30] *Vote* (29 July 1921) would have agreed:

> For reasons known to themselves (and also to us) men are very anxious to bar women from all cases which concern the relations of men and women with each other, and it is especially these cases in which, in the interests of Right, it is most essential that equal numbers of women and men should deliberate together.

It is impossible to know what effect, if any, the challenging of two female jurors may have had in a case that led to a change in English law. Unmarried Edith Roberts' plight was, a century ago, all too familiar. This 'Girl-Mother' as inter alia *Leicester Mercury* referred to her throughout extensive coverage of the August 1921 trial, was charged with the murder of her newborn infant. Her far from competent counsel, Mr. G.W. Powers, challenged all the women jurors.[31] Whether this was because he thought that women would be harsher towards his client than men or because he, like many of his peers, believed that women made inadequate jurors was never revealed; he strongly denied feeling that 'men would be more sympathetic'.[32] To the expert medical witness, Dr Basil Taylor, the case was clear cut: infant strangulation. Mr Justice Avory (known as 'the Hanging Judge') advised the jury to 'steel their hearts against being led astray by sympathy for a woman, informing them 'infant life must be protected'.[33] With the verdict in, and faced with no choice, the judge donned the black cap and 'went through the usual farcical horror of sentencing the girl to death, she collapsed into the arms of a wardress, and was removed'.[34] A Miss Mackintosh aired her views in 9 June 1921 *Leicester Mercury*, 'if ever there was a case which should have been tried by women it is such a one as this'. *Vote* (29 July 1921) agreed, 'Women, in this terrible position have a right to trial by women.' Arguing that in cases such as this one, both the (unnamed) father and the mother should stand trial, it saw the verdict (irrespective of the jury's strong recommendation to mercy) as another of the 'miserable cases of "Blind" Justice that make women so furious'.

That the last execution for the maternal killing of a newborn had occurred in 1848 was no guarantee of reprieve. This doubtless lay behind the 'great public meeting' of 18 July, reported in *Leicester Mercury*. 'Four magistrates (two men and two women), a canon, and many other speakers stood upon a wagon in Leicester's Market Place and called for mercy, and for alterations in the law.' A petition sent to Queen Mary and Nancy Astor MP for the reduction of the sentence garnered over 30,000 signatures in Leicester alone. Questions were asked in Parliament. On 25 July, the Court of Criminal Appeal rejected Edith Roberts' appeal that the verdict should be altered from murder to manslaughter. *Leicester Mercury,* keeping the case in the public eye, stressed the difference between crimes committed by hardened murderers and this crime, committed postpartum, frequently by young, terrified, unmarried mothers, and yet the penalty was identical. The year-long campaign was ultimately successful; the death sentence was first commuted to penal servitude, and finally a reprieve. After a much-publicised homecoming in July 1922, Roberts herself, if not the ramifications of her action and the possible consequence of the challenge to women jurors, gratefully returned to obscurity. Her actions and the outraged public debate resulted in the 1922 Infanticide Act: no longer could the death penalty be applied to 'biological mothers who killed their newborn child as a consequence of having "not fully recovered from the effect of giving birth to such a child so that the balance of her mind was then disturbed".'[35]

By the time of Roberts' trial, the words 'Ladies and Gentlemen of the Jury', had finally been uttered. On 29 July 1920 in Bristol, a slightly nonplussed Recorder, Dr Odgers K.C., told the six men and six women that this phrase had not previously been used 'in the annals of the jurisdiction of this country'. ('Members of the Jury' was the correct form of address.) So momentous was this that his words were reported verbatim in the subsequent *New York Times*. This first case tried by a mixed panel was a relatively trivial one, Henry Ayrton was found guilty of stealing parcels from Weston-Super-Mare station. Pleased by the verdict, Counsel for the Prosecution congratulated 'the women jurors for at last taking their proper place in the administration of justice in England'. The second case was more delicate for female ears, a 31-year-old riveter was accused of assaulting two girls. These women, who had just made legal history, comprised three milliners, a draper, a tobacconist and a hat manufacturer. One told reporters that she had had to close her shop in order to fulfil her civic obligations. Other newspapers reminded readers that women jurors had to be aged between 21 and 65 years and fulfil both nationality and householder requirements or, as *The Times* succinctly explained, be 'from the middle classes'.

In early January 1921, the press had another field day. Fifty women were summoned to the Central Criminal Court at the Old Bailey, empanelled by the Common Serjeant, Sir Henry Fielding Dickens K.C. Several women requested exemption from serving. Dickens tried to calm those who appeared 'nervous' explaining that all they had to do was 'sit and listen'. This first mixed jury at the Old Bailey finally included two women; one, the redoubtable Mrs Taylor Bumpstead, 'a veteran of public life', having been a Member of the Board of Guardians in the North of England. She may have struck some fear into the heart of defendants, the first of whom was acquitted, the second found guilty. Named foreman, her picture adorned the *Illustrated London News*. Taking her place on the jury caused Bumpstead no concerns but she was understandably aggrieved that no refreshments were provided throughout the day, nor were expenses – 6*s* a day for seven days (£90) – refunded. The *Yorkshire Post and Leeds Intelligencer* (7 April 1924) pointed out how everyone else in the court was paid, 'even the prisoners in the dock score over the juror, as they are provided with food and lodging'.

If the Scottish newspapers are to be believed, those north of the border were equally interested in jury service's feminisation. *Dundee Courier* advertised a Miss Spence's 'Talk' on 'Women Jurors' on 21 March 1921; this would have been directly relevant to Scottish readers whose first female jurors had sat on 10 March 1921; Scotland notched up the first female solicitor, Madge Anderson, ahead of England in December 1920. In December 1922, unsure as to which of four female applicants to the Law Society the privilege of becoming the 'first' English solicitor should go, the women were told to run down Chancery Lane, the winner of the race, 34-year-old Carrie Morrison known for her determination, achieved the accolade.

Renowned for its satirical journalism, 12 January 1921 *Punch* poured scorn on female jurors. 'Trial by Jury – New Style', implied that rather than leaving feminine concerns at the courtroom door, women brought their knitting into the jury box; considering their verdict, 'Six said Guilty, Four said Plain and Two stuck out for Purl.' This coincided with the next day's opening of the first murder trial heard by women jurors. At Bucks Assizes, milkman George Bailey was charged with murdering his pregnant wife Kate and concealing the body under the bed of their young daughter Hollie. There was the further complication of his attempting 'carnally to know' the young girl sleeping in the room adjoining where his murdered wife lay.[36] The jury (to whom neither side objected) included middle-aged Matilda Tack, Annie White, and dairy-worker Maud Stevenson who expressed concerns to Mr Justice McCardie as to whether she was up to the job; he rejected her request not to serve. She soon mastered her nerves and, even allowing for press attention and hyperbole, the three females took their responsibilities seriously, making notes whenever they required clarification. McCardie, furious at the press scrummage and attempts to take unauthorised photographs of the (women) jurors, pointed out, 'It's a cruel thing to try to depict in the public press a prisoner who is undergoing the agony of a trial for life.'[37] The Defence claimed Kate had committed suicide; Rex that she had been murdered. Bailey's previous conviction for forgery and fraud (his desertion from His Majesty's Army during the war could not be mentioned) did not assist him. When so many hundreds of thousands of supposedly 'good' young men had been killed, the possible fate of this undoubtedly 'bad egg' worried neither the crowd nor the press.

McCardie's hoped-for completion of the case by Saturday 15 January proved optimistic. The jurors had to spend a fourth night at Aylesbury's Bull's Head Hotel, placed in its entirety at the disposal of the jury. '[S]pecial arrangements were made for the women's comfort' – it is unclear what these were. Anxious to keep the three women out of the limelight, their 'minder' Mrs Norman checked if they could attend divine service. They were understandably 'alarmed when told that kinema operator Pathé intended to picture their march to church'; after being 'taken out in a two-horsed coach', dinner was served at 7.30.[38] No detail was too trivial for the paparazzi who flocked around the women. Before directing the jury, McCardie acknowledged that, knowing that the death penalty would ensue, women may feel more reluctant than men to bring in a guilty verdict. He reminded all twelve,

> You must not allow yourselves to escape from a verdict you may dislike merely because you dislike it. ... A jury with women in it has to vindicate the difficult law of guarding the security of human life as when the jury was composed of men alone. ... I shall now ask you as a British jury of men and women to arrive at your verdict with certainty and to deliver [this] with unswerving firmness.[39]

They complied.

Inevitably, several newspapers recounted the event through the female gaze. Miss Stevenson in a purple costume was 'grimly attentive'. Miss White 'sombrely dressed, sad-faced, grey-haired', with her outfit lightened by a 'colourful toque'. This in dreadful contrast to the black cap and white gloves laid adjacent to McCardie's seat as the jury deliberated their verdict. In contrast to the long drama so recently played out, barely thirty minutes after filing out, the twelve returned, eyes downcast. Court hacks correctly guessed the verdict: 'Guilty'. The ensuing *Daily Express* praised the women's,

> unmoved faces and well-scheduled nerves while all the grim business of the judge's black cap and the chaplain's "Amen" to the sentence was in progress. They had strung themselves to that point

with deliberate fortitude. They came through the ordeal of verdict and sentence as bravely as any one of the men.

Although no record has yet been traced of any of the jurors expressing sorrow for Bailey – nor for motherless Hollie who spent over fifty years not knowing what had happened to either parent and being lovelessly raised by her grandparents, one woman juror was distressed by a later 'Guilty' verdict handed down in March 1922. George Robinson's case of murdering his wife was less cut and dried than that of George Bailey. Mrs Lizzie Buskin recounted to the *Yorkshire Evening Post* how the jury had retired three times,

> We knew the man's life hung on a thread which would be snapped by the verdict we couldn't help but bring in. We were utterly helpless but we had to do our duty. So reluctantly we found the man guilty but strongly recommended him to mercy. The worst part was to follow. ... We all stood up. The Judge put on the black cap. The Court was so still. The Judge said to the prisoner he would have to be hanged by the neck ... and someone said "Amen". I couldn't help a gulp coming from my throat, and I saw another lady in the box crying ... The Judge said lunch was provided for us but I couldn't take much. I didn't feel like eating.

Maybe this lack of appetite was unsurprising having come face to face with the condemned man's sons on leaving the court. She was relieved that Robinson was reprieved the following year.

Debates over whether women should serve as jurors in murder trials, or indeed cases that might offend delicate female sensibilities, continued.

> [Some] Counsel have protested that they could not be expected to address a mixed jury on certain topics. Last week, in the Lord Chief Justice's Court, the Judge, at the suggestion of counsel, gave women jurors the option of leaving the jury-box at the outset of a case which promised to be complicated and heavy.[40]

Seeing this as partly a slur on women's intelligence, 'an official at the Hendon Women Citizens' Council wrote, "I read about the incident, and totally disagree with such suggested exemptions of women, [who are] quite well able to apply their attention to such cases as men.'"[41] McCardie may have applauded her views, presiding over a male-only sexual offence trial at King's Bench in 1922, he offered the three women the opportunity to withdraw. He congratulated the two who remained for their 'courage'; one tartly replied, 'We think that if we are called at all we ought to sit, whatever the nature of the case.'

Women's groups continued to push for women's inclusion in every type of trial, the argument that women were better placed to understand women's emotions gained some traction. If women were originally imagined to be easily swayed by male jurors, it was becoming obvious that this was not necessarily the case. Two novelists entered the fray, Marie Belloc-Lowndes' (1926) *What Really Happened* depicts Eva Raydon arraigned for murdering her husband. The two female jurors, one a 'quiet mouse-like little lady with a peculiar horror of any form of crime', the other 'in a maze of anxious doubt and uncertainty'. Yet the men, bombastically confident that their 'Guilty' verdict will be echoed by the women, discover when they retire that not only does the 'anxious lady' unequivocally state: 'Nothing would induce me to declare, as in my opinion, the prisoner undoubtedly guilty', she carries four of the jurors and 'Not Guilty' is returned.[42] Dorothy L Sayers' (1930) *Strong Poison* has 'Miss Climpson' categorically refusing to bow to male jurors' pressure to [wrongfully] find Harriet Vane guilty of murdering her lover, thereby denying the unanimous verdict necessary for the death penalty. While both are works of fiction, these feminist novelists are staking a claim for women's presence on murder trials as they may be 'better at judging the testimony of women and children'; excluding them increased the chance of miscarriages of justice.

The press had a field day when popular actress Marie Studholme was summoned to the Divorce Court in 1922. As happened in the George Bailey trial, newspapers eagerly commented on her appearance – 'Pretty as a picture', 'wearing brown furs, a smart black hat with a drooping feather', she and her two female co-jurors were duly sworn in. With the story covered in fifteen local papers, her view 'that women should take their place on the jury' gained wide coverage. Serving on a divorce panel, Studholme had been spared the possible need to condemn a fellow human being to death; she expressed empathy for women called to serve on cases such as the recent 'Ilford Murder' case that had so rocked the country, whose final act still remained to be played out, and whose shock waves would ripple down the century.[43] Like most female jurors, she was unconcerned about potentially being 'publicly subjected to the revelation of the most revolting and degrading indecencies as a necessary part of a public duty'.[44]

Debates about women's suitability continued in both the national and local press throughout the 1920s, but by the close of the decade it was obvious that women jurors were part of the legal landscape. A woman's personhood had been extended and her ability to 'solemnly, sincerely and truly declare and affirm that I will well and truly try the accused and give a true verdict according to the evidence', remained enshrined in British law.[45]

Kate Meyrick, 'The law's an ass'[46]

While thousands of women were embracing their gender's inclusion in the legal process, others continued to fall foul of the law. Apart from allegedly being the first woman in Dublin to ride a bicycle, Kate Meyrick's early life in Ireland and subsequently England gives no hint that she would ever be anything other than 'respectable'.[47] Married to a doctor who worked with nerve-damaged patients during the First World War, her first deviant action occurred in 1919 when she gathered up her eight children and left her philandering husband for good. As he had spent all of her money, as well as his own, she and her children were dependent on her wits for survival.

With the war over and thousands of survivors intent on having the good time so long denied them, London was rapidly becoming a site of hedonistic pleasure. Soon part of the demi-monde, Meyrick initially became manager then part-owner of Dalton's Club in Leicester Square. Under wartime licensing laws (reinforced by the 1921 Licensing Laws Act), London's closing time was 10pm. With Meyrick denying that politicians should determine both where, and up to what time, alcohol could be consumed, the stage was set for multiple confrontations between her and the strong arm of the law. Her tenure of Dalton's was short-lived; reputed to be a 'pick-up' place favoured by soldiers recently returned to Civvy Street, it was closed after a police raid in late November 1919. Summoned for knowingly permitting the premises 'to be used as an habitual resort of women of ill-repute', the prosecution claimed Dalton's was a 'sink of iniquity and noxious fungus growth'.[48] Her defence that her women were both 'respectable' and 'bringing comfort' to the horrifically disfigured and mentally scarred young men who had come back from the war, was rejected. Fined £25 (£1,350) for keeping a disorderly house, the club was, and remained, closed.[49] Several newspapers reported that, prior to the raid, Police Sergeant George Goddard had been invited to dance; Meyrick and Goddard's paths would cross again.

Undeterred by this setback, and with her children's education at Harrow and Roedean increasingly burdensome, in 1921 Meyrick opened "the 43", at 43 Gerrard Street, Soho. Her ninth 'child', it turned her into the doyenne of nightclub owners, a jailbird, and one of London's most loved or loathed women. She excelled at knowing how to provide her clients, including officers of distinguished regiments, the war weary, the disillusioned, the wealthy and the famous, with a good time. Both Meyrick and "the 43" appear in Evelyn Waugh's *Brideshead Revisited* and *A Handful of Dust*; Augustus John, JB Priestley and Joseph Conrad were among her 'regulars'.[50] Despite a 'sink of iniquity' accusation – and the undoubted use of drugs – "the 43" was, within the meaning of the 1920s jazz and nightclub scene, respectable.

Meyrick's memoir, *Secrets of "the 43"* (suppressed in order to protect a number of Establishment personalities), provides a wealth of insight into the running of the club, the clientele and the women who worked there, 'Meyrick's Marvellous Maids', who were la crème de la crème, 'superb dancers' who 'knew how to wear their clothes', a generous salary (and bonuses) ensured that these were always the height of fashion.[51] Aware that after leaving her husband, she could easily have fallen into prostitution, Meyrick saw women's financial 'independence' as crucial to their well-being. She believed that she was providing her girls, whose 'average weekly takings [were] at least £14 to £15 (£700) ... many made considerably more than this', with autonomy.[52] Over her ten-year tenure, 'my dance hostesses received gifts to the value of £20,000 (£936,000); many staff remained with her for the duration. Some who came seeking a job had had their 'wings burnt in London' and had no one to whom they could turn; she paid their fares home.[53]

If the staff were earning well, so too was Meyrick. It has been estimated that some £500,000 (c.£28,000,000) passed through her hands, literally; her net worth at death was £758 (£50,558). Outgoings, which she lists in fascinating detail, were inevitably high with significant amounts spent on 'lipstick, powder, rouge, hairpins and soap for the clubs. ... Nowhere more than in a nightclub is it necessary to spend money to make money.'[54] She also paid the legal fees of employees caught in the multiple police raids while her own legal fees ran into thousands of pounds. Led by Goddard, the first raid on "the 43" occurred in February 1922, resulting in a £250 fine (£11,600) and 35 guineas costs (£1,720).[55] So far, the worst that had befallen her was hefty fines. Things would change.

In late 1924, Sir William Joynson-Hicks was appointed Home Secretary. His jolly-sounding nickname Jix belies his reputation as 'the most prudish, puritanical and protestant Home Secretary of the twentieth century'.[56] Determined to suppress what were becoming known as 'The Roaring Twenties', the Nightclub Queen was within his sights. If, despite the repeated police raids, "the 43"'s clientele refused to abstain from visiting nightclubs, Jix would teach them a lesson. In late October 1924 the Vice Squad, led by its new head Sergeant Goddard, struck in 'one of the biggest night club raids London has ever known', descending on "the 43", barring all exits and rounding up miscreants.[57] Meyrick, one of her sons and two other defendants were arrested for the crime of 'selling liquor without a licence'. Determined not to submit to those whom she called 'killjoys', Meyrick, 'the best known figure in the night club world', appeared before Sir Charles Biron at Bow Street Magistrates Court.[58] Sending her for trial, he remembered her as a 'very remarkable woman [with] charming manners, [who] conducted her various clubs with more decorum than many'.[59] Decorum or not, the trial jury did not take pity on her plea of having to raise eight children on an allowance from her estranged husband of 15s per week. Drawing attention to her having previously paid fines and costs totalling £1,300 (£74,750), Prosecuting Counsel labelled her as 'treating the law with contempt'. Dismissing King Ferdinand of Romania and the Crown Prince of Sweden's pleas for leniency, the Guilty verdict resulted in six months in Holloway in the second, therefore less harsh, division.

Secrets describes in detail her first detention at His Majesty's Pleasure, 'The long, long hours of solitude, the nerve-racking deadening restrictions that are perpetually enforced. Visitors never gain even a glimpse of the real horror and sadness of prison life.'[60] She soon realised that whispered conversations still 'centred around the tragic ill-starred figure of poor Mrs Thompson', many prisoners having had 'personal contact with her' – and wardresses speaking well of her.[61] Hinting at things to come, Meyrick completed her sentence in the prison hospital. Holloway had damaged her health but it had not dented her reputation as London's premier club owner, her clubs now included the Silver Slipper, the Manhattan and an interest in the Folies Bergères; she had become adept at accurately judging what clients were prepared to pay for their pleasures, 'our prices were not extortionate'.[62] Proving Jix's attempts to stamp out vice were failing miserably, indeed that the opposite was happening, the upper classes were openly embracing top-end providers of a fast lifestyle. Meyrick's investment in expensive education was reaping social rewards; in 1926 her second daughter married the twenty-sixth Baron de Clifford, who was undeterred by his wife keeping the businesses running during his mother-in-law's periods of imprisonment. With Meyrick epitomising the new hedonistic order that those in power appeared intent on stamping out, Jix's morality campaign against nightclubs was becoming a personal vendetta against the most successful of all female proprietors.[63]

Meyrick was fortunate not to be behind bars for her eldest daughter's 1928 marriage to the fourteenth earl of Kinnoull. With her 'fine contempt for the law', she and Magistrate Charles Biron were meeting more times than either would like; she was sent down for breaking the licensing laws, which to her mind were insulting to adults who did not wish their evening's entertainment to end at 10pm. Parliament, she argued, cannot legislate on what time people go to bed. After all, if there were 'no people who wished to carry on their amusements after midnight, there would be no night-clubs'; she was merely satisfying an existing demand, why then label her as 'notorious?'[64]

Barely released from prison, in November 1928 she was charged under the *Prevention of Corruption Act* for bribery of a police officer, a serious charge. Following a tip-off and a raid on Goddard's 'freehold house', over £12,000 (£71,640) was discovered in a safe box, his police salary was under £7 (£418) a week. It transpired that Meyrick had been paying him £100 (£5,970) a week in return for her clubs not being raided. This was potentially not the only sweetener extorted from her. Gender, she claimed, left her 'open to continual attempts at cheating and extortion. Since the beginning of time, blackmailers have regarded women as their easiest prey. "Pay up or we make a complaint to the Police." Open to suspicion of being a lawbreaker myself therefore I could not turn to the law for help.'[65] The bribes had worked, up to a point, 'between October 1926 and February 1928', under Goddard's direction "the 43" was raided four times. Although the ensuing reports were 'unfavourable, they were not unfavourable enough to warrant proceedings'.[66] When the CID as opposed to the Vice Squad struck, they found 'drink everywhere' and Meyrick was charged in what became known as 'the Goddard Case'.

Meyrick anticipated little leniency. Examining the court drama from the perspective of those who, rather than handing out justice, were hoping to receive mercy,

> I see the whole picture so clearly. Over there sit the jury, a stolid-looking body of middle-class men and women. No sympathy or kindness to be read in any of their faces. Mr Justice Avory, looking so stern, so cold, so forbidding. ... Then the minor actors in that immense drama we call the Law ... The counsel ... all dressed up in their wigs and gowns to play their part in the performance. ... And then the fashionably dressed throng in court, the main crowd packed in the gallery. Smart people and shabby alike all waiting like human vultures to gloat over the spectacle of a fellow creature going through the depths of agony and degradation.[67]

Meyrick, whose clubs had provided so many with spectacles, was now herself the spectacle and although some would have flocked to see a policeman brought down, the star attraction was the Queen of the Nightclubs. The case dragged on. Experienced at listening to judges' summaries and directions, she realised that Avory was 'dead against us' – the 'us' implying that in this strange underworld, she now sided with Goddard. Either she had lost her sense of time, or the jury were surprisingly unsure of their verdict in what appeared a cut and dried case; 'Time dragged on!' for those waiting in the cells. Eventually, 'the jury file slowly in and settle themselves in their seats. The foreman rises to his feet and it seems to me as though he were savouring with a sort of ghoulish delight of anticipation the pronouncement he is about to utter. "Guilty".'[68] Goddard got two years with hard labour. Meyrick fared little better; the days of the more lenient Second Division were long past; this time it was fifteen months with hard labour for bribery and corruption, an unsurprising sentence from Avory, known to be humourless and nicknamed by his peers 'the Acid Drop'.[69]

Secrets recounts the dreary monotony of prison life and her fascination with imprisoned members of 'The Forty Elephants' who sometimes visited her clubs, 'a jolly crowd full of exciting experiences which they were quite ready to impart whenever we could manage to get into conversation and I think that they were also the best-looking collection of women I ever saw in prison.'[70] She expressed great sympathy for women serving years of penal servitude for performing 'illegal operations' (abortions). She empathised with those who performed such acts and those who, in desperation, sought them. Could anything justify the 'living death' to which these women were condemned? Despite moving in a superficially glamorous world, the fate that could easily have been hers when she left her husband had left its mark and she knew that those without her guts and worldliness could get drawn into prostitution and backstreet abortions. *Secrets* reveals a different Meyrick to the glamorous nightclub owner who, to the outraged Hubert Angell of *The People*, was on release, 'met with a rapturous welcome at the prison gates', bouquets and a 'champagne breakfast'.[71] He could muster no enthusiasm for her 'restoration to the privileges of citizenship', forfeited while incarcerated. His lengthy post-release article depicted her 'as one of the most dangerous women in London'.[72]

Everyone in the justice system may have hoped as fervently as she did that this would be their last encounter. This proved optimistic. With Lord Byng of Vimy appointed Commissioner of the Metropolitan Police, Jix's vendetta against London nightlife and its club scene intensified.[73] It was only a matter of time before many of the clubs, including Meyrick's, were throttled. No longer tipped-off or under the dubious protection of ex-Sergeant Goddard, raid followed raid – Meyrick considered these 'vindictive, as though I had been carrying on some shameful traffic'. She was not some sort of madam, nor were her clubs 'some species of "spiders' parlours" into which the flies were invited to walk for their undoing'.[74] Two more custodial sentences followed. Her fortune dented by her endless legal fees, the Goddard case alone was reported to have cost her £1,500 (£89,500), was now at risk through mismanagement. Each incarceration further weakened her health, but not her determination to provide those who still flocked to her clubs with the good time they craved. Her last brush with the law was at Marlborough Police Court. Although she would have been furious at his description, she would have been relieved by the outcome. Remarking that prison had 'signally failed to prevent a repetition of the offence', the magistrate stated, 'I do not want to send the old woman to prison'.[75]

However much she hated calling 'Time', hers was running out. She died on 19 January 1933 aged 57, of complications of bronchopneumonia at the home of her son-in-law, the Earl of Kinnoull. Mourners, eager to say farewell to the woman who had taken night clubs to a new level of sophistication, flocked to her funeral at St Martin's-in-the Fields. Wreaths from peers, actresses and the Association of London taxicab-drivers were piled up around the altar; the traffic ground to a halt to accommodate those who wished to pay their last respects to this 'New Woman' who epitomised the free spirit of the Roaring Twenties.[76]

For Jix, Meyrick pandered to, and profited from, the decadent lifestyle he yearned to suppress, and those who had either survived or attained adulthood in the wake of the Great War were intent on pursuing. To London's homeless, among whom were many ex-soldiers, she was the kindly figure who, when the clubs shut, toured the Shaftesbury Avenue area, giving 2*s* 6*d* (c.£10) to each.[77] Drawing on her experiences of working with her husband's nerve-damaged patients, hers was a listening ear; she offered sympathy to the homeless, to former officers, to peers, to prisoners and to chorus girls. As the lights dimmed across Clubland to mark her passing, many felt London was the poorer for the death of its greatest Nightclub Queen.

CHAPTER 5

Murder Most Foul?

Queens of Crime: Menace, murder and shell-shock

From the mid-nineteenth century, British readers had devoured crime fiction, both in books and serialised in magazines. Popular crime authors included several now overlooked women. Anna Katharine Green's (1878) *The Leavenworth Case* 'had fascinated' 8-year-old Agatha Miller (Christie), who developed a crime obsession, considering herself and her elder sister Madge 'connoisseurs of the genre'.[1] A challenge by Madge resulted in Christie becoming the 'world's best-selling fiction writer and the most translated author of all time'.[2] Having told Madge that to 'write a detective story' would be simple, Madge retorted, 'I bet you couldn't', Agatha vowed, 'some day I would'.[3] The outbreak of war placed the writing plan on hold.

Like so many young women from the leisured upper-middle-class, before the war Christie had undertaken some genteel Red Cross training via the Voluntary Aid Detachment (VAD). In 1914, she progressed rapidly from 'ward-maid' to auxiliary nurse at nearby Torquay Town Hall, rapidly transformed into a hospital. To her surprise, she enjoyed nursing, although the veneration with which doctors expected to be treated irritated her and may even account for doctors making up the largest group of murderers in her 101 novels and short stories, one even being a quadruple killer. Precipitously married to RFC subaltern Archie Christie on 24 December 1914, 'Nurse Christie' returned to work and the war 'settled down into a grisly stalemate'.[4] She loved nursing, even thinking that had she not married she may have considered becoming a professional nurse; Archie, however, loathed her 'filthy job and I hate you doing it'. She did not spot potential warning signs in his comment, nor in his obvious desire to have a wife who was an adjunct to him as opposed to an independent equal.

Recovering from 'flu, in 1916 she was sent to work in the newly opened hospital dispensary where she trained for the Apothecary Hall Examinations. Although she confessed to preferring nursing to dispensing, she was nevertheless intrigued and, after having 'blown up our Cona coffee machine ... progress was well on the way.'[5] Increasingly knowledgeable about 'the Power of the Drug, for good or ill', over thirty of her subsequent victims were dispatched using poisons ranging from the everyday arsenic, cyanide and strychnine, to the less common coniine and thallium, explaining to readers, where necessary, their toxic properties.[6] *Dame Agatha's Poisonous Pharmacopia,* lauded in the scholarly pharmaceutical press lists her (accurate) use of some ninety toxins.[7] She also noted that doctors had their own personal drug preferences; their rather cavalier approach to prescribing features in several novels, not always with the desired effect for the patient.[8] Having successfully passed the three-part examination in chemistry, materia medica, and compounding, she was legally qualified to dispense medication for a medical officer or pharmacist and from January 1917 until September 1918 she continued at the Red Cross Torquay Hospital dispensary at an annual 'salary' of £16 (£1,054). She returned to pharmaceutical work at University College Hospital in London during the Second World War.

Life in the dispensary was less pressurised, leaving her time to think. Remembering Madge's challenge, she began to wonder if she could write a detective story with a murderer that no one would deduce. Surrounded by multiple drugs, an idea of death by poisoning grew in her fertile imagination.[9] She now needed a detective with preferably a sidekick to act as 'Watson' to her nascent 'Holmes'. Like so many seaside resorts, Torquay had welcomed an influx of Belgian refugees. 'Why not make my detective a Belgian?'. Many affluent Torquay families arranged soirées to raise money for the refugees and Christie remembered attending an event organised by a neighbour with a retired Belgian gendarme, Jacques Hornais, billeted with her. She subsequently deeply regretted having opted for an elderly gentleman, 'my fictional detective must be well over a hundred by now'.[10] Hercule (originally Hercules with the 's' subsequently dropped) Poirot, a 'quaint dandified little man', burst upon the world of detective fiction in 1920.[11]

As the detective story developed, Christie became increasingly absent-minded at home – although fortunately not in the dispensary where every prescription had to be meticulously followed and a slip could prove fatal. Heeding maternal advice, she spent a fortnight's holiday alone on Dartmoor completing the novel, 'I was reasonably satisfied with it. ... It could be much better ... but I didn't see how *I* could make it better.'

The Mysterious Affair at Styles 'was duly sent off to publishers Hodder and Stoughton'. They returned it. 'It was a plain refusal, with no frills.'[12] Perhaps *Styles,* with its characters embedded in the Great War including a convalescing solider, a VAD nurse training in dispensary (modelled on Christie) whose handbook on pharmacopeia left lying around revealed how the murder weapon strychnine was used, Dr Bauerstein, 'one of the greatest living experts on poisons', and its country house setting, not to mention its egg-head Belgian detective, did not chime with the mood of the times – although it soon would.

With the war nearly over and the now much-decorated Archie still miraculously alive and posted to an Air Ministry job, the Christies found a small London flat, and Agatha began a course of 'book-keeping and short-hand to occupy my days'. She discovered that boredom and loneliness were the uninvited guests for newly married wives of her social class, followed by pregnancy. The post-war world into which Rosalind Christie was born in August 1919 seemed a precarious one, power had shifted, uncertainty abounded. Readers longed for an obvious demarcation between Good and Evil, the reassurance that eventually the former would triumph, offering at least hope that the world, or at least the one that the reader shared with the characters, would resume if not its former glory then at least a recognisable stability. What greater evil might there be than murder and what greater proof that all could be made well than the unveiling of the murderer who would suffer for their dastardly deeds? Guilt relating to capital punishment does not trouble Christie's detectives, although this became much more problematic for the other Queen of the Golden Age of Crime, Dorothy L Sayers. If, before the war, guns and knives were the standard murder weapons, Christie would use poisons, especially ones readily available in a pharmacy or garden shed, to devastating effect. Settings with clear boundaries such as a closed community, a long-distance train, a country house, played a vital part. With country-houses threatened by the death of heirs, inflation, taxes, and real and metaphorical bankruptcy, this setting may have attracted publishers John Lane to *Styles.* Emphasising the risks involved in publishing an unknown author, they demanded multiple alterations and offered an exploitative contract including a hidden clause which bound the author to four more novels; to Christie, 'none of it meant much'. That she would only receive £25 (£1,062), including the serial rights which John Lane said would be good for her prestige while omitting to mention it would be good for their bank balance, did not matter. 'The whole point was the book would be published.'[13]

Published in America in October 1920, *Styles* gained significant praise; the 26 December *New York Times Book Review* believed this first novel, 'betrays the cunning of an old hand, [readers] will most certainly never lay down this most entertaining book.' In England, the *Sketch* (21 January 1921) found this 'quaint' Belgian detective with his 'little grey cells', 'the most fascinating character any novel-reader could wish to meet'. If the 3 February *TLS* review was short, the praise was heartfelt, referring to 'the bet about the possibility of writing a detective story in which the reader would not be able to spot the criminal, every reader must admit that the bet was won.' Knowledgeable critics praised Christie's use of the pharmaceutical and medical reference books which remained her constant companions. This 'finest detective novel since the war', created a 'sensation'.[14]

Now Christie had her contractual arrangement to fulfil. The sinking of the *Lusitania,* demobbed men and women desperately hunting employment in Civvy Street, the perceived Bolshevik threat, seismic societal changes, form the backdrop to her second novel, *The Secret Adversary*.[15] One of the two detectives, 'Tuppence' Cowley, is recently unemployed, some of her VAD experiences are based on Christie's ward-maid ones, 'First month: Washed up six hundred and forty-eight plates every day,' the litany of her mundane tasks is endless. After various familiar war roles Tuppence landed in an office where, after the Armistice, 'I clung to the office with the true limpet touch for many long months, but, alas, [with the culling of women], I was combed out at last. Since then I've been looking for a job.'[16] Her co-detective a young demobbed officer, Tommy Beresford, also faces unemployment. Unlike Poirot or the later Miss Marple, young Tommy and Tuppence aged with their creator who considered them her favourite detectives. Even the germ of Christie's *Adversary* idea being planted in an A.B.C. teashop is redolent of the immediate post-war era. A.B.C.s had opened in the 1860s, giving women somewhere where they could either dine alone or with female friends without a male escort; reaching their heyday in the 1920s, in 1923, there were 150 in London alone. An avid listener to others' conversations, when two women talking at an adjacent table mentioned a 'Jane Fish', Christie felt she would make 'a good beginning'. More spy than detective story, Christie considered this a pleasant change. A doubtful John Lane offered £50 (£2,325) and Christie sold the serial rights to *The Weekly Times*. She still did not see herself as a professional writer, money was short in the household which, inevitably for a family of their social background, included both a full-time nanny for Rosalind and domestic staff.

Murder on the Links (1923) tied her irrevocably not only to the detective genre (although she would write non-crime as 'Mary Westmacott') but also to Hercule Poirot about whom the press remained ecstatic. Countless references to him and, inevitably, his brain power, not to mention photographs of his creator, adorned British newspapers. If *Styles,* with its cast of predominantly female wartime workers and the dying country house, reflects its wartime and immediate post-war roots and *Adversary* uses the employment crisis facing the demobbed, *Links'* opening owes much to men, including Archie's fear and dislike of women's increasing independence. Christie novels feature strong, independent women prepared to act in their own interests, 'using trickery and violence if necessary, and occupy any of the traditional male roles without fearing for their femininity'.[17] Her women can be ruthless murderers and cunning sleuths. It is the much-feared 'new' woman who opens *Links*. Daring to use the word, 'Hell', Dulcie Deveen bursts into a carriage of the Calais-express and Captain Hastings' life. As he smugly explains, a 'woman should be womanly. I have no patience with the modern neurotic girl who jazzes from morning till night, smokes like a chimney, and uses language which would make a Billingsgate fish-woman blush.' Fuelling his disgust, 'her face was covered with powder, and her lips were quite impossibly scarlet.'[18] Hastings' view would have been shared by many of Christie's male (and older female) readers. As Christie recognised that novels need a love interest, which she always found irritating to write, Hastings becomes fascinated by this archetypical modern young woman, while Poirot with his egg-shaped head and fussy ways identified the murderer. If, before the war, detectives were supposed to be what would now be called 'Alpha Males', Golden Age Crime readers who had seen their sons, and in many cases their wealth, sacrificed by an authority which had betrayed their trust, were more receptive to a less aggressively dominant sleuth whose fascination with, and understanding of, the criminal's psychological make-up chimed with the times. In *The Murder of Roger Ackroyd* (1926) – her first for publisher Collins and voted in 2013 the best crime novel ever by the British Crime Writers' Association, Christie daringly broke some of the unwritten rules of the detective genre. Significantly, the character Caroline Sheppard contains the germ of Miss Marple.

Despite *Ackroyd*'s success, 1926 proved Christie's annus horribilis. The family was now extravagantly installed in Sunningdale (Berkshire) buying a house they could ill-afford which Archie suggested they call Styles, close to several golf courses about which he was now obsessed. With an unhappy past, this house would bring the Christies no greater luck than its previous owners. When her beloved mother died in spring 1926, Archie seemed unable to comprehend the depths of her grief. Although subconsciously aware that he 'had a violent dislike of illness, death and trouble of any kind', she had not anticipated his inability to comfort her. Suffering from increasing melancholia, she yearned for his support as she undertook the onerous task of clearing out the much-loved, by now near derelict, family home in Devon. Having temporarily let Styles to help ease their financial burdens and moved into his gentleman's club, Archie rejected her suggestion that he should come down some weekends to assist her and see their daughter whom he adored, arguably more than she did. When he finally visited in early August, he requested a divorce. Her disbelief, refusal, fears about the implications for Rosalind and perhaps the potential effects of divorce on her writing career, consumed her. A product of her age, however much Christie might be starting to incorporate 'new', powerful women, the idea of divorce appalled her. She felt that 'my happy successful life [had] ended'. Nor did she see why his mistress should be shielded.[19] No longer recognising this 'hostile stranger' as the man she had married, with the benefit of hindsight, she ultimately realised that 'because his conscience troubled him he could not help behaving with a certain ruthlessness.'[20] Writing as 'Mary Westmacott', her semi-autobiographical (1934) *Unfinished Portrait* reveals her mental trauma; she reveals the depths of the problems that had overwhelmed their marriage including how Archie, a product of his class and era, found being overshadowed by his wife a bitter pill to swallow.

On 3 December, following a violent evening row, Christie walked out of Styles where they were once again living. The next morning, her car was discovered, abandoned. The newspaper headlines relating to the 'missing' crime writer were incessant. Surrey and Berkshire Police forces, assisted by thousands of volunteers (warned to 'wear stout shoes and not expect remuneration'), including fellow authors such as Dorothy L Sayers and her husband, and *News of the World* crime and motoring reporter Mac Fleming, combed the surrounding countryside. The nearby Silent Pool was dragged. It was as though Christie had stepped into the pages of one of her own novels and provided the press with a gold mine. 'AEROPLANE FLIES LOW ROUND THE COUNTRYSIDE: Search For Missing Novelist', screamed *Lancashire Evening Post* (7 December), supplementing its extensive previous day's coverage. Using language that could refer to one of her own plots, every possible explanation and outcome – including suicide and potential murder with Archie temporarily a suspect, were analysed just as the countryside was scoured daily by those advised by *Sunday Pictorial*, to avoid 'patent leather shoes'. A 'mysterious message in a cylindrical tin' (*Daily Herald*, 9 December), a letter to Archie, 'I am going away, I cannot stay in Sunningdale any longer', seemed to provide the types of clues beloved by the Queen of Crime. Pathos was provided by a photograph of Christie, 'with her little daughter'. 'Important fresh clues' were constantly reported, as was the promise of a 'find'. The press were having a field day. By 14 December, Superintendent Kenward was warning the public to fear the worst – although some newspapers were now shifting away from sympathy, wondering if this disappearance were staged and she would be found alive and well having garnered miles of newspaper publicity.

Writing for *The Sketch*, 'Candidus' (13 December) captured a changing mood. Sayers was 'shocked to the marrow' when her kindly vicar father jumped 'to the most scandalous explanation of the Christie business', but he was not alone. [21] Was this a cynical novelist 'hoaxing a kindly public for reasons her own?' Was she 'hiding somewhere and perhaps enjoying the fuss and ado?' If so, it would be a 'crime against society more heinous than many a homicide'. He and the journalists who followed his lead were partly right. Christie was indeed hiding at the expensive Swan Hydropathic Hotel, Harrogate, taking the waters and mingling incognito with other guests using Archie's mistress's name, Neele; when she was eventually discovered, the name was on every page. After two interviews, a bad-tempered Archie refused to speak further to the press as Christie was whisked away to her sister Madge to recuperate from a significant breakdown. She subsequently suffered (or claimed to suffer) from complete amnesia relating to the episode which is not mentioned in her *An Autobiography*, nor was her official biographer given access to any private papers which may have shed some light on what had occurred.

As the 'lost eleven days' continues to be trawled for clues, novelists, TV drama producers, psychologists and psychiatrists offer theories. Medically, it is purported she was suffering from 'dissociative fugue' or psychogenic amnesia, a rare psychiatric disorder characterised by reversible amnesia which can last days, months or longer, in this instance probably triggered by her (overly) beloved mother's death and Archie's incessant, increasingly cruel psychological pressure as she refused to consent to the divorce. Ill-prepared for her resistance, her desire to protect Rosalind who she felt loved her father more than her mother, and her own belief that marriage was for life, his pressure on her appeared relentless.

Press interest, at least until the next nine-day wonder developed, was relentless, the media's power to intrude into lives was increasing. Angry at having been 'hoodwinked' into believing Christie was dead either by her own or someone else's hand, arguably regretting the constant promises of a 'breakthrough'. There was fury at the time wasted by the two constabularies, 'diverted for more than a week from their ordinary duties, while both in London and Berkshire exhaustive and not inexpensive investigations have been set on foot', with searchers travelling long distances to assist. The *Leeds Mercury* (15 December) headline, 'The Woman Who Caused All the Mystery' leaves the reader in no doubt as to that journalist's antipathy. This and other papers emphasised the cost, £1,000 (£57,800). For the first time in a missing person case, aeroplanes were used, tractors, bloodhounds, around 15,000 volunteers with charabancs 'lent free of charge by their proprietors', had scoured the countryside; this had been a manhunt on an unprecedented scale only to discover not a corpse, but a woman skulking under an assumed name in a Harrogate hotel. Henceforth crowds, the press and journalists would be anathema to Christie.[22] It is likely that her dislike of psychiatrists also dates from this period; psychiatrist Rebecca Lawrence points out, in her novels, 'Mrs Christie maligns us enough'.[23] Still today, psychiatrists seek to analyse her actions, modern diagnoses include bi-polar and depression. While her novels result in solvable crimes the answer to her disappearance remains elusive, one she ensured would never be fully revealed.

Arguments about the divorce continued. Further antagonised by Archie's determination to fabricate evidence to protect Nancy Neele's name, Christie was determined to drag this through the courts. Eventually, in mid-April 1928, 'Mrs Agatha Christie, the novelist, was petitioner in a divorce suit in the Divorce Court to-day …. She alleged that her husband

Colonel Archibald Christie had committed adultery with woman not named at the Grosvenor Hotel, London.'[24] Despite demonstrably unreliable 'evidence' being offered which could have resulted in the divorce's refusal, the decree nisi was granted, custody of Rosalind assigned to Christie who now had to resume writing in order to keep afloat financially. The three novels completed between 1927 and 1929 were not ones that Christie herself was enthusiastic about, although fans, particularly of Poirot, welcomed his reappearance. Her shame, which led to her never again taking Communion in church, was out of kilter with the times. After 1926, the annual divorce rate never fell below 3,000, although the cost prohibited countless less-affluent unhappy couples to sever the marriage bond.[25]

As the 20s became the 30s, with Christie happily remarried to Max Mallowan, the classic village spinster materialised into sleuth. Although American author Mary Robert Rhinehart's female detective Hilda Adams appeared in *The Buckled Bag* (1914), and older British readers may have been familiar with Mrs Gladden, Andrew Forrester's *The First Female Detective* (1864), Miss Marple was innovative. Christie herself did not quite know how she entered her imagination, except she resembled 'some of my grandmother's Ealing cronies ... expecting the worst of everyone and everything.'[26] First appearing in the short story collection *The Thirteen Problems,* her creator was unaware that she would come to rival Poirot and they would be together for life. Considered ignorant of the world and its wickedness, it is fluffy 'Aunt Jane' who unravels crimes, unmasks murderers often with a click of her knitting needles, and her devastating 'I told you so look'.

Poirot was a product of the war years, gently laughed at for his Belgian ways; such was his popularity that he is the only fictional character to have been granted an obituary in the *New York Times,* 'Hercule Poirot Is Dead', 6 August 1975. Miss Marple is rooted in the inter-war years. Aged around 65 to 70, yet in many ways ageless, her type, like Sayers' Miss Climpson – no sleuth but integral to several plots, was part of the post-war landscape. A generation of spinsters, approaching or having entered middle age when the war broke out, had seen any remaining hopes of matrimony dashed and now eked out a genteel existence in villages like 'St Mary Mead' – itself instantly recognisable in 1930s England. Marple also reflects the life that so many of Christie's age and class contemporaries were living; the life she and Archie had hoped to secure when they first bought Styles and one she may have relished if she were not constantly chewing her pen, trying to get started on the next book, reassuring readers that evil would be uncovered and the world move on securely.[27] Shopping at department stores, admiring glass, china, linens, sipping a cup of camomile tea or a glass of Marple's restorative homemade cowslip wine after witnessing a murder, the English rural life with peonies and scones, established families, the vicar, the doctor – who knew everyone – the occasional newcomer who has to be tolerated, and of course the aged spinster, provided reassurance as the world hurtled towards another global conflict. There was something deeply comforting about the novels set around St Mary Mead – even the name providing a sense of continuity – as well as the promise that whatever foul deeds were perpetrated, the murderer would be uncovered by the sleuth and perhaps by the attentive reader, and all would be well. Christie had kept faith with her fans and they in turn with her, resulting in her ranking at third place after the Bible and Shakespeare as the most published writer of all times.

But Miss Marple is more than an arthritic elderly spinster whose sweet peas win prizes at village flower shows, with vivid memories of village doctors' medicinal concoctions. She is also a product of an age in which women were grasping new opportunities. Seemingly deferential to male authority, she is operating both within and outside the imposed societal restraints. There is something subversive about this spinsterish female sleuth, the grandmother of the intuitive, psychological detectives of the late twentieth and twenty-first centuries who, using the supposedly traditional feminine attributes of intuition and observation, achieve the resolution that has eluded the male police.[28] It is to Miss Marple and her creator that today's detective writers owe a debt. The Golden Age of Crime was indeed that, not only for its female writers but for the female as well as the less masculine male detectives they created.

With public appetite for crime writing remaining voracious, in 1930 Agatha Christie and Dorothy L. Sayers became founder members of The Detection Club, formed to provide crime writers with mutual support and a series of rules that the occasional reviewer chided Sayers with breaking. Dubbed Queens of Crime, their backgrounds differed educationally, socially and in their experiences of the Great War. Unlike Christie, Sayers saw no war service. In France when war broke out, 'which is frightfully thrilling', she returned to England on 25 August 1914 and subsequently Oxford, soon temporary home to a number of

Belgian refugees – none of whom, other than their perceived class-consciousness, made any impression on her.[29] Writing to a friend, she mentions two relations home from the Front with 'nervous breakdowns'. 'I'm rather glad they've gone', undoubtedly her first personal exposure to this condition which was mentioned 367 times in newspapers in 1915.[30] Her reaction was not unusual, for most civilians, shell shock or PTSD was incomprehensible, threatening, poorly understood. Nevertheless, her wartime life was as near normal as it could be for a woman studying in a university denuded of male students; 14,561 current and former Oxford University members served, 19 per cent (2,767) were killed.[31] She began to 'hate ever-lasting war-talk', rejected both nursing, 'I should hate nursing, hard labour and horrors', and 'working with the Quakers in France', and pursued her studies, achieving equivalent First Class Honours (Oxford only conferred degree status on women in 1920, Sayers was among the first graduands).[32]

If in 1915 Sayers had been perturbed by her kinsmen's 'breakdown', by 1918, no month passed without the press mentioning 'shell-shock'. With demobilisation, searching questions needed to be asked about the condition, with its far-reaching consequences and profound social and economic implications. The post-war world was a harsh one for veterans and disabled personnel but for none more so than neurasthenics. The 1916 Lunacy Act remained the definitive statutory provision under which in 'appropriate circumstances', traumatised veterans would be incarcerated in asylums.[33] The 1919 Mental Treatment Amendment Act stipulated that 'all ex-servicemen confined in mental war hospitals under martial law, should be committed without right of appeal to asylums operated under the Ministry of Pensions, making many sufferers and their families hesitant about seeking help. Aware that some 65,000 men were drawing disability pensions for neurasthenia, 9,000 were still hospitalised, and high numbers of veterans (including nursing personnel) remained deeply traumatised by their war service, in April 1920, Lord Southborough proposed an inquiry. The June 1922 *Report of the War Office Committee of Inquiry into "Shell Shock"* featured in several newspapers. Although the Committee recognised that 'the term "shell-shock" was wholly misleading ... it had been established and the harm was already done' – and used it.[34] Notwithstanding the acknowledgement that 'many healthy young males had suddenly begun to develop symptoms of neurasthenia', some medical witnesses remained sceptical. An extreme view was that 'any soldier above the rank of corporal seemed possessed of too much dignity to become "hysterical".[35]

Long before Southborough raised his concerns, on 1 November 1918, a group of women chaired by a Mrs Waddingham had formally gathered, determined to apply their considerable energies to providing some relief for nerve-shattered veterans. With the un-catchy name 'The Fellowship of Reconstruction and Welfare Bureau for Ex-servicemen of all Ranks and Services, their Wives, Widows and Relatives including the Merchant Marine', changed in July 1919 to the 'Ex-Services Welfare Society' and then after the Second World War to 'Combat Stress', the charity campaigned tirelessly for these damaged men. Within three months, it resolved to make provision for those cases of acute mental breakdown that would otherwise have been committed to asylums, which it vehemently opposed, instead seeking to support veterans to acquire employable skills and offer residential care for those who could not. Still campaigning to this day (sometimes politically unpopularly) for veterans' improved treatment and care, on Armistice Day 1924 a pamphlet publicised the fact that several thousand ex-servicemen were in institutions which, until recently, were described as 'pauper lunatic asylums'.

Shell-shock would underpin Sayers' work. In October 1920, facing a bleak future with little employment, she moved to London. By July 1921, Lord Peter Wimsey had 'walked in' to her imagination; despite subsequent efforts to rid herself of him, he refused to depart.[36] Needing to earn her living, wanting to write and an admirer of Conan Doyle, detective fiction may have seemed the obvious choice; the insatiable middle-class appetite for the genre offered the prospect of a ready market. The idea for *Whose Body?*, in which Wimsey and shell-shock make their début, had been in her head since her Oxford days.[37] Following publication in America, the *Leeds Mercury* of 18 October 1923 offered praise and surprise that 'a woman writer could be so robustly gruesome'. The *Northern Whig* of 3 November praised her 'remarkable skill' and commented on her use of 'puzzles', which became a prominent feature of all Golden Age Crime novels. Simply commenting on Wimsey as detective, the reviewer hoped to 'hear from this noble sleuth again'. Although less widely reviewed than Christie's *Styles*, 100,000 copies were sold in seven weeks; Sayers and Wimsey had made a favourable impression. While Christie's skills with poison were instantly recognised, Sayers' understanding of neurasthenia was overlooked. Although in this first novel, 'the noble sleuth' is something of a foppish ass, owing (too) much to Bertie Wooster, she had presented a character flawed not, like Sherlock Holmes, by his opium addiction, but by his own internal wounds. While Christie's Poirot entertains, Wimsey, who ages with his creator, challenges and disturbs.

Sometime around August 1925, Sayers met Mac Fleming, a divorced 'archetypal Fleet Street man'.[38] How aware she, or even he, was of his neurasthenia is unclear. They married on 13 April 1926, only informing her parents when it would be too late for them to attend. In a July 1926 letter, she tells her mother Mac had been 'badly gassed' in the war, adding that in such a situation, 'one cannot expect to go on quite as usual'. Time would reveal that 'Doctors don't seem to be able to do much' about his condition.[39] The marriage was not her only secret, she had also concealed the January 1924 birth of her son Anthony. Fostered near Oxford by her cousin Ivy, she never revealed his father's name. Anthony's birth would have both shamed and devastated her parents. Nursing her secret, she continued working in both the advertising firm Benson and on her second (of eleven) Wimsey novel, *Clouds of Witness* – where shell-shock, dreams and memories of Belgium, play a significant role and reveal more about the relationship between Wimsey and his valet Bunter. In a rare self-revealing line, she confesses that one character has the 'misfortune to become disagreeable when she was unhappy'. Sayers herself may have had good reason to be 'disagreeable', the 1920s were unkind to unmarried mothers and their offspring. In 1918, wartime welfare worker Lettice Fisher had founded The National Council for the Unmarried Mother and Her Child to provide help without stigmatising these women for whom contraception was unavailable, abortion illegal and who 'are no more blameworthy than men'.[40] It would be decades before such stigma was removed. The Council's Piccadilly headquarters were close to where the fictional Wimsey resided.

When Sayers began writing about her shell-shocked sleuth, she may have understood the condition in theory, but its impact upon her life would become apparent. Unlike the fictional Wimsey, cushioned by wealth and protected by Bunter who, like Christie's country house settings, is a throwback to a former age, Sayers had to confront Mac's disability which rendered him ever less reliable at work. Her being the main breadwinner affronted his masculinity while his 'fits of temper' meant 'it isn't easy for me to get any work done'.[41] Her most devastating account of a wife's reality of neurasthenia occurs in *The Unpleasantness at the Bellona Club* (1928), 'unpleasantness' stretching far beyond the club where the murder

121

occurred. That this is a novel steeped in the Great War can be adduced by the relevance of Armistice Day to the plot. The character of George Fentiman more closely resembles Mac than the idealised Wimsey. Cruel to his wife Sheila who supports him financially, Fentiman is bitter about 'the modern girl … that's what we fought the war for – and that's what we've come back to', and is delusional, leading him to confess to a crime he has not committed (recognised neurasthenic behaviour). Although in the innocent Fentiman's case this was 'the old trouble come back again', a plea of 'shell-shock' for criminal actions had become an acceptable defence. The scenes between the Fentimans, undoubtedly drawn from the Fleming household, even details such as Fentiman's 'tummy … feeling rotten', are among the most bitter in the canon. The reader admires the beleaguered Sheila and, at one remove Sayers, who stood by Mac. For Sheila, for Sayers, and for thousands who have lived with a shell-shocked veteran, anger is the third member of the relationship. There are strong hints that on these occasions Sayers was frightened, Mac could 'go into such a frightful fit of rage that one gets really alarmed', advising Ivy, 'Don't refer to this openly.'[42] A decade after the Armistice, men like Mac, the fictional Fentiman and Wimsey were constant guilt-inducing reminders of the gap between those who had served and civilians. While the physically maimed were visible, mental wounds could be more frightening as these could erupt at any moment, even in the most charming of sufferers, Wimsey's 'heart-breaking courtesy was punctuated by fits of exigent and exhausting passion'.[43]

In his bitter 1918 'Glory of Women', Siegfried Sassoon poeticised those 'wounded in a mentionable place'. Sayers dares to foreground what it was like both for those wounded in less 'mentionable' ways, and for those whose lives were blighted by others' wounds. If fictional Sheila's brother-in-law 'doesn't know how she puts up with' Fentiman, one wonders the same about Sayers, with Mac's 'increasing dependence on the bottle' and his temper, which had 'always been capable of violence'.[44] Like their creator, both Shelia Fentiman and Harriet Vane, Wimsey's eventual wife, whose razor-sharp intellect mirrors Sayers' own, are helpless bystanders as battle is waged in this endless, exhausting struggle. Unlike Fentiman and indeed Mac, in the last full-length Wimsey novel *Busman's Honeymoon,* the 'noble sleuth' and flawed hero finally reveals his weakness, 'It's my rotten nerves, I've never been really right since the war.'[45] It has taken eleven novels for this confession. But Vane still has to discover how to reach him. Despite being forewarned by her mother-in-law and Bunter, she was 'becoming less and less a person to him'.[46] She and their marriage are now on trial. The reader is dragged into the claustrophobic world of a neurasthenic veteran who, in his 'caged pacing to and fro', acknowledges he is a 'tormented devil'; every word she utters has to be right; if they cannot 'see it out together', the month-old marriage is doomed. To his, 'I tried to stick it out by myself', she gently asks, 'Why should you?' When he admits, 'You're my corner and I've come to hide', putting his head in her lap and weeping, Sayers can let the couple go.[47] They have been offered the resolution that eluded her own war-damaged marriage.

As a writer of detective fiction, Sayers is, in terms of plot, less 'satisfying' than Christie. But to overlook the shell-shock leitmotif of the Wimsey novels is to underrate her achievements and understanding of her world. Crimes may be reassuringly detected and murderers hanged, but the peaceful pre-1914 England to which readers longed to retreat would prove as illusory as the 25 October 1914 *Times'* belief that the 'heroic values of Agincourt' would be revived on the killing fields of France and Flanders.

Edith Thompson: The 'cool workings of authority'[48]

In December 1922, in the presence of Mr Justice Shearman and a jury of eleven men and one woman, Edith Thompson and Freddie Bywaters were charged on two counts with the murder of her husband Percy 'on the 4th day of October 1922 in the County of Essex' and of 'conspiring to murder'. Thompson had three additional counts of causing to 'be taken a certain destructive thing'.[49] The murder and subsequent trial rocked the nation. It filled miles of newspaper columns and remains one of the twentieth century's most contentious murder trials. Its ramifications reached far beyond three individuals hopelessly trapped in a love triangle.

On 15 January 1916, Edith Graydon reluctantly left her home, 231 Shakespeare Crescent, to marry Percy Thompson. She had just told her father William, 'I can't go through with it, I don't want to go.' Aware of the embarrassment of having to explain that his daughter had changed her mind, William reminded her that everyone was 'waiting' at St Barnabas Church, Manor Park.[50] Like so many of their (lower-middle) class, the Graydons dreaded community disapproval. The stage was now set for a Shakespearean tragedy whose ramifications continued long after the principal players were dead. Other than shunning disapproval, why William insisted upon his daughter going through with the marriage is not clear, although it may have had something to do with the heightened atmosphere of 1916. The Derby Scheme had just been passed into law and it was only a matter of time before Percy was called up.

Theirs had been a long courtship, having met on their commute into London to their respective workplaces, Percy as a shipping clerk and Graydon an increasingly successful office worker at wholesale milliner Carlton & Pryor, Aldersgate. It was obvious that she would be the more successful with, unusually for the time, her wages outstripping his. Office work gave intelligent girls from the working and lower-middle class an entrée into a respectable occupation and the chance of moving up the social scale, which she craved. Her boss, who stood staunchly by her, could not speak highly enough of her skills and her prospects. Whether her acceptance of Percy's proposal was influenced by the wholesale slaughter that had occurred throughout 1915, the feeling that any husband was worth having, and the likelihood that soon to be conscripted Percy would be elevated to 'national hero' status, is not impossible. There is ample evidence that she lived partly in a fantasy world, and popular novels – which she adored – depicted gallant heroes in uniform. A magazine 'Agony Aunt's warning words that a girl 'should remember that great events bring out the best in people and that the man who is a hero in a national crisis may be anything but that in an ordinary everyday home', proved prescient.[51] There was nothing heroic about Percy. Out of uniform almost as quickly as he donned it, overweight and a heavy smoker, he seemingly successfully hoodwinked the Army Medical Board into believing he had a heart condition and was honourably discharged.[52]

From 1917 they lodged in Westcliffe-on-Sea, safe from Zeppelins raids which reduced Percy to a wreck; this gave Edith time to indulge her love of reading while commuting into London. She continued working at Carlton & Pryor (war work such as munitions making as opposed to a frivolous office job may have garnered jury sympathy). With the war over, they lived with Percy's sister and her family in Mansfield Road, Ilford. Signs that all was not well in the Thompson marriage were visible. With Percy becoming violent towards Edith, they were asked to leave and barely saw his sister again. The Thompsons, largely aided by her £6 (£395) per week salary plus bonuses – larger than both Percy's and her father's at a time when women were automatically paid less for the same job as a man, were purchasing their own home, 41 Kensington Gardens, in the desirable suburb of Ilford. They planned to evict their sitting tenants Mrs and Miss Lester as soon as possible – this never materialised. Mrs Lester remained staunchly on Edith's side, although the women were not close. She remembered assisting Edith when, on 1 August 1921, her arm was 'black from the shoulder to the elbow from having been thrown across the room'.[53] A subsequent Home Office Memorandum framed this so that Edith was seen as having provoked the row and therefore 'deserved' the violence. The concept of domestic violence, like rape in marriage, simply did not exist in the official male brain. Edith's lawyer, Sir Henry Curtis-Bennett K.C, did not even bring such episodes to the court's attention. Mrs Lester told the 17 December 1922 *Sunday Post*, 'Mrs Thompson should have left her husband long ago.' She wondered why this 'sprightly, life-loving girl, full of fun, and always anxious to sample the joys the world could offer', had married Percy, 'a difficult, morose sort of man, with scarcely a laugh in him for whole days'. Lester had pinpointed the issues that dominated this miserable marriage, Thompson being a 'fun-loving girl' helps explain the judge's barely concealed antagonism.

The national stage upon which Edith Thompson would soon burst assumed women would resume their pre-1914 status. There was the unfortunate fact that some had been enfranchised (Thompson being under 30 was too young), but the sooner ideas of empowerment were dropped and the jobs into which they had stepped vacated, the better. Married women should embrace the joys of domesticity and motherhood and in no way compete with men in the job market. Pro-natalists, popular magazines including 'Problem Pages', and sexologists were united in presenting motherhood as the supreme achievement of a woman's life. In 1922, even childless women trapped in unhappy marriages could do little to extricate themselves. 'Till death us do part' meant that. William, aware that all was not well in his daughter's marriage, was a frequent visitor, sometimes staying overnight; the Graydons remained a close-knit family.

Concerns about women's morality, their dress and their working lives abounded. While the term 'Flapper' pre-dated the war, 'the "Jazzing Flapper", the social butterfly type … scantily clad … to whom a dance or a new hat [is] more important than the fate of nations', constantly appears in 1920s print media.[54] 'Fast young women even powdered their noses in public', married women were a particular source of opprobrium, 'hussies with three inches of powder on their faces'.[55] Nevertheless, the 'use of makeup, rouge, eyebrow and eyelash colouring, and lipstick were all made available', for women like Edith who also enjoyed a spot of gambling ('I've got 10/- on a horse each way'), times were changing.[56] Edith was almost the prototype of this new era. Retaining her maiden name at work, she had no intention of leaving her job which was enabling her not only to buy a house, but furnish it with the pretty things she craved. Nor was she going to settle down to her pre-ordained role as child-bearer, even though women who 'refused motherhood in order to continue with their work or study were castigated', and not only in the pages of the popular press, psychiatrists joined the opprobrium.[57] She had not inherited her parents' belief in conformity.

In 1920, Edith's sister Avis (b.1896) whose fiancé had been killed in 1917, had renewed her acquaintance with her younger brother's handsome friend Freddie Bywaters. Born in 1902 and too young to enlist, he had joined the Merchant Navy at 15; now he was experienced beyond his 18 years. With the 1914–18 slaughter having wiped out around one in seven of her male contemporaries and wounded a million more, the Graydons overlooked the considerable age difference when he started courting waitress Avis. This may have prompted her to suggest that with his ship laid up for repairs, he lodge at Shakespeare Crescent rather than with his widowed mother in Upper Norwood. The third actor in the tragedy had made his entrance. Edith was a regular visitor and, more savvy than Avis with her smart clothes, well-paid City job and vibrant personality, she fascinated him. A summer holiday (1921) was planned on the Isle of Wight. The Thompsons would escort Avis and Bywaters, who was clearly everything that Percy was not: witty, fun-loving and unable to resist the alluring Mrs Thompson; her defence counsel considered her, 'one of the most extraordinary personalities that you or I might ever meet'. [58] Avis paled into insignificance. At the end of the holiday, Percy seconded Edith's suggestion that Bywaters occupy their spare bedroom; he would be cuckolded under his own roof, a point which the prosecution would seize upon, quoting her 27 August 1922 'anniversary' letter to Bywaters, 'Fourteen whole months have gone by ... Neither you nor I thought we should have to wait all that long time.' Book-lover Edith's fictive and real worlds had collided; she would elevate what outsiders saw as a tawdry little affair into a great love worthy of the heroines of her fantasy world.

If he were previously in any doubt, Bywaters soon realised that the Thompson marriage was troubled and sought to defend Edith, further antagonising Percy. With twenty-first century eyes, one feels bemused that she remained in this loveless, violent relationship. Yet beyond the sheer cost of divorce lay other ramifications: the house and its contents were largely her purchases; she would have been fearful of dismissal from her job, which she loved, and realised the difficulty of finding a new one in the harsh 1922 economic climate (harshest for married women). In addition, 'respectability' would have been dinned into her throughout her childhood and divorce may even have jeopardised her family's love and certainly their pride in her. Bywaters may have advised her against this irrevocable step. On 13 March 1922 she wondered why he said, 'Never run away, face things and argue and beat everybody', replying, 'Do I ever run away? Have I ever run away? And do you think I should be likely to now?'[59]

Seemingly concerned about how long she, eight years older, could retain his love and that a sailor may have a girl in every port, she asks about possible lovers. Nor was she above provoking his jealousy, she had been to 'their' Holborn Restaurant and had a drink with another man, 'You're not cross are you darlint? No, you mustn't be.' She may even want to make Bywaters jealous of Percy: 21 September 1921, 'He has the right by law to all that you have the right to by nature and love' – although a different interpretation could be she is seeking his pity for her husband forcing himself upon her. Trial judge, Mr Justice Shearman twisted this against her, to him this indicated, 'that the love of a husband for his wife is something improper'.[60] Nevertheless, on 3 January, fearful she may be pregnant with Bywaters' child, she hopes that Percy will do just that, 'I think it the best way to disarm any suspicion.'

Maternity may have been Thompson's perceived destiny, but she was so determined not to embrace it that she took matters into her own hands. On several occasions, she asks Bywaters, the knowledgeable sailor, to procure her an abortifacient. At the trial, such refences were constructed by the prosecution as referring to her intention to procure poison. With abortion illegal, referred to coyly in the courts as a 'certain thing', Curtis-Bennett dared not reveal to the jury that she was seeking a termination. On 23 January, she told Bywaters how she eventually had to be taken home where 'something awful happened'. Recounting her ordeal in graphic detail, 'I don't know for certain what it was, but I can guess, can you, write, & tell me.' Desperate to arouse no suspicion, (that she suffered from endometriosis worked to her advantage) within a very few days, she 'dressed & went out & really enjoyed myself' – this capacity for enjoying herself would be used against this 'new woman'.

Bywaters and Edith's affair was above all epistolary; he travelled the world with P&O, always writing to her work address from exotic places; 15 February, 'Miss Prior took it in & examined the seal [Aden].' Living primarily through the fantasy of romance literature, clandestine letters may have helped her to escape the humdrum Ilford-Liverpool Street-Aldersgate routine. She was always careful to destroy his letters; he, against her instructions did not, keeping them in his sailor's 'ditty box'. That there was much that a prosecution lawyer could use to her detriment in the letters and which Curtis-Bennett fought hard and unsuccessfully to conceal, is beyond question; 'Mr Justice Shearman ruled that they were admissible, both as evidence of intent and motive.'[61] Had Bywaters destroyed them, the case against her would have collapsed with no evidence to prove she was an accessory to the crime, nor that poison had supposedly been discussed. He may have kept them with the germ of an idea that they could provide useful blackmail in the future, there was something of the thug about him, although he did his utmost to protect her at the trial, denying her complicity even on the scaffold.

On 15 February, she wrote, 'it's heart breaking to think all the scheming – all the efforts are in vain. But we'll be patient.' This, Counsel for the Prosecution Mr Travers Humphreys claimed, was one of the many times she was inciting her lover to assist her in poisoning Percy. No matter that Home Office pathologist Bernard Spilsbury found 'no indications of poisoning and no changes suggestive of previous attempts of poisoning', nor even of 'glass in the contents of the intestine', which a letter had mentioned: 'I'm going to try the glass again.'[62] The admonition, 'Don't keep this piece' was, in the Crown's eyes, further evidence of guilt as opposed to of a bored, unhappy woman who lived through novels such as 'Bella Donna'.

While the Thompson marriage was inwardly an unhappy one, to many outsiders it appeared peaceful enough. Percy, aware that the cuckolded husband was frequently a figure of fun, kept his fears enclosed within the walls of Kensington Gardens: 4 April, 'He knows or guesses something – how much or how little I can't find out.' Mrs Lester would testify to frequent, sometimes violent, bedroom rows. With Bywaters at sea more than he was in England, life continued its drab round; her one great pleasure was to curl up reading his letters by the light of the fire while her husband lay asleep. 24 January 'I stayed up in front of the fire until 10.30 with you darlint – thinking of you & thinking of us & thinking of that "Glorious Adventure" that you are helping me with. You are, aren't you?' The rhetorical question and elevating their affair to a 'Glorious Adventure' suggest she wondered if she were losing her hold on her 'darlingest boy' – such language, novelist Rebecca West cruelly claimed, demonstrated Thompson's 'mental furniture was meagre'.[63] Mrs Bywaters, whose husband had died in 1919 from the effects of gas, fearful of 'that woman's' influence over her son, was desperately trying to warn him off, explaining in her subsequent appeal to King George, 'he fell under the spell of a woman much older than himself'. With his father's guiding hand, she believed Freddie would not have erred, but his father had 'made the supreme sacrifice'; she included documentary proof, but the Home Office felt that the father's war service was not grounds to reprieve 'cold-blooded murder'.[64]

The Thompsons enjoyed the theatre, their choice of play may have appeared lowbrow to the intelligentsia but both were looking forward to an October evening performance of 'The Dippers' at the Criterion Theatre with her relatives, Lillie and Jack Laxton. As always, Edith dressed with care, a 'slate-grey crêpe-de-chine frock, and over it the expensive brown musquash fur coat with its heavy boa collar, light silk stockings [a sign of affluence], black patent shoes, and a brown velvet hat to match her coat', an ensemble that a successful 1920s woman would have enjoyed being seen in.[65] She may also have dressed to impress Bywaters, whose home leave ended the next day and whom she had arranged to see near her work before meeting Percy, dining, and going to the theatre. Anyone who saw her would have agreed with Thomas Hardy (who supported the verdict and the penalty) that she was 'Comely and capable' yet, as he also recognised, 'Plain yet becoming.'[66] The evening over, gratified to see how content the younger couple appeared, they parted company, the Laxtons rather 'envy[ing] their youthful happiness'.[67]

Edith, sensing Bywaters would be depressed that she was not around for his last evening ashore, had been overheard in a teashop, telling him 'to do something'. He had remained on excellent terms with the Graydons, who welcomed him to Shakespeare Crescent; despite suspicions of an affair with their married daughter, they still hoped that Avis would land him which would have resolved any potential adultery and removed the stigma of 'surplus woman' from Avis. He left at 11pm and, with a knife in his pocket, headed to Ilford; he knew at approximately what time the Thompsons would arrive to walk the 0.8miles from Ilford station to Kensington Gardens. At a street intersection, Bywaters pounced and a short and bloody fight ensued. Stabbed eleven times, Percy collapsed, the street awash with blood. A nearby, resident, John Webber, heard Edith screaming in 'a most piteous manner', 'Oh don't; oh don't.' Although this testimony should have helped exonerate her, little attention was paid to it at the trial. Having cradled her dying husband, covered in his blood, near hysterical, she rushed for Dr Maudsley who lived close by. Bizarrely missing the multiple stab wounds, he asked if Percy had been taken ill on the train and summoned a police ambulance. Meanwhile Edith, catching a glimpse of a fleeing figure, realised to her horror this was Bywaters making a headlong dash, attempting to put as much distance between himself and the scene of the murder. Nevertheless her thoughts were with Percy who, despite her pleas to Maudsley to 'Do something', was dead.

The police took control; Edith was seen home and subsequently gently requested to go to the Police Station to shed any light she could on what had happened. Accompanied by her mother, a policeman's daughter who had due respect for 'the Law', there seemed nothing to fear. No suggestion was made that a solicitor should be present. CID Detective Frederick Wensley who wrote up the case in *Detective Days*, giving himself due credit for superb detection in what was a straightforward case with a suspect soon rounded up, affirmed 'no real suspicion of Mrs Thompson crossed my mind. There was no doubt that her distress was genuine.'[68] A cooperative witness, yet aware that she should conceal Bywaters' name, denied knowing anyone who could have wished to harm her husband. This seemingly meaningless attack did not totally surprise Wensely, 'It was not many years since the war and during that time there had been a few cases of people doing extraordinarily motiveless things'; this may have been another such incident.[69] The neighbours having asserted that the Thompsons were a perfectly happy couple, there was no reason to suspect Edith. It was Percy's brother Richard, who loathed his sister-in-law and drip-fed venom about her for the rest of his life, who first mentioned Bywaters but believed him to be 'at sea'. It did not take the police long to discover that he was due to sail the next day. He was apprehended and brought to Ilford. Wensley considered him 'a conceited and dictatorial young man full of self-assurance, and there was a kind of studied arrogance in his tone.'[70] Bywaters confirmed that he and Edith had exchanged 'one or two letters' which had been 'destroyed'. A search of his room revealed the truth. Not only had he lied, the letters cast the widow in a different light, 'couched in passionate terms that left no doubt of their relationship. ... I could not fail to remark a sinister under-current in some passages ... "darlint be jealous, so much so that you will do something desperate".' Wensley overlooked the reference to domestic violence, 'I could be beaten all over at home and still be defiant.'[71] It is probable that, despite neighbours (but not lodger Mrs Lester) seeing them as a 'happy couple', Edith hid this from the outside world – so often the victim sees herself as deserving of the violence and she may, in the cold light of day, have recognised the 'Great Adventure' for the adultery it was. If witnesses came forward eager to confirm hearing the line written on 2 October, 'Don't forget what we talked in the Tea Room. I'll still risk and try if you will,' this would provide the damning evidence against her that Wensley now seemed determined to unearth.[72] He felt that the case had moved on nicely with Percy barely twenty-four hours dead. With neither suspect supported by a solicitor, whether by coincidence or contrived, Edith caught sight of Bywaters, 'Oh God, ... what can I do? ... Why did he do it? I did not want him to do it ... I must tell the truth'; the warning, 'You realise what you are saying Mrs Thompson? It may be used in evidence,' was (intentionally?) delivered too late.[73] She had almost convicted him. With the evidence against him irrefutable, Bywaters himself was astounded when he learnt that she too was being charged, 'Why her? ... Mrs Thompson was not aware of my movements'.[74]

The drama being played out inside Ilford Police Station soon riveted the country. The genteel 'Ilford suburb' figured in almost every national and local newspaper as the pair were charged and remanded at Stratford Police Court. 'Ilford Murder' shrieked the headlines as the couple were tried by the court of public opinion long before they appeared at Old Bailey's Court No. 1. A more sympathetic *Times* (6 October) reported how Thompson, widowed only seventy-two hours earlier and now charged with a capital offence, was helped into court by a female attendant. 'She was provided with a chair and sat with her limbs trembling and hands clutching her garments.' When she left court, she 'had to be practically carried out'. At the end of the hearing, Bywaters requested 'legal assistance', which surely should have been advised at the beginning.

The Times was almost alone in reserving judgement. It was as though male proprietors were unleashing all their pent-up fury at the 'New' emancipated women that Thompson epitomised: fun-loving, flirting, dancing, putting the war years behind them and revelling in their freedom seemingly bought with the blood of those who, like Detective Wensley's sons, lay in Flanders Fields. Having dared to glory in her femininity, now she would pay the price. *Sunday Express* editor Sir James Douglas claimed she was the 'creation of an hysteric and hectic age', rather than the pathetic creature she had become.[75] A selection of her letters to Bywaters, in which it is obvious that she was conflating her daily diet of cheap fiction with their tawdry love affair, would be laid before the public, read out in stentorian tones by the Counsel for the Prosecution in front of a moralist judge; all she could do was hold her head in her hands. Legal opinion deemed that her luck ran out when the case was listed for Mr Justice Shearman.

The Graydon family, shaken to its roots by the unfolding tragedy, were determined to purchase the best defence money could buy, retaining Sir Henry Curtis-Bennett K.C. What Edith seemed unable to understand was that she should follow his advice. Without her in the witness box, the prosecution's case would be weakened. Headstrong, believing that she could convince judge and jury of her innocence, she refused. Modern lawyers argue that with her disregarding his counsel, he should have refused the case. Dressed carefully in sombre colours, with her cleaned musquash coat and 'black velvety hat with black quills' as befitted her widowhood, she was the principal player in this melodrama which crowds struggled to attend – even paying the unemployed £5 (£232) to stand all night to reserve them a place when the doors opened; this, several newspapers considered, 'the decadence of public taste'.

After five long days, which consisted 'of sordid dullness and squalid boredom', but which newspapers reported in breathless detail, Shearman summed up.[76] Despite a moment of sympathy for Thompson and admiration for Bywaters, who was doing everything in his power to protect his co-accused, it would have been obvious to Curtis-Bennett, as it was to all legal observers, that the jury was being forcefully directed towards a 'Guilty' verdict for both defendants. Only two and a quarter hours were required. Avoiding the defendants' eyes, 'the jury file back into court, 'the woman comes in last. She is white to the lips.'[77] Less white than Thompson who had to be almost carried to the rail by two wardresses. Black-capped and white-gloved, Shearman twice pronounced the dreadful sentence, both were to hang, their bodies 'buried within the precincts of the prison', ending with the comfortless words, 'May God have mercy on your soul'.

Almost blaming all societal ills on this female black-clad representative of the rising lower-middle class which was threatening the social order, *Sunday Express* editor James Douglas' 'Case For and Against a Reprieve' (17 December), captured the mood of the trial. Edith Thompson embodied what is 'fatally corrupt in a society which breeds this frame of mind in the respectable, drab, dull soul of ordinary, commonplace folk.' How dared she, a product of the 'underworld of the humdrum clerks and the humdrum milliners where life is lived on a few pounds a week', ache with romantic longing for release from her 'duty' to her 'long-suffering husband and cosy home'. No mention of his violence or her financial investment in this unhappy home.

Having bayed for blood, awareness that Edith might end the twenty years hiatus during which no woman had been hanged, now dawned on Grub Street. No matter. If women wanted the equality of the vote, they would have to accept the equality of the rope. The official line that she could hardly be reprieved if Bywaters was not, was promulgated despite his having incontrovertibly wielded the knife while the only flimsy evidence against her were melodramatic letters from which only carefully selected portions had been read. The new Home Secretary, Sir William Bridgeman (who had recently replaced the liberal Sir Edward Shortt who, during his tenure, had reprieved a female co-defendant also tried by Shearman) was distressed by the verdict. Writing to his mother, he had hoped Edith would not be found guilty because 'I shall be flooded with petitions to let her off.'[78] In this he was wrong. Public sympathy had swung completely away from her towards Bywaters and his gallant attempt to protect this femme fatale. Even feminist papers such as *Common Cause* did not mention her, merely condemning the death penalty in principle. The appeal on 21 December, that the verdict went against the weight of evidence, that the defendants should have been tried separately, that the judge had misdirected the jury, was rejected. Like Bywaters, she would hang. Lillie Laxton, the last member of her family to see Edith at liberty contacted the 'Gentlemen of the Cabinet', 'The punishment of years of confinement is bourne [*sic*] by the offenders but the punishment of hanging is bourne by the parents and relations.'[79] True, but that did not perturb these 'Gentlemen'.

With Edith held in the 'convicted cell' at Holloway where two wardresses would watch her round the clock – the state had to exact its revenge, no possibility of suicide could be entertained – the prison chaplain, Granville Murray, sought to extract a confession. This would ease the collective conscience. With nothing to confess, Edith refused. Prison visitor Margery Fry, an ardent campaigner against capital punishment, tried to extract a confession. With nothing to confess, Edith refused. Perplexed 'by the foolish girl', Fry got closer to the truth than anyone; Edith 'had romanticised her sordid little love affair and genuinely thought herself innocent, discounting her own influence on her lover'.[80] But she was found guilty of incitement to murder, not influence.

Outside the prison, the two desperate mothers were petitioning the Queen as a mother, Mrs Graydon's 'Most Gracious Sovereign', even sending a reply-paid telegram to Sandringham. The communications were passed to the Home Office and ignored. A Catholic priest, Canon Palmer, visited Thompson. He seemed to provide some comfort; she asked Prison Governor and medical doctor John Morton, that Palmer continue to visit her and be present at the end. The Prison Commissioners to whom Morton cravenly forwarded the request, which he subsequently regretted, refused. She was not Roman Catholic therefore the uncomforting Prison Chaplain Murray would be her spiritual comforter. Bywaters requested permission to write to her, the Prison Commissioners refused. Her solicitor travelled across the country to appeal to Bridgeman for a reprieve, he refused. Prison doctor Dora Walker was summoned on Edith's 29th birthday, Christmas Day, because she was hysterical and screaming, 'Why did he do it?' She sedated her.[81] Walker may have hoped that the rumour that would (and continues to) circulate that being pregnant Edith would automatically escape the gallows, was well-founded. It was not. Prison Governor Morton confirmed the (double) execution date: 9 January 1923 at 9am.

Public hangman John Ellis was offered the commission. It would involve his first flight – Manchester to Croydon; he returned by rail, the flight crashed on the return journey killing all on board. Ellis claimed that he was still expecting an eleventh-hour reprieve; he was convinced 'she had no actual part in committing the crime for which she was sentenced to death', and believed that by keeping the letters, Bywaters had inadvertently, 'led Edith to the scaffold'.[82] This man of little formal education but long exposure to condemned murderers and an innate understanding of crowd behaviour commented how, with the appeal rejected, 'the British public accomplish[ed] one of those remarkable voltes-face for which it is renowned. Up until this point, Edith had been execrated. Now 'a wave of revulsion swept the country from one end to the other. The authorities went calmly about their business.'[83] To some, Ellis may have appeared to be doing the same, whether the claim that he accepted the commission genuinely believing he could make her end as quick and painless as possible, or if this was self-justification after the event is a secret he took with him to his grave. He first attempted suicide in 1924 and succeeded in 1932.

The final scene in the tragedy or, as some claimed, melodrama, was due to be enacted. Ellis had gained the necessary measurements to 'manage the drop'. Drugged by an increasingly irresolute Morton with the most powerful combination of sedatives and stimulants – no condemned (wo) man could be comatose as they faced the noose, she had to be carried the seven yards from her cell to the execution shed. A 4,000-strong crowd gathered outside Holloway, the newspapers had helpfully reminded readers, 'Ilford Execution Today'. A woman paraded outside the jail 'carrying two sandwich boards. One read, "If this woman is hanged the judge and jury are murderers also." The other read "you cannot abolish murder by murder".'[84] Mounted police were necessary for crowd control. Nine o'clock struck, the throng expected the prison governor to appear within minutes. No one. Then 'very pale and distraught [chaplain] Murray left the great gates and entered the vicarage which is in the prison courts.'[85] He would henceforth campaign tirelessly for the abolition of the death penalty. At 9.33am, 'the official notice stating that the execution had been carried out was posted outside the prison.'[86] Purged of the emotions which drove them to the walls of Holloway, bystanders wandered back to their mundane lives. They may have thought that catharsis achieved, the curtain had descended after the final act. It had not, the epilogue would drag on for close on a century.

Later that afternoon, Edith's parents and sister were informed that they should view the body and formally identify Edith Thompson née Graydon. If they hoped that at least she could now be released for burial, that minor comfort was denied them. She would, as per the sentence, be buried in an unmarked, unsanctified grave within Holloway. Kate Meyrick subsequently noted, 'poor Mrs Thompson's grave was in our exercise-ground, its position clearly indicated by a clump of bushes'.[87] Mrs Graydon requested the 'mourning suit' her daughter had worn for her execution be returned. It was not. The Home Office file reports it was 'burned' possibly because Thompson haemorrhaged as she dropped (which gave rise to the pregnancy rumour); Mrs Graydon was told that she had been buried in the suit which, no longer meek, she refused to believe. Every request was met with obfuscation. So far, the authorities must have felt any anger was containable, the *Daily Mail* of 8 January (previously delighted with the verdict), had already helpfully published a letter from T.S. Eliot praising the paper's attitude, 'which was in striking contrast with the flaccid sentimentality of other papers I have seen, which have been so impudent as to affirm that they represent the great majority of the English people.'

This 'flaccid sentimentality' now became thunderous outrage. Newspapers which had rushed to condemn her, urged readers to be appalled. Details of her final minutes leaked out, each more disturbing than the previous one; Margery Fry's evidence included statements that she had 'never seen a person look so changed ... by mental suffering as the Governor; ...Miss Cronin [wardress who had attended the execution] was very greatly troubled by the whole affair ... I was greatly struck by this as Miss Cronin ... was not a sensitive or easily moved person.'[88] Questions were tabled in Parliament; newspapers kept the case alive. *The Sphere* (17 February 1923) reported that the author of the damning December Pamphlet, 'Mr James Douglas's dissection of the letters not read in court [now] vindicates her innocence.' Newspapers inferred that reported bluster in the Commons indicated parliamentary discomfort. Surmising that this was the reaction of a nation that, having bayed for blood, discovered that it did not like what it had wished for; the authorities still hoped the public could be distracted.

Yet Thompson refused to lie still. Principal actors or bit players in the drama raised their voices. The 1923 *Notable British Trials* asserted her innocence in unemotional terms, arguing that the claim of 'incitement to murder' had never been proven in court.[89] Eighteen months later, the National Council for the Abolition of the Death Penalty (NCADP) was formed (merging in 1948 with the Howard League for Penal Reform).[90] In 1930, prison chaplain Granville Murray, who had left the prison service shortly after the execution, gave evidence to a Select Committee on Capital Punishment; Edith's refusal to confess to a crime that she had not committed had left its mark, the death penalty was 'torture'. Furthermore, 'there is always the possibility that an innocent person may suffer the gallows. ... A fallible tribunal should not confer an irreparable penalty.'[91] Thinly disguised, the case featured in fiction, twice unsympathetically with her lower-middle-class roots demeaned and her business acumen ignored, E.M. Delafield *Messalina of the Suburbs* (1924), and Dorothy L. Sayers *The Documents in the Case* (1930).[92] The mood shifted with Fryn Tennyson Jesse's searing *A Pin to See the Peepshow* (1934), whose dramatisation Richard Thompson successfully petitioned the Lord Chancellor to ban. Others followed: Alfred Hitchcock's *The Paradine Case* (1947) (Hitchcock knew Avis and had caught glimpses of Edith); Agatha Christie's *Crooked House* (1949), Jill Dawson *Fred and Edie* (2000); Sarah Waters *The Paying Guests* (2014). In the 2018 BBC1 'retrial' *Murder, Mystery, and My Family,* 'His Honour Judge David Radford, a recently retired Senior Circuit judge, concluded that the conviction of Edith Thompson for murder was unsafe.'[93] No such doubts surrounded the nine women who followed her to the scaffold, although the hanging of women continued to arouse strong feelings.

Even the Second World War did not lay Edith's ghost; questions about both capital punishment and her case returned with accusations of mendacity laid against *Daily Express* editor Beverley Baxter MP, who in 1948 had reported to the Select Committee on Capital punishment. His 1922–23 leader columns had tried to rally popular opinion against the imposed penalty as much as it had demanded it beforehand, 'If I had those days to live over again I would have thrown my protest day after day on the front page, not in the leader column, and roused the entire country.'[94] In 1956, Arthur Koestler's *Reflections on Hanging*, serialised in *The Observer*, provoked lengthy discussions and repeated denials of a miscarriage of justice. With public interest growing, a now very elderly Dr Dora Walker, whose mental breakdown was attributed to having been present at the execution, was warned that she was bound by the Official Secrets Act and 'must not discuss with anyone events that happened while I was in the prison service at Holloway', events which, following the execution, she had discussed with her young lodger.[95] Edith may have been dead for thirty-three years but she still haunted the Corridors of Power.

Irrespective of how the case changed attitudes towards capital punishment, particularly the execution of a woman, for the Graydons and Bywaters it was and remained an ever-present personal tragedy. Using the intermediary of a 'prison visitor' (possibly Fry), the Graydons again requested the authorities permit the reburial of their daughter's body. Refused. Edith Thompson 'was and must remain buried within the precincts of the Prison'.[96] Then in April 1971, with her parents long dead, her remains and those of three other hanged women were exhumed and reburied in an unconsecrated pit in Brookwood Cemetery, Surrey. Avis, who died in 1977, was never informed.

On 20 November 2018, following unstinting efforts by René Weis, the Home Office allowed Mrs Graydon's wish to be fulfilled. Following a Christian funeral service, Edith Thompson was reinterred with her parents at Manor Park, close to the home she had reluctantly left on 15 January 1916 to marry Percy Thompson. The final wrong that a vindictive Government had visited upon this vibrant 'new woman' who had embraced all the opportunities that the post-war world seemed to offer, who through her own efforts was rising from lower to property-owning, financially secure middle class; who, denying her preordained destiny of drab motherhood, loved clothes, dancing, a flutter on the horses, had been righted. After ninety-five years and 'with benefit of clergy', she lies in consecrated ground. The curtain has finally fallen on the Thompson/ Bywaters tragedy.

If Christie's fiction provided comfort with its ultimate unmasking of evil, Sayers' work is bleaker as she lifts a curtain on those living with a war-damaged mind. But the devastating Thompson case laid bare the social tensions at play between the 'new' woman and those determined to destroy her using a misogynistic, patriarchal, hierarchical system of [in]justice.

CHAPTER 6

The Paris Peace Conference: Promises to Keep

Queen Marie of Romania: Enlarging a Kingdom

When Marie Alexandra Victoria ('Missy'), Princess of Great Britain and Ireland was born in October 1875, the country where her destiny lay was little more than a vassal state. The ending of the Russo-Turkish war (1877–1878) resulted in a smaller Romania than we know today gaining independence from its Ottoman overlords. In an age of kings, it began looking around for one of its own, settling in 1881 for the German Prince Karl of Hohenzollern-Sigmaringen. Crowned Carol I, he reigned until October 1914. In 1893, his nephew and heir Prince Ferdinand married Missy, the 17-year-old granddaughter of Queen Victoria and Tsar Alexander II. Obeying her mother, Missy had recently rejected a marriage proposal from her first cousin, George, Duke of York, third in line to the British throne.

Playing on the new King Ferdinand's strong familial ties with Germany and eager for another strategically placed ally, the Central Powers had unsuccessfully courted Romania since war broke out. However, on 27 August 1916, thanks to significant behind-the-scenes manoeuvring by Marie, dubbed 'the Allies best ally', Romania signed the Treaty of Bucharest, throwing in her lot with Queen Marie, as opposed to King Ferdinand's native land. The British and French press enthusiastically praised their new Gallant Little Ally. Once Romania entered the war, Marie, beloved by many of her subjects, was now adored. Politicians and diplomats had long recognised her as the power behind her weak and vacillating husband. Writing in her diary on that August 1916 day, she noted her privileged insider position as 'One of the only ones to have known ... it is going to be war'; she was worried about her own role, 'What can a woman do in a modern war? It is no more the time of Joan of Arc.'[1]

Things soon turned sour for Romania. Caught in a pincer movement by crack German and Bulgarian troops led by General August von Mackensen, with promised Allied ammunition not arriving, the late August euphoria of the British press gave way to despair, predicting that Romania would soon disappear off the news agenda. It might have done, had Marie, who had long ago learned how to work the press, not still captured the limelight. Having found a role for herself and her two elder daughters as Red Cross nurses, she adorned the pages of multiple Allied publications, lauded for her humanitarian and compassionate actions. On 24 October 1916, the front page of the *Daily Mirror* featured 'Rumania's Beautiful Queen Tending The Wounded'; she was the star of numerous Pathé news features and, when America entered the war, *Century Magazine* dubbed her 'The Soldier Queen' despite her non-combatant status. For the *New York Times* she was 'Rumania's Heroic Soldier Queen' and 'The People's Idol'.[2] Romania's direct involvement in hostilities may have been short-lived but the suffering of civilians and soldiers, including those sent to Germany as POWs, was horrific. In terms of ratio of men killed, Romania ranks third behind Serbia and Turkey, losing over 25 per cent of her men under arms.[3] Russia's 1917 collapse left Romania ever more perilously exposed and in May 1918 she reluctantly accepted draconian peace terms from Germany as the Allies' promises of men and matériel remained unfulfilled. The brutality of the subsequent German occupation of more than half the country, including Bucharest, makes harrowing reading. In early November 1918, the German army retreated, stripping Romania of every movable asset. With the Allies paying only lip service to the suffering, the American ambassador pleaded for 'aid in the name of humanity'.[4] However, post-war, famine in Romania was never seen as a priority by the Western Allies (nor even by those Fighting the Famine in Austria, Germany and Russia). *Punch* ran a cartoon contrasting starving abandoned Romania with Central Powers' countries whose children received some food aid.[5]

Encouraged, at least from the wings by Marie, Romania was determined that the Allies' considerable territorial promises which formed part of the 1916 Treaty of Bucharest, would be honoured and Romania's sufferings acknowledged at the Paris Peace Conference where, from January 1919, delegates from thirty-two victorious and neutral countries, most with their own agendas, were converging. Somehow a consensus would have to be reached that satisfied the conflicting demands of the representatives of millions of people, lands formerly held by the crumbling Austro-Hungarian, Russian and Ottoman Empires reassigned and a lasting peace brokered which would make good on the wartime mantra that this really had been 'the war to end war'.

Complicating Romania's claims at the Conference were the terms Germany had forced upon her in May 1918. Although never ratified, this Peace Treaty with Germany counted against her in the eyes of the victorious allies. Insultingly, Romania was only awarded two Conference delegates, while Serbia and Belgium had three each. With the Great Powers disinterested in the fate of the Balkan nations, about whose geography Lloyd George was not alone in being culpably ignorant, it was soon obvious that Romania's demands were being ignored. Exacerbating the country's woes, 'there was a strong force of mutual repulsion' between her two delegates, Chief of Government Ion Bratianu and his main political rival Take Ionescu, 'They moved on different planes ... and Rumania, in the person of her delegates, was treated like Cinderella by her stepmother[s Clemenceau, Lloyd George and Woodrow Wilson].'[6] It was obvious that the Supreme Council were intent on ignoring the Romanians, deemed secondary people who should submit themselves to the will of their superiors. America even threatened potential loss of her [not very] active assistance if the country did not grant industrial concessions to a pushing body of financiers. As a further insult, Romanian delegates only received drafts of the proposed treaty with Austria the evening before its ratification and their comments were ignored.[7] Geographically situated between Bolshevik Russia and Hungary, now in the grip of revolution that was already spilling over into Romania, politicians decided a better statesman was needed to plead the country's cause.

The biggest gun that Romania could send to Paris was undoubtedly their beguiling queen. Throughout the war, she had cultivated support for her adopted country via Allied Ambassadors while her cousinship with both George V and Tsar Nicholas were distinct advantages. Even in April 1914, the Austro-Hungarian ambassador had perceptively noted how Romanian policy could soon depend on Marie rather than (the then still) Crown Prince Ferdinand, informing Vienna that, 'her character and mentality is one of the most important reasons for putting relations with Romania on quite another basis'. [8] Now in early 1919, having experienced her statesmanship, France's Ambassador to Romania, the Comte de Saint-Aulaire championed sending her to Paris although, following accepted protocol, her husband put the idea to her. Claiming to have been initially overwhelmed by the mission entrusted to her, she was ecstatic and temporarily humbled, 'I'm flattered that they all think I can help.'[9] She was determined that where Romania's delegates were failing, she would succeed. She would ensure that the territorial promises made to Romania: the Banat, Bessarabia, Transylvania, Bukovina and the 'missing' part of Dobruja, would be honoured and the country's sufferings acknowledged and alleviated.

Marie was now coached in 'facts and figures'; she was instructed to make contact with all Conference leaders in order 'to persuade them to honour the 1916 Treaty and remind them of the validity of Romania's claims' – and the extent of her ongoing sacrifices.[10] Her family ties were considered crucial. With George V among Romania's outspoken critics, indeed she 'wondered how much he really understood about Europe outside the British Empire', she was to go home and speak to the same Lloyd George who had once been in love with and proposed to teenage 'Missy'.[11] Carefully paving the way, on 11 January 1919, Marie wrote to him about 'Disquieting rumours [that] have reached us that we are not to be treated as allies at the peace discussions'; he felt obliged to tell the representatives of the other powers that they could hardly go back on the promises made to the small Balkan nation which had made such sacrifices at a critical juncture during the conflict.[12]

On 1 March 1919, the royal train left Bucharest for Paris; Marie's goal, 'to talk the Western Powers out of Transylvania, the Bukovina, the Dobruja and the Banat'. A lesser character may have felt daunted. Marie simply noted in her diary, 'My Romanians have an almost mystic belief in my powers which flatters and upholds me but which makes me a bit anxious.'[13] The fate of her Russian relatives may also have preyed upon her mind. If she failed to deliver on Romania's hopes, would their starving, ragged subjects, many of whom were already subject to and receptive of Communist propaganda, turn on the Royal Family and at best exile and at worst murder them? Much was hanging on her foray into international diplomacy.

As the train steamed across the war-devastated Balkans, which seemed so unimportant to Western leaders, French journalist Colette – renowned for her 'scoops' – was considering how she could ensure the first interview with the royal arrival for her newspaper *Le Matin*. She ambushed the train as it paused before entering Paris. That the royal party was surprised is an understatement, but aware that this could be the media opportunity she needed, francophone, francophile Marie accepted Colette's lavish bouquet of orchids and was gratified to hear the journalist's view that all Paris would love her.[14] An interviewer's dream, Marie spoke passionately, candidly and occasionally tactlessly (telling Colette that she was merely a servant of her country and an unpaid one at that), Colette fell under her spell; countless other journalists would follow.

As well as being media-savvy, Marie could engineer an entrée. Republican France was fascinated by royalty. Reporters ran along the platform, elbowing each other out of the way in their attempts to get a glimpse of Marie, her three daughters, and their entourage as the train steamed triumphantly into the epicentre of the political world. The hopes and fears of millions lay on the shoulders of the great, the good and the not so good, politicians, negotiators and captains of industry. Now into their midst alighted Marie of Romania, granddaughter of both Queen Victoria and Tsar Alexander II, and the power behind the throne of a distant country on the very edge of Europe. What would both sides make of each other?

Despite being an 'unpaid servant', Marie's accommodation, a suite of twenty rooms in the Ritz hotel, reflected her royal status. Civil and military dignitaries, girls clutching bouquets and photographers lined the route and, as the Romanians settled into their luxurious accommodation, a constant stream of flowers arrived. So many that the Ritz ran out of vases and had to scour Paris for reinforcements. Hotel staff may have been more dismissive of the posy of wild flowers picked from the countryside around the war-ruined Chateau de Courcy with which Marie was presented when paying homage to fallen French soldiers (another press opportunity) in the nearby Oise.[15]

Throughout that first and all subsequent days, Marie 'smilingly passed through the rush, noise, confusion, doing my best to remain calm, not lose my head'.[16] With 'all the journalists of the globe seem[ing] to be circling round me, buzz[ing] like swarms of bees', there may have been some in the anti-Romanian camp who hoped that her celebrity status would go to the Queen's head and rather than fulfil her mission, she would allow herself to get swept along in the current of adulation.[17] Under twenty-four hours after her triumphal arrival, Marie was closeted with Romania's Prime Minister Bratianu. He 'came for a long talk to give me a picture of the political situation, to explain whom I must see … in what way I can be helpful'.[18] He warned her that the 'atmosphere was not favourable to Romania.'[19]

Marie assured Bratianu she would do what she could although her methods may initially have raised eyebrows. If her purpose were to take the conference by storm, she would do this sartorially as well as diplomatically. Aware of the power of a woman's dress, she had spent almost the whole war in Red Cross nurse's garb. Now, she arrived with,

> 60 gowns, 31 coats, 22 fur pieces, 29 hats and 83 pairs of slippers. Perhaps it seems a good many, Still I feel that this is no time to economise. You see Romania simply has to have Transylvania. We want so much Bessarabia too. And what if for the lack of a gown a concession should be lost.[20]

Her jewellery was somewhat depleted; having been initially sent for safekeeping to Russia, it had disappeared in the maelstrom of the revolution. Nevertheless, her gowns, chosen to flatter and appeal, must have stood out among the pin-striped, grey-haired male delegates. Her backstage diplomacy included close attention to her wardrobe, selecting, 'yellow silk for a reception given in her honour by the Chinese Ambassador, point de Milan lace for the Italian reception, embroidered cloth of gold for the US President and mousseline de soie with hand painted roses for Lloyd George'.[21] If the fate of Transylvania hung on cloth of gold or Bessarabia on mousseline de soie, Marie would not be found wanting. When clothes did not produce the desired result, she resorted to another supposedly feminine topic, her and her interlocutor's children or his favourite topic. Romania's position was much helped by her queen's 'ability to wrap her country's demands, which may have sounded too extravagant during acrimonious official discussions, in an attractive package of feminine charm, petulant worldliness, and hard politics'.[22]

Despite the press's interest in her clothes and her suite of rooms which she soon, according to the Spanish Infanta Eulalia (her sister's mother-in-law), turned into an Oriental seraglio – but as her bedroom in the Royal family's private retreat at Cotroceni was described as a cross 'between a church and a harem', this may have come as no surprise, Marie never lost sight of her mission.[23] She had told Colette, 'My beautiful country trampled by Germans [is] so badly known by the outside world'; she was going to remedy this ignorance and ensure its sufferings were understood by the so-called Big Four (France, Great Britain, Italy and the USA) who held the world's fate in their hands.[24]

Marie had a mountain to climb if the terms of the 1916 Bucharest Treaty were to be honoured. As she subsequently wrote, 'So many diplomats and officials were having their say that it was difficult to get a hearing. It needed an exceptional ambassador to plead for a country which did not enjoy special popularity.'[25] Assisted by her stunning wardrobe (extended by visits to Paris couturiers), she remained the darling of the anglophone and francophone press. What may have escaped both those who wrote and those who read the newspaper columns was that notwithstanding her self-deprecating remarks, she was an astute operator. Like Gertrude Bell, who was pleading the Arabs' cause, Marie believed that pledges made in return for Romania's wartime support must be honoured. Her dead soldiers and starving population must not 'be the end of our road'.[26] After the fall of Bucharest, she had noted in her diary there will come an hour, 'when one has a right to lift up one's voice'; that hour had now come.[27]

Coached by Bratianu and expressing the hope that she would keep her wits about her and be able to field the questions coming at her from all angles, Marie first lifted up her voice to the forty reporters at her 6 March press conference.[28] Suitably arrayed in blue, wearing her French Croix de Guerre and her other medals (neatly combining femininity with masculine war decorations) she held court, refusing to sanitise her country's former and ongoing sufferings. Not only were many Romanians starving, the departing Germans had denuded the country of all its assets, there was not one railway bridge left standing between Jassy and Bucharest; perforce these were being rebuilt with wood as there was no metal left. Doubtless missing the irony, the beautifully dressed queen also mentioned, but shrugged off, the shortage of clothing, 'we have always been rather a ragged little country'. In his fulsome 7 March *Pall Mall Gazette* article, the Reuters journalist assured worried readers that a meeting was scheduled for the next day with Mr Hoover to discuss provisioning the country. Although no fan of Romania or her flamboyant queen, Hoover sent provisions as did the American Red Cross. A decision based on pragmatism as much as humanitarianism. Romania's trump card, which Marie was never averse to playing, was her geographical position as a bulwark against Bolshevism

Forgetting that the Big Four were inimical to Romania's demands, the French press, covered her every move. What *Le Gaulois* deemed a 'pious pilgrimage' to the 'devastated areas' on 9 March further increased her popularity with the French public. Placing wreaths on tombs, empathising with those who, like Romania, had been occupied, attending the Opéra in a performance in aid of French orphans, Marie was becoming the queen of hearts and minds.

But she had sterner minds to capture than a press which had succumbed to her looks, her charm and the 'luminosity' of the piercingly blue eyes out of which apparently shone the 'soul of Romania'.[29] Her greatest test would be her encounter with 'the Tiger', French Prime Minister Georges Clemenceau. It was hard to know which was greatest: his loathing for Bratianu, for Romania in general, or her surrender to Germany. A trepidatious Marie arrived for the encounter. Aware of the courtesies due to royalty, welcomed with full military honours and the Romanian national anthem, Clemenceau then ran down the steps at the Quai d'Orsay to greet her before they retired to his private office. She countered his observation that Romania wanted the 'lion's share of the Branat' with the riposte that was why she had 'come to see the lion's first cousin, the Tiger.'[30] He accused Romania of having 'treated with the Boches before the Armistice', she retorted that her country was 'encircled by our enemy', including their erstwhile Ally, now Bolshevik, Russia. She had 'come to modify your attitude about Romania and I mean to fight now as I have fought my battles during our tragic war years'. Unsure to whom the final victory of this encounter went, she had nevertheless captured his interest and made definite headway; President Poincaré subsequently told her that Clemenceau had mellowed towards Romania, 'Your Majesty has given a face to Her Country.'[31]

The French papers sorrowfully noted her imminent departure for London on 12 March. She had been wined and dined by senior members of the British contingent, astutely commenting that although Lloyd George was witty and stimulating 'how much [does] he really underst[an]d about Europe outside the British Empire?'[32] He could never have read *Dracula*, referring to Transylvania he had asked, 'What is that place Romania is so anxious to get?[33] Throughout her week in Paris, Marie had fought against diverging from Romanian patriotism and reverting to being the granddaughter of Queen Victoria, at ease with her native land's politicians. She refused to adopt Western politicians' eyes and see her adopted country as a small unimportant kingdom in the Near East who had capitulated to Germany, another awkward Balkan country far from the powerhouse of Western Europe. Her next mission was to use her familial ties and friendship with cousin George to soften the British delegation's undoubted anti-Romania stance. This assault would take place from within the very bastion of British monarchy, Buckingham Palace.

At 7.40 pm on 12 March, Marie burst onto London's grey post war stage.[34] Cognisant of the success of her interview with Colette, before leaving Paris Marie granted an exclusive to *The Times*; she would court the British press and the British people as well as their politicians; that day's editorial, 'The Resurrection of Romania', was all she could have hoped for. It acknowledged the 'suffering, bravery and common sense of the people', while simultaneously paying tribute to their representative in Europe, the 'Queen of an Allied State who has done her full woman's part in sharing the sorrows and the suffering of her adopted country'. Newspapers across the land soon vied with each other for publishing 'rare and charming portraits' of HM Queen Marie, her young daughter Princess Ileana, and their mission in support of their 'Brave and Suffering Nation' which had been subjected to unimaginable horrors of deprivation, disease and slaughter. Ten-year-old Ileana prosaically enumerated these to Buckingham Palace's shocked and sheltered occupants. Marie acknowledged 'the war years had brought me face to face with a reality that had been spared my cousins'.[35]

Unaware of the polite storm squalling around the private apartments of Buckingham Palace, newspapers' enthusiasm mounted. The *Illustrated London News* eagerly reminded readers that at undeniable personal risk, Marie had served devotedly in her country's wartime hospitals; with nurses still figures of public adoration this was an astute move. For the *Daily Mirror* the erstwhile royal nurse was now, 'An irresistible Ambassador', whose overtures some politicians were determined to resist. Marie's charm offensive continued. If statesmen were too busy to see her during the day, no matter, she was an early riser. Assisted by her friends Waldorf and Nancy Astor, guests were summoned to breakfast at Buckingham Palace, calmly overlooking that her hosts deplored her methods, which were not restricted to politicians. Industrialists and anyone who could provide aid to starving Romania (not to mention tea for its queen long deprived of this essential commodity) flocked through the gates. Adding insult to injury, she continued to court the press. George V considered newspapers 'filthy rags', Marie delighted in her photograph appearing in national and local publications which favoured her image over that of the politicians she dismissed as 'tired, bored statesmen around a green table'.[36] She pleaded with George not to be shocked. In 'My Mission at Buckingham Palace', she remembered turning to him saying, 'Forgive me if I am different from what you think a queen ought to be.'

Inimical to both Romania and Marie, acting Secretary of State for Foreign Affairs (while Balfour attended the Paris Conference), Lord Curzon nevertheless honoured her with an official dinner, inviting her to present Romania's cause to attendees. She rose to the challenge of convincing 'each man to do what he could for my suffering country'.[37] She scored significant success with the then Secretary for War and Air: childhood sweethearts when they had both holidayed on the Isle of Wight, Winston Churchill may not have kept his juvenile promise to marry her, now he listened sympathetically to her pleas.[38]

Meeting people to whom one has little to say is the fate of royalty. King George hosted a reception for all foreign ambassadors and emissaries to the Court of St James. Claiming to dread the proposed encounter, Marie acquitted herself effectively. Aware that her English cousins 'were watching me, a little anxious as to what surprises I might bring into their well-ordered existence', she successfully hid her anathema to such gatherings. 'All the Countries of the world lined up in a row,' she wrote, 'and to have to find something not too idiotic to say to each in turn while the last spoken to always hears what I am saying to his neighbour.'[39] Despite also being coached in London, 'I did not always strictly obey their advice; I had my own ways and means which were often more efficacious than theirs if somewhat less conventional. It was a case of 'rushing in to win'.[40] Other hurdles which she cleared with similar aplomb included a press conference convened by the Romanian Ambassador – perhaps less of a hurdle than she implies with her continued ability to woo the press. *Punch* made Marie's claims for 'starving' Romania front-page news and the *Daily Mirror* framed her as an anti-Bolshevik feminist pin-up and most sections of the press were eager to comment on her flamboyant sartorial style which doubtless was on full view during her official appearances at the House of Commons and a luncheon hosted by the Lord Mayor.[41]

Soon it was the British press who sorrowfully announced the exotic queen's return to Paris (20 March); she remained hot news for weeks, with comments first passed days ago revisited in adulatory tones. She had undoubtedly taken the press by storm even if her acclaim in some corridors of power were more muted. *The Tatler* reminded readers that their 9 April 'Cover girl' HM Queen Marie of Romania, a 'welcome visitor to our shores', had returned to Paris having 'inspected a number of military hospitals'. Marie reported being filled with sorrow when she compared the makeshift, primitive facilities where she had battled infectious diseases, horrific wounds, and death, with those available in England.

The sternest task in Paris was still to come, initiating an interview with Woodrow Wilson. She was everything that the puritanical Democrat President was not, and indeed loathed. She wondered if, in his self-appointed task as 'Democracy's Saviour', he had time for a 'mere Queen' – and one of an obscure little country at the very edge of Europe with a still unenfranchised significant Jewish minority. Marie tended to brush aside legitimate questions about the plight of Romania's Jews, whose ill-treatment was growing into something of a cause célèbre – although anti-Semitism was not an accusation that could be laid only against Romania. Clinching a meeting with this prickly opponent was something of an achievement and she was keen to exert her influence over him.

Referring in *Later Chapters of My Life* to their meeting as an 'interesting episode', she shared her non-too-complimentary views about Wilson, 'The world had selected him as the great Arbiter of peace ... a sort of Messiah'. Arguably ironically for one receiving round-the-clock adulation, she commented that the 'world has an instinctive need of idols' and despite having 'feet of clay' Wilson had been elevated to this role.[42] Initially Wilson made it plain to this 'mere queen' that he had no time to see her, he had meetings scheduled every day from 9am. No stranger to breakfast meetings, she replied that she would gladly receive him at seven in the morning. Round One went to Romania, he agreed; he and Mrs Wilson would call 'at half past eight'.[43] A glimpse of the witty queen comes across when she recounts a pre-meeting discussion with Foreign Secretary Balfour. Knowing Wilson's desire to create a League of Nations, she asked Balfour whether she should also mention her recent fashion purchase to Wilson. He advised her, 'Begin with the League of Nations and finish up with the pink chemise. If you were talking with Mr Lloyd George, you could begin with the pink chemise.'[44]

On 10 April, the Presidential couple arrived, he wearing, 'the smile he has on his photographs'. Having avoided the chemise pitfall, initially the meeting went off adequately, with Marie astutely guiding the conversation round to the League of Nations which Wilson assured her, 'would be beneficial to the smaller countries'. Perhaps overconfident, she then made the greatest faux pas of her mission. As Wilson rose to leave, she picked up a photograph of Ileana. 'This Mr President,' she proclaimed, 'is a picture of my youngest daughter, Ileana. My love child.'[45] She had severely misjudged the opposition. The President's physician who had attended the meeting commented, 'in all my experience I have never heard a lady talk about such things. I ... did not know where to look', nor, reportedly, did the President.[46]

Initially predisposed to dislike Marie, Edith Wilson had been impressed by their encounter at an exhibition at the Grand Palais. Having inveigled Edith into extending an invitation to lunch, Marie and her unannounced entourage of ten arrived thirty-five minutes late. Fellow diners were appalled, one commented, 'Every minute we waited ... I could see from the cut of the President's jaw that a slice of Romania was being lopped off.'[47] Ignoring her own warning about feet of clay, Marie was convinced the lunch had gone very well. She even conceded that Wilson was 'polite, amiable ... although entrenched in his superior detached attitude which makes him soar above the average mortals'.[48] She, meanwhile, did not appreciate being treated as a 'rather ignorant beginner who could profit of his advice'. Always able to give as good as she got, when he began to lecture her on Romania's treatment of its minorities, she sidestepped the issue and 'mildly suggested that he was evidently well acquainted with these difficulties because of the Negro [*sic*] and Japanese question in the United States'.[49] She had, as she further commented, always enjoyed a skirmish, feeling that 'if there had been more time, I could do more with the president'.[50]

Knowing when to take a final bow can be an acquired art. The woman whom the French press now dubbed the 'Business Queen' demonstrated that her sense of timing (other than being so late for Wilson) remained impeccable. To the distress of French journalists, the sycophantic public, and the press pack who were still keen to lap up her every comment, either Marie or her advisors (though it is hard to imagine anyone overruling her), felt it was time to bid Paris farewell.

According to her diary of 16 April 1919,

Paris gave me a tremendous send-off from President Poincaré and Marshal Foch downwards. I ... had given every ounce of my strength to carry out the mission trusted to me. I was tired but I felt

I had done my best, ... relying entirely upon my own intuition. I had endeavoured to grasp situations ... intent upon lessening any prejudice entertained against Romania. I had brought forward the needs and aspirations of my people and had given my country a living face.

She had achieved more than giving Romania 'a face'. Along with the truckloads of flowers and the cheerful hysteria which accompanied her to the Gare de Lyon, 'several carriages with provisions for the sick and needy', not to mention ammunition to restock Romania's depleted arsenals (which would soon be fired in anger), were attached to the train. Five days later, the royal train steamed into Bucharest to a rapturous welcome.

Through Marie, Romania had punched above its weight. The Great Powers had reluctantly acknowledged her right to be heard. That relations soon descended into animosity was no fault of hers. She had successfully 'brought forward the needs and aspirations' of her people.[51] Playing on fears of Bolshevism, she had been quick to portray Romania as the bulwark protecting Europe from Communist Russia. One rune that she had accurately read would have disastrous long-term consequences for the 'Greater Romania' she had created. With her own first-hand knowledge of the 'overwhelming indignation and hatred' that an unjust peace can engender, when the deliberations of the Paris Peace Conference were complete, she noted her despair at the terms imposed upon Germany,

The wheel had turned full circle ... Reading through one clause after another, I felt that the conditions were ... exaggerated, inhuman. A country could not submit to such excessive demands. The foe had been overthrown, brought to his knees, but he had been brave, it had needed nearly the entire world to beat him; was it fair or even politic to want to strangle him altogether? I thought of the hideous suffering that would follow, of the seething hatred which would make many hearts fester with an undying desire for future revenge ... it was unwise.[52]

This prescience lay in a future she fortuitously did not live to see. When the dust had settled and the acclaim had died down, Marie's achievements were analysed. She had been given the task of ensuring

151

that the promises made in the 1916 Treaty of Bucharest were kept, that Romania was granted Transylvania, Bukovina, Bessarabia, the Banat and the Dobruja. Ultimately, Transylvania Bukovina, Bessarabia, part of the Banat and southern Dobruja, were included in Greater Romania. One observer noted, 'I know of no one who went away from Paris with more satisfactory annexations than did Marie of Romania ... [She] arrived at the Peace Conference from a kingdom numbering eight million subjects. She departed the ruler of eighteen million', then geographically the fifth largest country in Europe.[53]

A century later, although Romania lost some territory after the Second World War, she retains her greatest gain, Transylvania and it is here, adjacent to 'Dracula's Castle' (Bran, Transylvania) that Marie's own heart now rests. Lovingly restored by Marie, the castle remains both visual testimony to, and memory-keeper of, a British princess trapped in a loveless marriage to a weak king. As Queen Consort she deployed every weapon in her female arsenal to ensure that promises made to the country which years ago had taken her to its heart, were kept.

Gertrude Bell: Mapping a Kingdom

While Marie of Romania arrived in Paris determined to enlarge a kingdom, renowned 'orientalist' Gertrude Bell arrived to create one.

In 1916, Bell became a key member of the British wartime Arab Bureau. Her intimate knowledge of Arabia, across which she had travelled and written about extensively, her linguistic fluency, awareness of complex religious differences, knowledge of intertribal relationships, and her dealings with tribal leaders, outweighed the unfortunate fact that she was female. During the war, it was felt that if anyone could encourage the Arabs to rebel against their Turkish overlords (with whom Britain was at war) who administered great swathes of Arabia, it was Bell. Her title, 'Oriental Secretary', provided euphemistic cover for her role as 'Chief Intelligence Officer'. To enlist Arab support, promises were made about future self-governance, promises which Bell was determined would be honoured – albeit with significant weighting in Britain's favour. Having been based in Cairo, Delhi and Basra, she had lived in Baghdad since April 1917. She had formed relationships based on mutual trust and friendship with key Baghdadi leaders, information which she shared with A.T. Wilson (A.T.), British Governor of Baghdad from April 1918 to October 1920, informing her stepmother Florence (30 August 1918), 'I know I can do a good deal to help him.'[54]

Throughout her life Bell was a prolific, often indiscreet correspondent whose wartime and post-war letters provide insights into the workings of the Arab Bureau. On 28 November 1918, she told her father Hugh,

> I am having by far the most interesting time of my life ... The Franco-British Declaration (...) has thrown the whole town into a ferment. It doesn't happen often that people are told that their future as a State is in their hands and asked what they would like. They are all talking and mercifully they all come in to me with the greatest eagerness to discuss what they think.

This 'Declaration', which Bell thought had been published 'prematurely', was part of Woodrow Wilson's stated determination that 'countries or provinces which had been under German or Ottoman imperial control ought to be given the opportunity for self-determination' through a mandate system.[55] To safeguard its interests in Mesopotamia – which it had fought so hard, and sacrificed so many lives to protect – Great Britain accepted the mandate for 'Iraq', despite the country not then existing, no one knowing where its borders would be, and who would be the (titular) head of state.[56]

As far as British and French interests in Arabia were concerned, on 23 November 1917, the Bolshevik newspaper *Pravda* published a secret document which had fallen into Bolshevik hands when Bolsheviks overran the French Embassy in St Petersburg. This formed the Sykes-Picot Agreement. In the depths of the First World War, politician Sir Mark Sykes and his French counterpart François Georges-Picot had held a series of talks relating to how to carve up the Ottoman Empire (of which Mesopotamia formed a part) and broadly divide the spoils between their two countries, information shared with the French Ambassador to Russia. Now seen as an expression of imperial arrogance that created nations where none had existed, the Agreement had scant regard for tribal, ethnic, religious, or sectarian differences. Even in 1918, administrators in Mesopotamia considered it a betrayal of the Arabs who had supported the British on the understanding that when hostilities finally ceased, a single 'Arab nation' would be established. Bell was probably unaware of this

Agreement. However, by the time the Peace Conference convened, that Whitehall might be involved in some behind-the-scenes manoeuvring relating to Mesopotamia was undoubtedly in both her and A.T.'s heads. She informed Hugh on 17 January 1919, that acting as some sort of liaison officer,

> I may come home [to England] a little earlier. A.T. ... want[s] someone at home who can help to give a guiding hand, if that's possible; keep him closely informed of how things are shaping and at the same time represent the experience we have gathered here. ...
> I should perhaps ... come down through Syria, so as to see what's going on there, which would be an advantage.

Bell felt that 'one is more useful here [Baghdad] knowing what the pulse is like at home'. Her familial status, her wartime record, and her reputation as a leading expert on 'Arabia' meant that she moved more easily through the corridors of power than almost any other woman in England, enabling her to take useful soundings.

This plan (alongside her desire to 'learn to cook mutton chops' while 'home') did not materialise. Nevertheless, when Bell reached Paris in early March 1919, (A.T. arrived on 20 March), she and Marie were the only women to attend the conference in neither a journalistic nor administrative capacity. She was uncharacteristically pessimistic about what she might achieve, not because of her gender, but because she assumed conference leaders would 'go on the plan of not wanting to hear anything from the people who come from the place they are talking about'. A.T. despondently noted,

> no one except Miss Bell had any first-hand knowledge of Iraq or Nejd or, indeed, of Persia. The very existence of a Shia majority [about 50 per cent of the population] in Iraq was denied as a figment of [...] imagination by one "expert" with an international reputation and Miss Bell and I found it impossible to convince either the Military or the Foreign Office Delegations that the Kurds in the Mosul *vilayet*[57] were numerous and likely to be troublesome, that Ibn Saud was a power seriously to be reckoned with or that our problems could not be disposed of on the same lines as those advanced for Syria.'[58]

Ironically, A.T. himself seems to have overlooked how putting together these three distinct former Ottoman vilayets with no common history, religion or even geography made little sense and served only the interests of British administrators.[59]

There is ample evidence that Bell was aware of both the struggle that the Mesopotamia delegates would face in pleading their cause and the gargantuan issues facing them as they tried to carve a nation out of these disparate vilayets. Deeply aware of the weight of responsibility resting on her shoulders, 'Our Eastern affairs are complex beyond all words, and until I came there was no one to give the Mesopotamian side of the question at first hand'.[60] Certainly those who had contact with her recognised her underlying knowledge; however, had Mark Sykes not succumbed to the Spanish 'flu pandemic in February 1919 while staying in Paris, he may have been less enthusiastic. He had described her as a 'silly chattering windbag of conceited, gushing flat-chested, man-woman, globe-trotting, rump-wagging, blethering ass.'[61] Her 'Chief', may also have been unimpressed had he known she had arrogantly told her stepmother she would put A.T. 'into touch with my friends,' at which point, 'I can leave matters in his hands'.[62]

Awareness of delegates' lack of knowledge did not prevent Bell from immediately trying to influence outcomes, telling Florence on 5 March about 'an interesting evening at Mr Stead's house (editor of *The Times* – I don't like him but he was very useful)'. On 8 March she lunched 'with Mr Balfour who, I fancy, really doesn't care. Ultimately, I hope to catch Lloyd George by the coat tails and if I can manage to do so, I believe I can enlist his sympathies.'[63] More productive was her 16 March lunch with one of the architects of the League of Nations, 'Lord Robert, bless him, is such a help to me personally.'[64] Despite her experience she felt, 'I've dropped into a world so amazing that up to now I've done nothing but gape at it.'[65] T.E. Lawrence (*Lawrence of Arabia*), an old friend, was among the four lunch guests. He introduced her to Faisal ibn Hussein, third son of Sharif Hussein, a direct descendant of the Prophet Muhammed through his daughter Fatima, temporal rulers in Mecca for the last nine centuries. Faisal had been a key figure in the British-backed and -funded Arab Revolt (June 1916) against Turkey; in return, post-war support for national Arab governments had been promised. A man of enormous charisma, Faisal headed the Arab delegation to Paris only to find himself snubbed by not being on the list of official delegates. In the complex web being woven around Arab affairs, determined to stake a claim to over lordship of Syria, France saw Faisal as standing directly in their way. British intervention resolved the matter.

Bell fell instantly under Faisal's spell, remaining there for the rest of her life. He reciprocated her admiration. An undated paper in her archive relates to a private meeting. Recognising that she had the ear of powerful British delegates, he listened 'with surprise and dismay' as she confided, 'no power on earth would make France relinquish the Syrian Mandate [as per the Sykes-Picot agreement].' It is unclear whether Faisal knew that she had subsequently lunched with Balfour ... and 'begged [him] to clear Faisal's mind of illusions ... so that he might shape his course accordingly.'[66] Manoeuvring to strengthen the Arab cause, Bell believed 'the fate of Mesopotamia was linked to settlement of the [Franco-British] dispute over Syria,' explaining to Florence (16 March), 'I can't write or think of anything else but what we are doing with the East.'[67] With her head full of the not-to-be resolved questions surrounding 'Arabia', she left Paris convinced that Arabs should play a far more significant role in the government of Mesopotamia than she had thought prior to arriving in Paris, stating 'a Sharifian ruler was not only good for Syria it was the best answer for Iraq'.[68] This would now be her overarching aim, a course from which she never deviated and devoted all her energies.

Returning to Baghdad, she undertook a task which represented another in her long line of female 'firsts'. Having insisted on writing it 'in her own way', her November 1919 149-page White Paper "Review of the Civil Administration of Mesopotamia", was presented to Parliament, in November 1920, receiving a standing ovation.[69] Highly readable, it provided a view from the ground of Zionism, nationalism, the importance of the Arab nationalist cliques as well as the thorny questions of the vilayet of Basrah, the Occupation of Mosul, the Nationalist Movement and the 'Kurdish Question'. As the introductory 'Note' explains, His Majesty's Government called for a report on this difficult period from the Acting Civil Commissioner, who entrusted the preparation of it to Miss Gertrude L. Bell, C.B.E.[70] Always aware of her own brilliance, her fury that the press were more interested in the Review having been written by a woman than in its contents remains palpable. 'How dare the press be amazed that 'a female [can] write a white paper'.[71]

Even before its publication, this Review lay behind the rupture in her and A.T.'s working relationship. She was committed to self-rule for Mesopotamia; aware that controlling the oil fields was crucial to British interests, imperialist A.T. and his subordinates in the Baghdad office, would not risk letting this vital resource fall into the hands of any government potentially inimical to Great Britain. A.T. had even added a covering letter to the Review when it was dispatched to Whitehall. He considered 'erroneous' Bell's premise that 'An [Independent] Arab State in Mesopotamia and elsewhere within a short period of years is a possibility.'[72]

Aware of A.T's views, unafraid to pull strings to exert influence, Bell told Hugh (12 January 1920) that she had written to 'Edwin [Montagu, Secretary of State for India]. But the truth is I'm in a minority of one in the Mesopotamian political service – or nearly – and yet I'm so sure I'm right that I would go to the stake for it.' Her letter backfired. Montagu responded with a curt telegram (6 August), 'when the future of the country hangs in the balance, we should all pull together'. Her direct approach ran against all 'usual practice and convention'. He added that the Civil Commissioner [A.T.] was the correct channel for her views.[73] A lesser woman may have been cowed. She merely riposted, 'Colonel Wilson gives me every opportunity of telling him any conclusions which may occur to me.' A stormy meeting with A.T., cognisant of what he considered her latest, as opposed to her only, indiscretion, offered one welcome ray of light at the end of the dark tunnel of their deteriorating relations. He had informed his successor, Sir Percy Cox, with whom Bell had enjoyed an excellent wartime working relationship, that the position between the two of them 'would be untenable but for the fact that [he] was hoping before long to be relieved'; this occurred in the autumn of 1920.[74] In a relatively rare flash of humour, recounting the episode on 7 August, she noted, at the end of this interview, 'we shook hands warmly – you can't shake hands anything but warmly when the temperature is 115°'.

As anticipated, 1920 proved a difficult year. Her letters make plain the extent of both her personal and Mesopotamia's problems. She was determined not to be side-lined. In 1919 she had been given the moniker 'Umm al Mummin (Mother of the Faithful) and the last person who bore that name was Ayishah, the wife of the prophet', proof, if she needed it, of the esteem in which Arabs of differing branches of Islam held her.[75]

This may explain why she felt that she could not leave an area that would soon be on the brink of insurgency. Isolated in the office, she confided in letters her concerns about,

> which way [Mesopotamia] will go with all these agents of unrest to tempt it? I pray that the people at home may be rightly guided and realise that the only chance here is to recognise political ambitions from the first, not to try to squeeze the Arabs into our mould and have our hands forced in a year – who knows? perhaps less ... with the result that the chaos to the north and east overwhelms Mesopotamia also. I wish I carried more weight ... I'm in a minority of one in the Mesopotamian political service – and yet I'm sure that I'm right.[76]

She was undoubtedly 'in a minority of one'. Poor at socialising with the British political officers' wives – who knew she considered them to be her intellectual inferiors, she deprived herself of the support network that many women create for themselves and which enabled many of her female contemporaries to move forward in the new post-war world. It was only to her family in England, separated by the slow mail, that she opened her heart.

One area where she excelled was information gathering. On 1 February 1920, she told Florence, 'People are beginning to come down ... with news of Syria and Turkey and having now a rather satisfactory network of informants, I hear of the arrivals and send for them.' Proving her judgement correct and A.T.'s and his acolytes' wrong, 'It's a distressing story which they bring. We share the blame with France and America for what is happening.' Prophetically, 'I think that there has seldom been such a series of hopeless tangles as the West has made about the East since the Armistice.' Oscillating between optimism that a workable way forward would be found and despondency at the overwhelming task, on 1 February 1920, she was 'happier about the whole position', but on 7 March in a letter to Florence she wrote 'I've just written to Lord Robert giving an exhaustive criticism of the dealings of the Conference with Western Asia' – which again did not endear her to her superiors.

Perhaps the only Paris delegate fully cognisant of the depths of antagonism between the Sunni and Shia communities, Bell struggled to make contact with 'the grimly devout citizens of the holy towns and more especially the leaders of religious opinion, the Mutjahids who can loose and bind with a word,' summing up the issue,

> Until quite recently, I've been wholly cut off from them because their tenets forbid them to look on an unveiled woman and my tenets don't permit me to veil – I think I'm right there, for it would be a tacit admission of inferiority which would put our intercourse from the first out of focus. Nor is it any good making friends through the women – if the women were allowed to see me they would veil before me as if I were a man. So you see I appear to be too female for one sex and too male for the other.[77]

With little understanding of her character, some modern commentators admonish her for this refusal.[78]

This letter also informed Florence that Faisal had just been crowned King of Syria, (a throne which he would occupy for a matter of months as he was expelled by France on 24 July 1920). With the Arabs pushing for self-determination in Syria, Bell was quick to read the runes closer to home, writing on 10 April, 'I think we're on the edge of a pretty considerable Arab nationalist demonstration with which I am a good deal in sympathy. It will, however, force our hand and we shall have to see if it will leave us with enough hold to carry on here.' Despite sympathising with the Arab desire for self-determination, she was enough of a product of her race and class to believe that 'if Mesopotamia goes, Persia goes inevitably, and then [the jewel in Britain's Imperial crown] India. And the place which we leave empty will be occupied by seven devils a good deal worse than any which existed before we came.'[79] One of the 'devils' that existed before the British wartime victory in Mesopotamia was Turkey – for whom a significant number of Baghdadis had considerable sympathy; if nothing else, they were co-religionists, another was the extreme Wahhabi sect led by Ibn Saud. Despite her undoubted love of the Arabs among whom she had made her life, Bell's letters reveal more of her complexity than she perhaps realised.

With the clamour for self-determination growing ever louder, Whitehall refused to listen to those on the ground. By 1 June 1920, 'We are in the thick of violent agitation and we feel anxious'. This letter explains, 'It's largely the fault of H.M.G [in London].' With a Constitution drawn up, translated into Arabic and ready for distribution, 'A.T. begged

[H.M.G] to let us make it known before Ramadhan. They refused, for reasons unknown to us – we think for no special reason except that they always think they know better than we do,' concluding with justifiable Bell arrogance, 'They don't.'[80] What Whitehall seemed unable to grasp, and what was crystal clear to Bell and her colleagues, was that 'general declarations of our intentions of setting up Arab institutions', with little 'practical evidence' of these happening ... meant 'the extremists ... play for all they are worth on the passions of the mob'.[81] In a rare display of harmony, Shias and Sunnis were proclaiming, 'the Unity of Islam and the Rights of the Arab. And they are running it for all it's worth. ... the underlying thought is out with the infidel [i.e. Great Britain]'.[82] The situation, as Bell had acknowledged, was exacerbated by occurring during Ramadhan. That the Nationalists had 'created a reign of terror' may not have reassured her family.

Syria's continued attempts to promote anti-British feelings in Mosul (whose inclusion in the about-to-be-created Iraq remained unclear) peaked between June and September 1920. The British had continued to offend local cultural mores and demanded increasing Arab manpower. Displaying culpable ignorance and heedless of warnings about the realities on the ground, including that the British garrison was 'severely understrength', in March 1920, Churchill had arrogantly pronounced that between 2,000 and 3,000 troops would be sufficient to contain double that number of 'native' ones. In fact, these 'native' troops were well-armed thanks to looting matériel from retreating Turks as well as formerly anti-Ottoman tribes having previously received British arms. It has been estimated that these tribes possessed some 50,000 to 60,000 rifles – about which even Bell, with her network of informers, was unaware.[83]

Bell subsequently informed Hugh (4 June) about events in Tall'Afar when the Shammar tribe, 'urged by Sharifian propaganda', rose up against the British-officered local Arab levies and 'deliberately murdered the levy commander on the steps of his house', as well as other locally employed British personnel.[84] To her seeming satisfaction, 'A punitive expedition went out at once ... all the inhabitants of Tall'Afar are going to be turned out and told to go down into the villages in the plain, and every house is to be destroyed. Nor shall we allow the town to be rebuilt. I fully agree with the decision and so do the inhabitants of Mosul who say that if we are the Mandatory Power, we must protect them from the danger of such occurrences.' She could occasionally be an 'Arabist' only if Arabs conformed to her views of how an occupied population should behave.

Bell and A.T.'s relationship was now spiralling out of control. At the end of 1919, he had noted, 'I am having trouble with Miss Bell. On political questions she is rather fanatic.'[85] On 14 June she recounts, 'I had an appalling scene last week with A.T. We had been having a sort of honeymoon', but following an episode (which demonstrated that Bell could be over-generous with the information she shared with her 'Arab friends'),

> [he] was in a black rage that morning and he vented it on me. He told me my indiscretions were intolerable, and that I should never see another paper in the office. I apologised for that particular indiscretion but he continued: 'You've done more harm than anyone here. If I hadn't been going away myself, I should have asked for your dismissal months ago – you and your Emir!'[86]

Clashes between two such strong and frequently tactless personalities were perhaps inevitable. However, it is hard not to sympathise with A.T., with rebellion simmering near Mosul, Bell's sharing of information could be construed as a security breach. Having glossed over her 'indiscretion' and referring to her conviction that an Emir was the right way forward for Iraq, she concludes with her usual arrogance, 'I know really what's at the bottom of it – I've been right and he has been wrong.'

With the Arab insurrection temporarily quelled, Bell was information-gathering in the bazaars, testing local enthusiasm for Faisal as King, garnering views on the Mandate which, she reported, should 'work with goodwill on both sides.'[87] Either she was hearing what she wanted to hear or, with the [Sunni] Baghdadi political élite unsympathetic towards Shia tribal aspirations, she was told that as far as the political situation was concerned, 'a good many of our errors [were] more of omission than commission'.[88] Whitehall having finally granted permission for the calling of the (Sunni) longed-for constituent assembly, Bell threw herself heart and soul into turning this into a reality, taking pride in how the Sunni magnates explained that 'we've come to you because you're beloved. Everyone in Baghdad praises you.'[89]

Events then took a significant downward turn. On 23 July, Kifl station on the Euphrates River south of Baghdad was attacked by insurgents who held the railway staff captive. The local Political Officer requested a rapid show of force and the British commander at Hillah sent a small column, known as the Manchester Column, which was badly mauled, (199 men out of 400 missing). Bell misguidedly believed most of the missing would be 'safely in the hands of the tribes who are not at all vindictive'.[90] On 2 August Bell told Hugh,

> whatever our future policy is to be we cannot now leave the country in the state of chaos which we have created; no one can master it if we can't. If we decided to withdraw at once we should have to send at least two divisions from India to extricate the troops and personnel we have here. It is touch and go – I am quite unable to predict what will happen.

A rout similar to that suffered by the Manchesters could, she believed, sound the death knell for the British administration, adding that if that should happen, 'I shall stay peacefully here.' Her belief in the Baghdadis' love for her was never tested. By 8 August, 'the military position is growing more stable ... the [tribes] are said to be getting a little tired of Jihad.' She hoped that 'order must be restored but it's a very doubtful triumph to restore it at the expense of many Arab lives' – a different comment to her endorsement of the 4 June 'punitive' expedition.

Whatever his opinion of Bell as an 'intriguer' or a 'fanatic', A.T. both acknowledged and harnessed her skills, asking her to write a précis of the revolutionary movement. She also recognised that his political acumen might be correct, he had been forging a moderate constitutional party, taken action to damp down disturbances and generally acted with what she termed 'great wisdom', believing that he was not aiming to 'suppress Arab nationalist sentiment.'[91] The main stumbling block in their tangled relationship was Bell's support for Faisal as King with Iraq moving towards self-government following the terms of the Mandate; A.T. envisaged a dependent state within the British Empire. With Faisal recently deposed in Syria, the way was open for him to acquire the Iraqi throne. A.T. may have seen Bell as 'intriguing' in her endeavours to crown Faisal – although this was ultimately and enthusiastically endorsed both by his successor, Sir Percy Cox, and Winston Churchill at the March 1921 Cairo Conference.

Serious questions had been asked in Parliament pertaining to the cost to the British taxpayer of 'garrisoning large numbers of British forces' in Mesopotamia; 'we could no longer afford to be rulers and protectors of that part of the world'. Far from covering Great Britain in glory, the administration of Mesopotamia during the last two years had been 'a serious menace to the mandatory system and the prestige of our rule in the East'.[92] Questioning the Prime Minister [Lloyd George], Mr Asquith had pointed out that 'it was not incumbent upon the British people to take that burden [£33million] on their already overburdened shoulders.'[93] The Mesopotamian population being 2.8 million, the price tag appeared excessive.

On the ground in Baghdad, discontent rumbled on. 'We are now in the middle of a full-blown Jihad, that is to say we have against us the fiercest prejudices of a people in a primeval state of civilisation' – this latter comment sitting ill with Bell's frequent praise of Arab culture. Because of the war she continued, 'the credit of European civilisation is gone. ... How can we who have managed our affairs so badly, claim to teach others to manage theirs better? It may be that the world has need to sink back into the dark ages of chaos out of which it will evolve something, perhaps no better than what it had.'[94] At times a sense of despair descended on her although, still in the thick of things, she could shrug it off. Two weeks later and with Sir Percy Cox due to take up the helm in October, she perhaps disingenuously told Hugh (20 September), 'it is only quite recently that I have realised how prominent a place I have occupied in the public mind here as the pro-Arab member of the administration. ... I am quoted in the coffee shops as the upholder of the rights of the Arabs.' Although she responded that it 'is HMG which upholds the rights of the Arabs', she was certainly flattered. By the end of September,

> The agitation ha[d] succeeded. No one ... would have thought of giving the Arabs such a free hand as we shall now give them – as a result of the rebellions! Whether it will be to their ultimate advantage, whether it won't rather retard than advance the growth and development of the modern state ... is another question.

With Sir Percy in charge, Bell's life entered calmer waters. Her letters reveal her constantly taking the political temperature surrounding her, alert to the 'Shia problem, the tribal problem' and the ever growing criticism that, having promised 'an Arab Government with British advisers, [we] had set up a British Government with Arab advisers'. Baghdadi leaders were placing 'feelers' as to whom the British might be prepared to accept as head of state.[95] Sir Percy was charged with transforming the administration from British led to (at least nominally) an Arab led one, and although rebellion still broke out among some sections of the tribes, by February 1921, this was considered extinguished. A Provisional Government and a Council of State with eight portfolios were established under the leadership of the widely respected elderly Naqib, a close friend of both Cox and Bell.

In London, Winston Churchill, now at the Colonial Office with special responsibility for the Middle East, was determined to lower the cost of the Mesopotamian administration which Cox believed he could reduce from £37 to £20million. Plans were afoot for what became known as the Cairo Conference, to take place between 12 and 22 March 1921. With her magisterial *Review* fresh in everyone's mind, no one questioned Bell's inclusion among the 'Forty Thieves' (Churchill). Did the six members of Sir Percy's party know that for Churchill 'the essential condition of reduction [in cost to the taxpayer] ... [w]as my paramount object'?[96] What Churchill may not have realised was that Cox, Bell and T.E. Lawrence (attending as Churchill's Arab adviser) were determined to return with the authority to promote, even engineer, the candidature of Faisal as King of Iraq who, as Bell had stated in her Christmas Day 1920 letter, was 'very very much the first choice'.

Placing Faisal's name before Churchill as the electorate's front runner had taken months of manoeuvring, cajoling, persuading; Bell spearheaded the effort. Sunnis' fears of 'being swamped by the Shias ... who are in a large majority', recurred constantly. She acknowledged that 'there are a number of leading Shias ... who would prefer British administration (which they can't have) to an Arab Sunni administration.... But when it comes to the point the Moslem never dares to raise his voice against the Moslem, even if it's a kind of Moslem he hates. I believe if we could put up a son of the Sharif at once, he might yet sweep the board' but time was against them, 'if we hesitate, the tide of public opinion may turn overwhelmingly to the Turks'.[97] Criticisms of acting as kingmaker are levied against Bell but it is hard not to feel that she understood that, with his impeccable ancestry Faisal was, if nothing else, the least bad option.

As the Baghdad contingent embarked for the Cairo Conference which would make or break the new Iraq, even though its borders were not yet defined and uncertainty over the vilayet of Mosul's inclusion remained, they left a relatively peaceful situation with the January-February uprisings quelled. Cox was as determined as his paymasters to find a workable solution including independent government under King Faisal who, to Cox, Lawrence and Bell's relief, had bowed to French insistence that he revoke all claims to Syria and his father's claim to Palestine. On arrival, Bell carefully took Churchill through the main contenders. Impressed by Faisal's war record, his family connections which 'would give the British leverage over both his father Sharif Hussain and his brother Abdullah', he also represented, (a big plus) 'the hope of the best and cheapest solution'.[98] Churchill was jubilant at the expected reduction in the cost of initially £5,000,000 and then £12,000,000. But the final geography of the new country was still uncertain. Indeed, on 4 December 1921, Bell wrote about a well-spent morning at the office making out the southern desert frontier of Iraq; she as much as anyone drew the lines in the sand of the new kingdom.

Returning from Cairo in early April 1921, Cox and Bell had to make good on their undertaking with Churchill that they could ensure Faisal was 'chosen locally' via an election that at least appeared to represent the will of the indigenous population.[99] Bell was on the small committee charged with both the timing of Faisal's arrival in Iraq, where he had never previously set foot, and his election. With her well known anti-female suffrage past and her disparaging views of Arab democracy expressed in *Review* as 'the rank and file of the tribesmen ... could hardly be asked who should next be the ruler of the country', she had few qualms about ensuring her chosen candidate romped home.[100] She genuinely believed that minorities had to be protected under the new administration and was striving to bring about as equitable an outcome as she could in a country split by religious, racial, cultural and economic differences. She believed she could guarantee Faisal toed the line. As the terms of the Mandate stipulated Great Britain should prepare Mesopotamia for self-rule, her being 'careful to keep my private opinion [about who should be king] to myself' may have been self-delusion, her 'private opinion' was public knowledge.[101]

It is unclear whether she was pre-warned that the other serious contender (at least in his own eyes), Basra politician Sayyid Talib, the Interior Minister who had been canvassing hard while the delegates were in Cairo, would be, as Cox reported to Churchill in April, 'arrested in a public thoroughfare' and exiled to Ceylon.[102] At a dinner to which she was not invited, Talib had warned a *Daily Telegraph* journalist that if 'any attempt is made to influence the elections', he had powerful, heavily armed tribal chiefs waiting to step in. Apprised, Bell had immediately shared Talib's boast with Cox. Talib's arrest came back to haunt her. In the summer of 1924, Cox's Political Officer H. St John Philby, a firm Talib supporter and strongly anti-Faisal, blamed her for both his dismissal and Talib's arrest, leaking the insalubrious details to the *Westminster Gazette*.[103] The method of removal following a tea party given by Lady Cox may have been unsavoury, Talib's techniques involving blackmail and threats were equally so.

The leak lying three years in the future, Bell was elated, 'Lord! how glad I am that I gave in a careful report of that speech. I got it from [two sources] and collated the two accounts so as to have it absolutely right.'[104] The way was becoming ever clearer for Faisal's 'election'. Bell's Baghdadi informants kept her abreast of the local chat, triumphantly telling Hugh on 12 June, 'Things are at last beginning to move', adding, 'I don't for a moment hesitate about the rightness of our policy.' The following week, 'We here are now launched on our perilous way.' The British Cabinet having approved the choice of Faisal, Cox and Bell had to ensure that the election appeared if not 'free and fair' then at least not rigged.

Faisal's arrival into the newly created country over which he would (hopefully) rule required careful engineering. Referring to his pending 23 June entry into Basra, Bell prayed 'it will be the sign for a great popular ovation, it will immensely simplify matters for us'. Her concerns were well-founded. Once again seeing herself at the heart of Iraqi affairs, she reports on a deputation she received from Basra that had requested a 'separate Legislative Assembly' albeit under a common King. 'I said, "No".'[105] Opinions diverge as to the warmth of Faisal's welcome in Basra. Although the 'agent' Bell had 'sent down to bring me a report … gave a very glowing account', he may have told her what she wanted to hear. She described her part in the triumphal 30 June Baghdad welcoming party in excited detail. In the ensuing '6 to 8 weeks till the elections were over', Bell became Cox's righthand man, ensuring that the country declared itself in the way that they had promised Churchill and he in his turn Parliament, it would.[106]

A breathless excitement enters her correspondence. Rushing from receptions, political meetings, and intimate dinner parties, with the one objective of delivering an overwhelming YES to the question asking if the electorate supported Faisal's kingship. It was Bell with her Oxford training as an historian, her self-taught exemplary skills as an archaeologist, and her intimacy with the tribes who was given the additional mission of ensuring that the king presumptive was briefed on the long history of the territory over which he was to rule and was introduced to the desert tribes whose support would be crucial to his cause. A brief that she fulfilled admirably while simultaneously keeping her ear close to the ground in Baghdad, digesting the four local papers. 'If there's anything I think unsuitable I intimate the fact to the editors, directly or indirectly. Today I had to do it directly.' Not averse to 'dressing down' former leaders of rebellions, some wondered who was really in charge, Cox or Bell, although she applauded Cox's 'extraordinary' hold over the country. As she was known to hero-worship those whose opinions coincided with her own, it is hard to be sure of the statement's reliability.[107] The veracity of her 8 July comment about being involved in 'creating kings' is unquestionable. Her mission extended to furnishing his palace, requesting her long-suffering parents to place orders for furniture in England, organising the [English-style] education of his son who would succeed on Faisal's death in 1933, training his household, devising an Iraqi flag as well as Faisal's own standard. Unsurprisingly, on 27 July, Bell pronounced herself 'immensely happy ... if we can bring some order out of chaos what a thing worth doing it will be.' In Mosul, she was 'drawing up some directions for the guidance of the press', while awaiting the results of the referendum which resulted in 96 per cent of the electorate supposedly satisfied with Bell and Cox's choice.

On 28 August 1921, Bell explained to Hugh 'we've got our king crowned', describing the coronation in painstaking detail. Bizarrely, as no national anthem had yet been devised, the band played 'God Save the King'! Bell took pride in the sight of 'all Iraq from North to South gathered together'. She does not seem to have seen the irony of her comment, 'It's the first time it has happened in history' – the nation of Iraq had just been constructed – out of Bell's lines in the sand.

Faisal may have been edged over the finishing line, hints that he might not be as compliant as Cox and Bell had promised Churchill were visible prior to the coronation. On 21 August showing the type of indiscretion that had led to her being reprimanded by A.T., she informed Hugh of a 'secret' cable from the Colonial Office which advised that 'in his Coronation speech [he] must announce that the ultimate authority in the land is the High Commissioner.' However, 'Faisal urged from the first that he is an independent sovereign in treaty with us'; Bell expressed impatience with the Colonial Office who seemed not to understand that 'we can direct to a great extent', but that the new Kingdom of Iraq would have to be allowed to 'grow upwards'. Running counter to the loyalty that she claimed she always showed towards HMG, she indiscreetly added, 'We are going, as you know, to drop the mandate and enter into treaty relations with Mesopotamia.' Then the further indiscretion, significantly not included in the *Letters* published in 1927, 'Sir Percy, bless him, wobbled a little, but my view was that as it came to the same either way, in the end, there was no point in claiming an authority we could not enforce.'

All was not yet peaceful in the new country; its borders were still barely defined. Which lands belonged to Ibn Saud in Arabia and which to the new Iraq? Bell, now at the peak of her powers and influence, was busy in her office drawing lines on maps and trying to resolve competing claims to water and, importantly, oil wells, which she referred to as 'detestable' but which were becoming an issue; the fate of both Mosul and the Kurds remained unresolved. Similarly, the arguments of the Mandate being superseded by a treaty rumbled on. Even Bell was now struggling to fully control Faisal, partly due to his ability to change his mind. Acceptance of the mandate one day was replaced by refusal the next. Churchill was adamant that a treaty with Iraq would only be signed if the mandate were acknowledged. Bell, who had exerted all the influence and power that she had been able to muster over Faisal could only stand by and watch him destroy the bond which she had so painstakingly tried to create. Determined to at least appear to be his own man, Faisal was resolute, a treaty must be signed between the two nations. Despite his having told Bell, 'you're a Mesopotamian, a Bedouin', when the chips were down, her ultimate loyalties proved to be with Great Britain, 'we had no alternative'.[108]

A weariness began to creep into her letters. Her beloved Cox retired in December 1922, replaced by Sir Henry Dobbs with whom she had a good but not warm working relationship. While he admired her 'remarkable knowledge of this country and its people and her sympathy with them enabling her to penetrate into their minds', seeing her as 'a connecting link between the British and Arab races', she was slowly but steadily side-lined, no longer having the ear of her 'Chief'.[109] She told Hugh on 30 January 1923, 'Seven years I've been at this job of setting up an Arab state. If we fail, it's little consolation to me personally that other generations may succeed.' Faisal was increasingly less malleable 'seeing all the wrong people' (23 July 1924); state building was proving harder than king-making and although they remained on warm terms, she was fading out of the limelight and it was her companionship more than her political acumen that he sought.

In one area her grip over Faisal remained complete. In July 1922, he had appointed her Honorary Director of Antiquities. Taking her appointment seriously, she had been busy writing a Law of Excavations which, while recognising the excavator who funded digs had some rights, ensured that Iraq's treasures did not haemorrhage out of the country and into the museums of those nations who were now determined to resume digging in 'Arabia'. She began working on a proposed Museum which would house Iraq's treasures for Iraqis to view. That this was also part of nation building is undeniable; giving Iraqis a sense of their past would help them to see themselves as one people. Bell performed her appointed mission with dedication. Bringing her remarkable brain and work ethic to the task, she soon had 'the richest collection in the world of objects representing Iraq's early history displayed in a few rooms near the palace in Baghdad – these would be transferred to the National Museum.[110] She was, however, aware that some excavated finds were too delicate to be stored in the far from optimum conditions of the Museum and, prioritising conservation over heritage, allowed these to be transferred to European institutions – a policy for which she has been criticised. She also visited sites to which excavation permits had not been accorded. Giving 'backsheesh' for illegal finds, she scoured Iraq looking for objects 'I *must* have for my museum.'[111] On one occasion, 'As I rode round I espied half an elephant planted on top of the courtyard wall over the door. It's unusual to see half an elephant standing on a wall so I rode into the courtyard' and reclaimed it.[112] Bell was 'changing the way archaeology was managed' in order to protect Iraq's heritage.[113] Nevertheless, despite being retained as 'Oriental Secretary', since Dobbs' arrival she had been increasingly assigned a back seat. She told Hugh on 26 May 1926, 'Politics are dropping out and giving place to big administrative questions in which I'm not concerned.' She confided on 16 June 1926 to Florence, 'It's too lonely my existence here.' Even the opening of her National Museum was reported as 'a nice little ceremony'.

Time was running out. Subject to deep depression, with her fragile health deteriorating (it is possible chain-smoking Bell had been diagnosed with lung cancer during her 1925 trip home), on 11 July 1926, she took an overdose of (prescribed) sleeping pills and turned out the light. The next day, striving to quash rumours of suicide, Sunni and Shia, Jews and Christians, Britons and Iraqis, lined the streets as the coffin of the woman who had long ago been dubbed 'Khatun' (Queen) was escorted with full military honours to her final resting place in the capital city of the country which she, arguably above all others, had created out of the rump of Kurdistan and the Sunni and Shiite areas of Mesopotamia.[114]

Conclusion: Changing Roles?

Although 1996 marked women's football's debut as an Olympic sport, it was 2012 before Team GB fielded a women's team. Although no British team participated in 2016, success in the 2019 World Cup assured an English team's presence at 'Tokyo 2020'.[1] Delayed until 2021, it will mark the centenary of the FA banning the unsuitable women's game. If women's football's rising popularity is a cause for celebration, other teams of girls have hit the headlines in more disturbing ways: there is 'evidence of a new wave of girl gangs emerging from the shadows'; 'committed to violence and crime', many members hail from similarly chaotic backgrounds as the Forty Thieves and their Elephant and Castle patch.[2]

Ninety-eight years after the IWGC's incorporation under Royal Charter, Victoria Wallace became its first female director. Determined that the Commission would reflect twenty-first-century interests and educate the public about its mission, the 'CWGC Experience, Beaurains, France', opened in June 2019, subsequently achieving First Place in the 'Best Tourism Project in Europe, British Guild of Travel Writers' International Tourism Awards'. 'Remembrance' must assist the living as well as honour the dead; for a century, thousands of volunteers have sold poppies. One who did so at the first fundraising effort in 1921 was 6-year-old Rosemary James (now Powell). In 2018, aged 103, Britain's longest-serving 'Poppy Girl' received the MBE. 'Getting old', she subsequently retired. Over the years, the material from which the tokens are made, as well as the charity's name, has changed, but the poppies' purpose, to help survivors and their families to 'Live On', remains.[3]

Previously confined to charitable clinics such as the Family Planning Association and Marie Stopes, in 1974, free contraception, regardless of age or marital status, was formally incorporated within the NHS.[4] Harnessing the power of the image of the child, Save the Children Fund's mission remains dedicated to the youngest of citizens. Still responding to the needs of children when disaster strikes, in 2020 SCF launched its 'Coronavirus Appeal', striving to prevent the lives of the world's children being blighted by the pandemic, lobbying governments on behalf of those with no voice.

CHANGING ROLES - WOMEN AFTER THE GREAT WAR

Ninety-seven years after Normanton was called to the Bar, on 24 September 2019, wearing a spider brooch, the first female President of the Supreme Court, Lady Hale, delivered a 'bombshell court ruling' informing an outraged Government that its 'decision to suspend Parliament was unlawful'; her Spider brooch T-shirt went 'viral' raising over £18,000 for the charity Shelter.[5] Three months later, Hale issued another warning to the Government, this time against attempting to politicise the judiciary.[6] In 1955, having freely admitted her guilt, murderer Ruth Ellis was the last woman to be hanged in Britain. Edith Thompson's ghost haunted the multiple decades-long deliberations, which resulted in the 1969 UK abolition of the death penalty. An October 2018 report estimated that globally 'at least 500 women' were currently on death rows. In the USA, sixteen women have faced execution since 1984, forty-nine are currently under sentence of death. With exact global figures unobtainable, it is estimated 'that over 100 women have been executed in the last ten years – and potentially hundreds more'.[7] While some women's alleged crimes are undoubtedly horrendous, other condemned women are believed to be innocent or provoked by years of domestic and sexual abuse, often their abusers are never brought to justice.

Following the 1919 Paris Peace Conference, the 1920 Treaty of Trianon stripped a humiliated Hungary of Transylvania, thereby honouring the 1916 Treaty of Bucharest. On 29 April 2020, Romania's President Klaus Iohannis accused the opposition Social Democratic Party, of scheming to cede 'Transylvania to the Hungarians'.[8] Days later, Hungary's President Viktor Orbán's Facebook page included a map of 'Greater Hungary'; Transylvania, still home to many ethnic Hungarians, lies inside these re-drawn borders.[9] Significant tensions relating to Transylvania sour relations between these two Balkan states and NATO allies.[10] The 1921 Cairo Conference seemingly honoured some of the wartime promises made to the Arabs relating to self-determination. Since the beginning of the 2003 Iraq War, few months pass without Iraq featuring in the Western media. The complexities of the area appear as intractable as Bell predicted when drawing her lines in the sand. The psychological cost of that and the related Afghan War remains considerable, a 2018 study noted that 17 per cent of British veterans deployed in combat roles reported symptoms of probable PTSD, the figure excludes those who do not seek help, and also serving personnel who fear presenting with 'shell-shock' will blight their military career. Like Sayers in the 1920s, their families continue to share, even bear, much of their burden.[11]

This book sought to explore to what extent women's lives were altered by the peace which they had done so much to win. When I started the research, I wondered whether, notwithstanding the job losses, the pro-natalist pressures, the undoubted misogyny and the monstrous miscarriage of justice, I would find evidence of increased female empowerment. What I had not anticipated was how much the actions of the women featured, and the countless ones whom I reluctantly excluded, did change society. For good or ill, they helped to shape our world. That is their continuing legacy.

Endnotes

Introduction
1. L.K. Yates (1919), *The Woman's Part: A Record of Munitions Work*, George Doran, New York p.13
2. Parliamentary Papers 120, Vol. XVI p.9
3. See Pamela Horn (1995), *Women in the 1920s*, Allan Sutton, Stroud p.24
4. J.F. Kennedy Inaugural Address 20 January 1961

Chapter 1
1. Alice Norris Dick, Kerr Ladies player
2. *The Week* 6 June 2020 p.53
3. *Portsmouth Evening News* 7 September 1916. There are 23 references to Ladies Football in 1916 in *British Newspaper Archive,* 290 in 1917, 235 in 1918 and 36 in 1919
4. *Georgetown Gazette* 2, no, 8 (May 1918)
5. *Nantwich Guardian* 11 January 1918
6. Alice Norris quoted in Gail Newsham (1994 edition), *In a League of Their Own!*, Wheatons, Chorley p.42
7. *Lancashire Evening Post* 26 December 1917
8. *The Guardian* 26 December 2017
9. Newsham p.18
10. Newsham p.19
11. See Tim Tate (2016), *Girls with Balls*, John Blake p.159
12. 1911 census
13. Althea Melling *'Ladies' Football': Gender And The Socialisation Of Women Football Players In Lancashire C.1916 – 1960*. PhD thesis University of Central Lancashire 1999 p.242
14. https://api.parliament.uk/historic-hansard/commons/1919/jun/02/restoration-of-pre-war-practices-no-3
15. Melling p.242
16. Tate p.138
17. Tate p.162

18. https://www.britishpathe.com/video/women-footballers
19. Tate p.172
20. *The Times* 7 May 1920
21. Tate p.183
22. Jean Williams (2014), *A Contemporary History of Women's Sport, Part One: Sporting Women, 1850-1960,* Routledge p.126
23. *Football Favourite* 1 September 1920
24. *Lancashire Daily Post* 28 October 1920
25. Tate p.188
26. With no known grave, both are remembered at Le Touret, France
27. Private Joseph Walmsley is remembered at La Ferté-Sous-Jouarre Memorial
28. Newsham p.45
29. *La Vie au grand air: revue illustrée de tous les sports* 17 June 1920 « Une tournée triomphale »
30. *Lancashire Daily Post* 4 November 1920
31. *Lancashire Daily Post* 4 November 1920
32. Tate p.193
33. Williams p.126
34. Newsham p.51
35. Newsham p.58
36. Melling p.144
37. Melling p.122
38. *Dundee Evening Telegraph* 29 June 1921; Birmingham *Gazette* 28 June 1921
39. Tate p.241
40. Tate p.239
41. *Dundee Courier* 22 November 1930
42. *The Leeds Mercury* 7 December 1921
43. http://libraryblogs.is.ed.ac.uk/hcalibrarian/2017/07/28/why-football-banned-women/
44. Tate p.235
45. Williams p.130
46. https://www.oldpolicecellsmuseum.org.uk/content/learning/bad-girls/victorian-girl-gangs
47. https://www.oldpolicecellsmuseum.org.uk/content/learning/bad-girls/victorian-girl-gangs

48. https://www.crimeandinvestigation.co.uk/crime-files/london-gangs/key-figures
49. See for example *The Times* 7 August 1919
50. Clara Neilding pleaded neurasthenia *The Times* 7 August 1919; Brian McDonald (2015) *Alice Diamond and the Forty Elephants: Britain's First Female Crime Syndicate* p.169
51. Horn p.63
52. William M. Meier "Going on the Hoist: Women, Work, and Shoplifting in London, ca. 1890–1940" *Journal of British Studies*, Vol. 50, No. 2 (April 2011), pp.410-433 p.428
53. *Lancashire Evening Post* 25 August 1926
54. Meier p.423
55. *Ministry of Reconstruction Report on Domestic Service Parliamentary Papers 1919* XXIX p.22
56. Jean Rennie (1977 edition), *Every Other Sunday,* Coronet p.18
57. Meier p.431
58. McDonald p.160
59. 29 September 1927 *Morning Bulletin* Rockhampton Australia
60. Lilian Wyles (1952), *A Woman at Scotland Yard*, Faber and Faber pp.174-175
61. https://www.dailymail.co.uk/news/article-3366655
62. See *The Tatler* 1 January 1919
63. *The Tatler* 1 January 1919
64. In the UK in 2019 goods to the value of some £4billion were stolen https://www.retailresearch.org/crime-costs-uk.html
65. *Daily Herald* 7 February 1920 (The case was covered in multiple papers)
66. *The Times* 7 February 1920. Accounts differ slightly, some claiming that one of them wore a smart cloth coat
67. Accounts of the trial are widely available via British Newspaper Archive
68. *Leicester Daily Post* 7 February 1920
69. *Leicester Daily Post* 7 February 1920
70. *The Times* 30 October 1920. No trace of the outcome has been found
71. McDonald p.164
72. See for example *Nottingham Journal* 23 December 1925; Maria was killed in 1940, during the Blitz
73. *The Guardian* 27 November 2019 (the true number is believed to be higher)

74. https://www.occrp.org/en/daily/11232-thousands-of-girls-caught-up-in-gangs-in-england 29 November 2019
75. https://www.headliners.org/girl-gangs-in-south-london

Chapter 2

1. 'Mother of Two of Them' *The Scotsman* 16 April 1919
2. Philip Longworth (1967), *The Unending Vigil*, Constable p.29
3. Sir Frederic Kenyon (1918), *How the Cemeteries Abroad Will Be Designed*, HMSO p.3
4. *Warwick and Leamington Gazette* 15 February 1919
5. *The Scotsman* 17 April 1919 (68 letters in newspapers available via the BNA Archive discuss this topic in April alone)
6. *Chester Chronicle* 14 August 1915
7. *The Scotsman* 16 April 1919
8. Kenyon p.7
9. *Sheffield Daily Telegraph* 10 April 1919. The Selborne's 'Missing' son's grave was never identified
10. https://hansard.parliament.uk/Lords/1919-04-09/debates/35758c81-20bc-41cd-a52b-bbe4efe9791c/WarGraves
11. *The Scotsman* 17 April 1919
12. Some 960,000 Frenchmen were returned to a home community. See Dominiek Dendooven, "Bringing the Dead Home: Repatriation, Illegal Repatriation and Expatriation of British Bodies During and After the First World War," in Paul Cornish and Nicholas J. Saunders, eds. 2014, *Bodies in Conflict: Corporeality, Materiality and Transformation* (New York: Routledge), p.71
13. *New York Times* 18 November 1918
14. Lisa Budreau "Mourning and the Making of a Nation: The Gold Star Mothers Pilgrimages 1930-1933" *Stand To September 2004* pp.5-8 p.6
15. https://api.parliament.uk/historic-hansard/commons/1920/may/04/imperial-war-graves-commission
16. See Great War, the Commonwealth War Graves Commission online exhibition "Shaping Our Sorrow" https://shapingoursorrow.cwgc.org/
17. https://hansard.parliament.uk/commons/1920-08-10/debates/e7f77edc-1ed0-40ad-a983-176f5e25b926/WarGraves
18. The original plan had been for 2ft by 1ft 3in by 6in according to *The Graphic* 19 April 1919 p.12
19. Kenyon p.8

20. http://archive.cwgc.org/Record.aspx?src=CalmView.Catalog&id=
    CWGC%2f1%2f1%2f5%2f4&pos=2
21. Longworth p.47
22. Kenyon p.7
23. Kenyon p.8
24. *Daily Herald* 24 July 1920
25. Richard van Emden (2012), *The Quick and the Dead,* Bloomsbury
    p.255
26. Nurse Edith Cavell was repatriated in May 1920
27. *Leeds Mercury* 11 November 1920
28. *Leeds Post and Yorkshire Intelligencer* 8 November 1921
29. *Leeds Mercury* 11 November 1921
30. *Yorkshire Evening Post* 6 September 1923
31. *Yorkshire Post and Leeds Intelligencer* 9 January 1928
32. *Sheffield Independent* 7 August 1929
33. *Sheffield Independent* 9 July 1930
34. https://shapingoursorrow.cwgc.org/anger/rallying-the-opposition/
35. Winston Churchill Commons Debate May 1920 https://shapingoursorrow.
    cwgc.org/anger/the-commission-defends-itself/
36. Kenyon p.12
37. Edwin Lutyens (rep. 2009) *Cemeteries of the Great War* Uitgeverij p.16
38. It is possible that Ware accepted both architects' ideas to ensure that
    they did not carry their bitter rivalry into the design of the cemeteries.
39. Lutyens p.31
40. https://www.oxforddnb.com/view/10.1093/ref:odnb/9780198614128.
    001.0001/odnb-9780198614128-e-37597 - they quote - F. Jekyll,
    Gertrude Jekyll: a memoir (1934)
41. Quoted in the Oxford Dictionary of National Biography https://www.
    independent.co.uk/property/gardening/a-little-piece-of-england-the-
    horticultural-surprises-in-a-french-war-cemetery-2304323.html
42. Jekyll p.179
43. See Jane Brown (1985), *Gardens of a Golden Afternoon*, Penguin
    pp.137-138
44. https://chaumierelesiris.com/tag/commonwealth-war-graves-
    commission/
45. https://www.parksandgardens.org/places/winchester-college-garden-
    of-remembrance At that time, the school roll was 450 boys. The garden
    has since been redesigned but the plans remaini n the school library

46. Quoted in the Oxford Dictionary of National Biography https://www.oxforddnb.com/view/10.1093/ref:odnb/9780198614128.001.0001/odnb-9780198614128-e-37597 - G. Jekyll, 'Garden design on old-fashioned lines', *Black's Gardening Dictionary* (1921), pp.383-4

47. https://livesofthefirstworldwar.iwm.org.uk/story/65060

48. Anna Durie, 'A Soldier's Grave in France' 1920, *Our Absent Heroes*, The Ryerson Press p.19

49. See *Toronto Star* 17 May 2014

50. In 1919, the information about Corkscrew was not 'common' knowledge so it is very likely Chanter did work for the Commission; James Garratt, PhD thesis University of Western Ontario 2018, "Tribute to the Fallen: The Evolution of Canadian Battlefield Burials during World War One", p.273-4

51. Veronica Cusack (2004), *The Invisible Soldier: Captain W.A.P. Durie, His Life and Afterlife*, McLelland & Stewart p.150

52. *Toronto Star* 17 May 2014

53. Cusack p.150

54. Garrett p.275

55. *Toronto Star* 17 May 2014

56. *Toronto Star* 17 May 2014

57. Garrett p.276

58. *Toronto Evening Telegram* 7 February 1925

59. Early cemetery record

60. https://shapingoursorrow.cwgc.org/anger/anna-durie-a-mothers-defiance/63

61. https://shapingoursorrow.cwgc.org/anger/anna-durie-a-mothers-defiance/

62. *Toronto Star* 17 May 2017

63. https://psychcentral.com/lib/the-5-stages-of-loss-and-grief/

64. https://yougov.co.uk/topics/politics/explore/not-for-profit/Royal_British_Legion (the figures fluctuate with each survey)

65. Guerin features in countless American papers see newspapers.com. The website https://poppyladymadameguerin.wordpress.com provides an in-depth view of her work

66. *Port Arthur News Chronicle* July 1921 (Meuse Argonne American cemetery)

67. Dianne Graves (1997), *Crown of Life: The World of John McCrae* p.267-8

68. Intensive coverage by *Baltimore Sun* continued until after 11 November 1919

69. Held on the last Monday in May, this day commemorates American veterans of all wars and was formerly called Decoration Day. It was observed on 30 May until 1970

70. *Logan Republican* 22 April 1920

71. https://poppyladymadameguerin.wordpress.com/chapter-6-madames-childrens-league-usa-poppy. Quote from 'The Student Life' publication (of Logan) on 30 April 1920

72. https://poppyladymadameguerin.wordpress.com/chapter-6-madames-childrens-league-usa-poppy. Quote from *Salt Lake Telegram* 5 April 1920

73. https://poppyladymadameguerin.wordpress.com/chapter-6-madames-childrens-league-usa-poppy. Letter 22 May 1920 Madame Lebon, American and French Children's League's Chairman in France to Guerin

74. See Nicholas Saunders (2014), *The Poppy: A History of Conflict, Loss, Remembrance, and Redemption* p.120

75. https://www.vfw.org/community/community-initiatives/buddy-poppy/

76. South Africa's enthusiasm declined with the onset of the Apartheid era see https://samilhistory.com/2017/11/07/legions-and-poppies-and-their-south-african-root/

77. Saunders pp.111-112

78. https://en.wikipedia.org/wiki/Madame_Gu%C3%A9rin

79. Sarah E. H. Moore (2008), *Ribbon Culture*, Palgrave Macmillan p.46

80. *Yorkshire Post and Leeds Intelligencer* 26 October 1921 Letter from the Lord Mayor

81. Moore p.46

82. Lee Karen Stow (2007), "She Bought Poppies not Bandages: Moina Belle Michael's Appropriation of the Flanders Fields Poppy", MA by research University of Lincoln p.53

83. Moina Michael (1941), *The Miracle Flower: the Story of the Flanders Field Memorial Poppy*, Philadelphia, Dorrance and Company p.79

84. Michael p.79

85. See Saunders p.104

86. Stow p.14

87. Michael p.71

88. Stow p.62; Saunders p.123

89. Citation, May 1940

ENDNOTES

90. https://unc-lefolgoet.pagesperso-orange.fr/bleuet.htm

Chapter 3
1. *Yarmouth Independent* 11 January 1919
2. *Montrose Standard* 17 January 1919 is the most outspoken in its condemnation
3. http://theworldismycountry.info/posters/lift-the-hunger-blockade/
4. Angela V. John (2009), *Evelyn Sharp Rebel Woman 1869-1955*, Manchester p.91
5. Ruth Fry (1926), *Quaker Adventure: the Story of Nine Years Relief and Reconstruction*, Nisbet & Co. Ltd p.313
6. Angela V. John (2009) *Evelyn Sharp Rebel Woman 1869-1955*, Manchester p.92, p.93
7. Fry p.304
8. Fry p.304
9. Fry p.304
10. See Francesca Wilson (1945), *In the Margins of Chaos Recollections of Relief Work in and Between Three Wars*, Macmillan p.107
11. Sian Lliwen Roberts, "Place Life Histories and the Politics of Relief: Episodes in the Life of Francesca Wilson, Humanitarian, Educator, Activist", PhD thesis p.91; see Fry p.193
12. Wilson p.109
13. Fry p.195
14. Fry p.211
15. Roberts p.40
16. Fry p.209
17. Fry p.196
18. Wilson p.138
19. Wilson pp.122-123
20. Fry p.157
21. John p.128
22. See Charles M. Edmondson and R. Barry Levis: "Archbishop Randall Davidson, Russian Famine Relief, and the Fate of the Orthodox Clergy, 1917-1923" https://www.jstor.org/stable/23920418 pp.619-637 passim
23. John p.130, 132
24. Evelyn Sharp (2008), *Unfinished Adventure: Selected Reminiscences from an Englishwoman's Life*, Faber and Faber p.233
25. Fry p.167

26. Fry p.169
27. John p.99
28. Marceline Hecquet, « Nous… qui avons laissé faire », *La Mère Éducatrice*, 6, n° 6, juin 1923
29. John p.102
30. *Daily Herald* 14 February 1923
31. *Daily Herald* 13 February 1923
32. *Daily Herald* 6 August 1923
33. John p.106
34. John pp.106-107
35. John p.108
36. *Daily Herald* 16 May 1919; Mulley p.241
37. Mulley p.242
38. Mulley p.245
39. Emily Baughan, 'Every Citizen of Empire Implored to Save the Children!' Empire, internationalism and the Save the Children Fund in inter-war Britain.' *Historical research*. Volume 86:Issue 231 (2013, February); pp.116-137 p.131
40. Baughan p.121
41. Baughan pp.132, 124
42. 5 December 1919 *The Scotsman*
43. Linda Mahood (2008), "Eglantyne Jebb: remembering, representing and writing a rebel daughter", *Women's History Review* 17:1, 1-20 p.176
44. Mulley p.270
45. 11 September 1920 *Buckingham Advertiser and Free Press*
46. Mulley p.271
47. Privately published pamphlet April 1919 quoted in Mulley p.231
48. Mulley p.280
49. Mulley p.284
50. Mulley p.286
51. Roberts p.63 and *passim*
52. USSR joined in 1934; see James Muckle "Saving the Russian Children: Materials in the Archive of the Save The Children Fund Relating to Eastern Europe in 1920-23" *The Slavonic and East European Review*, Vol. 68, No. 3 (July, 1990), pp.507-511 p.509
53. Baughan p.133

54. Muckle p.510 (The distance between Buzuluk where FFC were working and Saratov is 950km)
55. Baughan p.116
56. Baughan p.126
57. See Baughan p.126
58. Mulley p.312
59. United States of America, Somalia and South Sudan
60. 18 December 1928 *Journal de Geneve*
61. *Common Cause* 7 February 1919
62. Entry in *Oxford Dictionary of National Biography* https://doi.org/10.1093/ref:odnb/36323
63. https://www.bbc.co.uk/news/science-environment-11040319
64. *The Vote* 31 October 1913
65. *Common Cause* 9 April 1914 (upon marriage, women were dismissed from inter alia teaching and medical posts)
66. Entry in *Oxford Dictionary of National Biography* https://doi.org/10.1093/ref:odnb/36323
67. https://blogs.ucl.ac.uk/museums/2014/05/08/war-love-and-coal-new-exhibition-from-ucl-museum-studies-students/
68. *Freedom* 1 November 1914; *International Women's Suffrage News* 1 July 1915 Comstock Laws made it illegal to disseminated information about birth control
69. June Rose (2007 edition), *Marie Stopes and the Sexual Revolution*, Tempus p.117
70. *The Guardian* 14 February 2018
71. Rose p.157
72. See Evelyn Underhill, *Saturday Westminster Gazette*, 21 November 1914 p.17
73. Rose p.156
74. Rose p.160
75. Quoted in Rose p.179
76. Rose p.184
77. See Rose p.181
78. See Rose p.181
79. https://hallidaysutherland.com/research/the-national-birth-rate-commission/

80. Isabel Hutton (1960), *Memories of a Doctor in War & Peace*, Heinemann p.81

81. Pauline Brand, PhD thesis (2007), *Birth Control Nursing in The Marie Stopes Mothers' Clinics 1921-1931*, de Montfort University, Leicester p.140

82. Anne Hardy and Lawrence Conrad (2001), *Women and Modern Medicine*, Clio Medical p.136, p.134

83. Quoted in Rose p.191

84. 1922 Congress of the Royal Institute of Public Health

85. See Brad p.213; Hardy, Conrad p.134

86. Sylvia Pankhurst, *The Suffragette Movement – An Intimate Account of Persons And Ideals* p.480; Brand p.65

87. Brand p.142

88. https://time.com/4065338/margaret-sanger-clinic-history/

89. Lesley Hall (2013), 'The Subject is Obscene: No Lady Would Dream of Alluding to It': Marie Stopes and her courtroom dramas, Women's History Review, 22:2, 253-266, DOI: 10.1080/09612025.2012.726114 covers this rift in interesting detail

90. *Common Cause* 27 May 1921

91. Hall p.255

92. See *The Women's Leader* 29 July 1921

93. *Nottingham Journal* 8 October 1921. See Rose p.200

94. http://ww1centenary.oucs.ox.ac.uk/body-and-mind/the-british-army%E2%80%99s-fight-against-venereal-disease-in-the-%E2%80%98heroic-age-of-prostitution%E2%80%99/

95. See Rose p.165

96. See Rose p.165

97. Rose p.193

98. McIlroy, appointed Dame in 1929, was the first medical woman appointed to a professorship; Rose p.197

99. https://www.catholicworldreport.com/2017/03/03/stopes-v-sutherland-the-legal-battle-between-a-eugenicist-and-a-catholic-doctor/; Brand p.296

100. Halliday Sutherland, *A Statement of Christian Doctrine against the Neo-Malthusians*, Kindle edition

101. Hall p.259

102. https://www.catholicworldreport.com/2017/03/03/stopes-v-sutherland-the-legal-battle-between-a-eugenicist-and-a-catholic-doctor/

103. Halliday Sutherland has a website which stresses his actions were driven by hatred and fear of eugenics www.hallidaysutherland.com; the story features periodically in the Catholic press. Brand p.297
104. Hall p.254
105. Quoted in Rose p.223
106. Rose p.232
107. http://mariestopes.org.uk/central-london
108. https://api.parliament.uk/historic-hansard/lords/1926/apr/28/welfare-centres
109. https://api.parliament.uk/historic-hansard/lords/1926/apr/28/welfare-centres
110. Audrey Leathard (1980), *Fight for Family Planning*, Macmillan p.35 (The Upper House vote was 57-41)
111. Brand p.185.
112. See Brand for dates and venues
113. Brand p.297
114. See Brand p.265 & p.300
115. See Brand for detailed information about Stopes as an employer.
116. *Nottingham Evening Post* 16 July 1929
117. Quoted in Rose p.246
118. Birth control. Memorandum 153/MCV. Ministry of Health, July 1930.
119. https://theconversation.com/how-the-catholic-church-came-to-oppose-birth-control-95694; https://catholicstraightanswers.com/what-is-the-churchs-teaching-on-contraception/
120. *The Guardian* 13 July 2019
121. *The Guardian* 14 October 2008
122. *The Guardian* 14 October 2008

Chapter 4

1. Bebb v. Law Society Court of Appeal [1914]
2. https://first100years.org.uk/eliza-orme-2/
3. *The Times* 3 December 1903
4. See https://ials.blogs.sas.ac.uk/2019/12/17/women-at-the-bar-the-sex-disqualification-removal-act-1919-and-the-admission-of-women-to-the-legal-profession/
5. See Judith Bourne (2014), King's College London PhD thesis, *Helena Normanton and the Opening of the Bar to Women* p.104
6. Bourne p.127

7. Bourne p.128
8. See https://api.parliament.uk/historic-hansard/lords/1919/jul/22/sex-disqualification-removal-bill-hl
9. Bourne p.133
10. https://first100years.org.uk/ivy-williams/
11. https://first100years.org.uk/ivy-williams/
12. Bourne p.173
13. *Belfast Telegraph* 22 December 1922
14. Bourne p.219
15. *Westminster Gazette* 29 December 1924
16. Maureen Beasley (2017), *Ruby A. Black: Eleanor Roosevelt, Puerto Rico, and Political Journalism in Washington*, Lexington Books, Washington DC p.35
17. Bourne p.228
18. Used in *Daily Herald* 24 August 1933 – it is unlikely that the newspaper intended to do her harm it was a journalistic ploy to attract readers.
19. https://archiveshub.jisc.ac.uk/data/gb106-7hln/7hln/a/12
20. *Edinburgh Evening News* 1 March 1930
21. *Leeds Mercury* 1 March 1930
22. See inter alia *Daily Express* 8 February 1924
23. Bourne p.254
24. *Sunderland Daily Echo and Shipping Gazette* 21 December 1932
25. https://castleassociates.org.uk/
26. https://www.lawteacher.net/
27. Letters in *The Times* 28 January 1921
28. Quentin Falk (2012), *The Musical Milkman Murder*, John Blake p.50
29. Nicola Goc (2016), *Women Infanticide and the Press 1822-1922* Routledge p.150
30. In Kevin Crosby "Keeping Women off the Jury in England and Wales in the 1920s", *Legal Studies* 2017 pp.695-717, p.713
31. For in-depth analysis see Gic
32. *Leicester Mercury* covered the story in unsparing detail between June 1921 and July 1922, for Powers see also *Nottingham Journal* 26 July 1921
33. *Nottingham Journal* 26 July 1921
34. *Vote* 29 July 1921; *Nottingham Journal* 8 June 1921
35. Mairead Enright (2018), "'The very antithesis of womanhood'; Edith Roberts and the Infanticide Acts" in *Gender and Legal History in Birmingham and the West Midlands*

36. Quentin Falk, *The Musical Milkman Murder*, provides a painstaking reconstruction of the murder and trial
37. Falk p.57
38. Falk p.130
39. Falk p.165
40. *Dundee Evening Telegraph* 7 January 1921
41. *Dundee Evening Telegraph* 7 January 1921
42. Marie Belloc-Lowndes, *What Really Happened* https://archive.org/details/novelsofmystery100lown/page/n639/
43. See British Newspaper Archive for coverage of her jury service
44. *The Times* 28 January 1921
45. Juror's oath
46. Charles Dickens, *Oliver Twist*
47. https://www.irishtimes.com/culture/heritage/queen-of-the-nightclubs-1.1607995
48. *Pall Mall Gazette* 28 January 1920
49. For an account of the trial and her defence See *inter alia Pall Mall Gazette* 14 January 1920
50. https://www.irishtimes.com/culture/heritage/queen-of-the-nightclubs-1.1607995
51. Kate Meyrick (1933), *Secrets of "the 43"*, Parkgate Publications p.210
52. Meyrick p.213
53. Meyrick p.213-214
54. Meyrick p.274
55. *Daily Herald* 20 January 1933
56. https://en.wikipedia.org/wiki/William_Joynson-Hicks,_1st_Viscount_Brentford#cite_note-Matthew_2004,_p39-13 (Joynson-Hicks was behind the 1928 suppression of Radclyffe Hall's lesbian novel *The Well of Loneliness*
57. *Shields Daily News* 20 October 1924
58. *Shields Daily News* 20 October 1924
59. C. Biron (1936), *Without prejudice: impressions of life and law* p.334
60. Meyrick p.106
61. Meyrick p.108
62. Meyrick p.271
63. See Heather Shore, ' "Constable dances with instructress" the Police and the Queen of Nightclubs in inter-war London', *Social History* Vol. 38 No. 2 (May 2013) pp.183-202 p.194

64. Meyrick p.193
65. Meyrick p.279
66. *Staffordshire Sentinel* 4 December 1929
67. Meyrick p.191
68. Meyrick p.192
69. *Brewer's Dictionary of Phrase and Fable* (Centenary ed., 1970), Harper & Row p.7
70. Meyrick p.176
71. *The People* 2 February 1930
72. *The People* 2 February 1930
73. *Oxford Dictionary of National Biography* Kate Meyrick https://doi.org/10.1093/ref:odnb/66827
74. Meyrick p.193
75. *Evening Telegraph* 10 May 1932
76. *Taunton Courier, and Western Advertiser* 25 January 1933
77. See *Sunderland Daily Echo and Shipping Gazette* 25 January 1933

Chapter 5

1. Agatha Christie (1993 edition), *An Autobiography*, Harper Collins p.216 https://crimereads.com/the-original-ladies-of-crime/
2. Christie p.217; https://www.mentalfloss.com/article/85723/15-mysterious-facts-about-agatha-christie
3. Christie p.217
4. Christie p.245
5. Christie p.255
6. Agatha Christie (1925), 'In a Dispensary' *The Road of Dreams*, Geoffrey Bles
7. See inter alia Bardell, Eunice Bonow. "Dame Agatha's Dispensary." *Pharmacy in History*, vol. 26, no. 1, 1984, pp.13–19.
8. Michael Gerald "Agatha Christie's Helpful and Harmful Health Providers: Writings on Physicians and Pharmacists" in *Pharmacy in History, Vol. 33, No. 1* (1991), pp.31-39
9. Agatha Christie, 'In a Dispensary' *The Road of Dreams*, Geoffrey Bles, 1925
10. Christie p.263
11. *Nottingham Journal* 4 June 1921 (the first day of the *Styles* serialisation)
12. Christie p.265-6
13. Christie p.285 her italics

14. *The Sketch* 28 February 1923
15. '"The Daughters of his Manhood" Christie and the Golden Age of Detective Fiction' Mary Anne Ackershoek in (1997) *Theory and Practice of Classic Detective Fiction*, ed Jerome H. Delamater and Ruth Prigozy Contributions to the Study of Popular Culture, Hofstra University p.120
16. Agatha Christie (1922), *The Secret Adversary*, available via Project Guthenburg
17. Ackershoek p.120
18. Agatha Christie (1923), *Murder on the Links*, available via Project Guthenburg
19. Christie p.362
20. Christie p.364
21. Letter to her mother 14 December 1926
22. Christie p.364
23. 'Agatha Christie's doctors' *BMJ* 2010; 341
24. *Leeds Mercury* 21 April 1928
25. See Pamela Horn (1995), *Women in the 1920s*, Allan Sutton, Stroud p.41
26. Christie p.449
27. Christie p.490
28. P.V. Geetha Lakshmi Patnaik 'An Unsuitable Job for a Woman'?: Woman as Writer and Protagonist in Detective Fiction IJELLH *International Journal of English Language & Literature* Vol 4 Issue 4 April 2026 pp.135-138 p.141
29. Letter to her parents 2 August 1914, 1 November 1914
30. Letter to Muriel Jaeger 27 July 1915; British Newspaper Archive From 1915 to 1918 shell-shock appears 2,747 times in the available newspapers
31. https://archive.org/details/oxforduniversity00univuoft/mode/2up
32. Letters 16 May and 27 July 1915
33. I am grateful for the information relating to shell-shock and its early treatment provided by 'Combat Stress'
34. The Report of the War Office Committee of enquiry into "Shell Shock" p.4
35. Ted Bogacz 'The Report of the War Office Committee of enquiry into "Shell Shock"' https://www.jstor.org/stable/260822 p.232
36. James Brabazon (1988) *Dorothy L. Sayers* Gollancz p.86
37. *Daily Express* 28 February 1934
38. Brabazon p.113
39. Letter to her cousin Ivy, 21 August 1934
40. Horn p.13

41. Letter to Ivy 21 August 1934
42. Letter 23 November 1933
43. Dorothy L Sayers (1937), *Busman's Honeymoon*
44. Brabazon p.143
45. Dorothy L Sayers (1937), *Busman's Honeymoon*
46. Dorothy L Sayers (1937), *Busman's Honeymoon*
47. Dorothy L Sayers (1937), *Busman's Honeymoon*
48. Laura Thompson (2018), *Rex v. Thompson*, Head of Zeus p.298
49. The complete account of the trial is available in Filson Young, *Notable British Trials*, (Glasgow, 1923) and can be accessed via https://edithjessie thompson.co.uk/ Letters quoted are from 1922 unless otherwise stated
50. Rene Weis (1990), *Criminal Justice*, London p.25
51. Robin Kent (1970) *Agony Aunt Advises*, W.H. Allen p.91
52. https://edithjessiethompson.co.uk/criminal-justice/chapter-1/
53. Thompson p.89
54. *Hartlepool Northern Daily Mail* 5 February 1920
55. Horn p.73
56. Robert Graves (1941), *The Long Weekend* p.39; *The People* 7 January 1923; letter 13 March 1922 Edith Thompson's letters are all available on https://edithjessiethompson.co.uk/primary-source-texts/letters-of-edith-thompson-and-frederick-bywaters/ Fatefully, he kept her letters, she destroyed nearly all of his
57. Horn p.54
58. Quoted in Thompson p.144
59. Edith Thompson's letters are all available on https://edithjessiethompson. co.uk/primary-source-texts/letters-of-edith-thompson-and-frederick-bywaters/ She used 'darlint' as opposed to 'darling'. All quoted date from 1922 unless stated otherwise
60. Filson and Young p.135
61. James Douglas (Editor), S*unday Express*, 'The Ilford Murder The Case For and Against a Reprieve'
62. Autopsy Report CRIM I / 206/ 58186; letter 8-10 April
63. https://edithjessiethompson.co.uk/criminal-justice/preface/
64. Quoted in Thompson p.114
65. https://edithjessiethompson.co.uk/criminal-justice/chapter-4/
66. Thomas Hardy, 'On the Portrait of a Woman about to be Hanged' in *The Works of Thomas Hardy* Wordsworth Poetry Library 1994 p.741

ENDNOTES

67. https://edithjessiethompson.co.uk/criminal-justice/chapter-4/
68. Frederick Wensley (1931), *Detective Days Cassell and Co.* p.223. Details about her time at Ilford Police Station are from this source
69. Wensley p.224
70. Wensley p.227
71. Wensley p.230
72. Wensley p.230
73. Wensley p.230
74. Wensley p.232
75. Douglas
76. Douglas
77. Douglas
78. Quoted in Thompson p.377
79. Quoted in Thompson p.383
80. https://edithjessiethompson.co.uk/criminal-justice/chapter-6/
81. Caitlin Davies (2018), *Bad Girls: A History of Rebels and Renegades*, John Murray, kindle edition
82. John Ellis (1996 edition), *Diary of a Hangman*, True Crime Library p.10
83. Ellis p.14
84. *Pall Mall Gazette* 9 January 1923
85. *Dundee Evening Telegraph and Post* 9 January 1923
86. *Dundee Evening Telegraph and Post* 9 January 1923
87. Meyrick p.108
88. Quoted in Thompson p.377
89. Filson Young, *Notable British Trials*, (Glasgow, 1923) and can be accessed via https://edithjessiethompson.co.uk/
90. https://www.deathpenaltyproject.org/wp-content/uploads/2017/12/DPP-50-Years-on-pp1-68-1.pdf p.29
91. https://babel.hathitrust.org/cgi/pt?id=uc1.$b47213&view=1up&seq=484
92. Sayers' only non-Wimsey novel
93. https://edithjessiethompson.co.uk/three-days-in-november-2018
94. Beverley Baxter (1935), *Strange Street*, Hutchinson p.155
95. Adrian Wright, *The Innumerable Dance: The Life and Work of William Alwyn*, Boydell Press p.27
96. https://edithjessiethompson.co.uk/three-days-in-november-2018

Chapter 6

1. Quoted in Tessa Dunlop, 'Romania's Wartime Queen' in *History Today* November 2018
2. *New York Times* 4 October 1918
3. Great Britain ranks 11th in this unenviable League Table with France 5th and Germany 7th J.M. Winter (2000 edition), *The Experience of World War One*, Greenwich p.207
4. Hannah Pakula (1985), *The Last Romantic: Queen Marie of Romania*, Simon & Schuster p.263
5. See Pakula p.282
6. Emile Joseph Dillon (1920), *Inside The Paris Peace Conference* https://www.gutenberg.org/files/14477/14477-h/14477-h.html (np)
7. Dillon (np)
8. Doina Pasca Harsanyi (1996) "Blue blood and ink: Romanian aristocratic women before and after World War I", *Women's History Review*, 5:4, 497-511 To link to this article: https://doi.org/10.1080/09612029600200125 p.503
9. Pakula p.270
10. Pakula p.270
11. Pakula p.279
12. John van der Kiste, *Crowns in a Changing World: The British and European Monarchies, 1901-1936* (Kindle edition)
13. Quoted in Pakula p.274
14. https://www.youtube.com/watch?v=sxfSXl_jPMM
15. *Pall Mall Gazette* 12 March 1919
16. Quoted in Pakula p.275
17. Marie of Romania, *Later Chapters of My Life*, edited Diana Mandache (2004), Sutton p.24 (Marie's personal diaries were written in English and kept from 1914 until her death (see Roxana Bălăucă "There is an hour of which I have never spoken" in *Philobiblon* – Vol. XVII (2012) – No. 1 pp.231-246
18. Mandache p.24
19. Mandache p.27
20. Julia Gelardi (2006), *Born to Rule: Granddaughters of Victoria; Queens of Europe*, St Martin's Publishing Group p.296
21. See Harsanyi p.505; Pakula p.296
22. Harsanyi p.506

23. Paul D Quinlan in *Balkan Studies* 1991 "The Importance of Marie in Romanian History" pp.35-41 p.37
24. Colette *Le Matin* 6 March 1919
25. Mandache p.xxxi
26. Quoted in Bălăucă pp.231-246 p.237
27. See Bălăucă pp.231-246 p. 240
28. Pakula p.277
29. *Le Gaulois* 5 March 1919
30. Margaret Macmillan (2002 edition), *The Peacemakers Six Months that Changed the World* p.143
31. Pakula p.278
32. Pakula p.279
33. Dillon (np)
34. *Pall Mall Gazette* 12 March 1919
35. Pakula p.280
36. Tessa Dunlop, 'Romania's Wartime Queen' in *History Today* November 2018
37. Pakula p.282
38. See http://www.tkinter.smig.net/QueenMarie/MammaRegina/index. htm Churchill's treatment of Romania in October 1944 which gave Stalin 99% occupation of country lay far in the future. Luckily Marie was long dead when this betrayal occurred.
39. Mandache p.47
40. Mandache p.33
41. See Dunlop
42. Mandache p.71, 72
43. Mandache p.72
44. MacMillan p.143
45. MacMillan p.143 Although Ileana's parentage was a badly-kept secret, King Ferdinand had recognised her as his own
46. MacMillan p.143
47. Quoted in Gelardi p.143
48. Pakula p.285
49. Mandache p.72
50. Mandache p.72
51. Mandache p.87
52. Mandache p.77-8

53. https://rebeccastarrbrown.com/2018/05/01/from-kent-to-bucharest-marie-of-edinburgh-queen-of-romania/

54. Many of Gertrude Bell's letters are available via the Gertrude Bell Archive at Newcastle University, http://gertrudebell.ncl.ac.uk/

55. Ann Wilks (2016), "The 1922 Anglo-Iraq Treaty: A Moment of Crisis and the Role of Britain's Man on the Ground", *British Journal of Middle Eastern Studies*, 43:3, 342-359 https://doi.org/10.1080/13530 194.2015.1102709 p.346

56. See Wilks p.346

57. The closest definition of vilayet is 'territory' but those on the ground used vilayet and I follow their example

58. Quoted in Janet Wallach (2005 edition), *Desert Queen*, Anchor Books p.230 – no source given

59. Bell always used the Arabic term

60. Letter to Hugh Bell 7 March 1919

61. Andrew Lycett *The Times* 13 August 2006

62. Letter to Florence Bell 16 March 1919

63. Letter to Hugh Bell 7 March 1919

64. Letter to her father Wed (nd) March 1919 see Gertrude.bell.ncl.ac.uk/letter_details.php?letter_id=349

65. Letter to Hugh Bell 7 March 1919

66. Quoted in Georgina Howell (2006), *Daughter of the Desert: The Remarkable Life of Gertrude Bell* p.381-2

67. Letter to Florence Bell 16 March 1919

68. Wallach p.230

69. Letter to Hugh Bell 17 January 1921

70. The Review is easily available on the internet from for example https://archive.org/details/reviewofciviladm00iraqrich

71. Letter to Hugh Bell 22 January 1921

72. Wallach pp.244-5

73. Quoted in Howell p.357-8

74. Howell p.359

75. Letter to Hugh Bell 7 December 1919

76. Letter to Florence Bell 12 January 1920

77. Letter to Florence Bell 14 March 1920

78. *Queen of Quagmire* Rory Stewart https://www.globalpolicy.org/iraq-conflict-the-historical-background-/british-colonialism-and-repression-in-iraq/48076-the-queen-of-quagmire.html

79. Letter to Florence 10 April 1920
80. Letter to Hugh Bell 1 June 1920
81. Letter to Hugh Bell 1 June 1920, 14 June 1920
82. Letter to Hugh 1 June 1920
83. See *Armed Forces and Insurgents in Modern Arabia* Kaushik Roy, Sourish Saha accessed via Google books
84. Letter to Hugh Bell 7 June 1920. See http://www.kaiserscross.com/304501/315743.html
85. Wallach p.248 no source given
86. This part of the letter is available online but not in the *Letters of Gertrude Bell*
87. Letter to Hugh Bell 4 July 1920
88. Letter to Hugh Bell 4 July 1920
89. Letter to Hugh Bell 26 July 1920
90. Letter to Hugh Bell 2 August 1920; see also http://www.kaiserscross.com/304501/315743.html
91. Letter to Hugh Bell 16 August 1920
92. Aberdeen Press and Journal – 26 June 1920
93. *Yorkshire Post and Leeds Intelligencer* 24 June 1920
94. Letter to Florence Bell 5 September 1920
95. Letter to Hugh Bell and Florence Bell 10 October 1920
96. https://api.parliament.uk/historic-hansard/commons/1921/jun/14/middle-eastern-services
97. Letter to Hugh Bell 22 January 1921
98. Howell p.397
99. Howell p.401
100. See Vivien Newman (2018), *Suffragism and the Great War* pp.78-83; Bell *Civil Administration* p.127
101. Letter to Hugh Bell 17 April 1921
102. Christopher Catherwood in *Winston's Folly How Winston's Created Modern Iraq* argues that the coup was aided and abetted by Gertrude Bell p.163
103. Philby's son, Kim achieved notoriety as one of the 'Cambridge Five' spies in the employ of the Soviet Union
104. Letter to Hugh Bell 17 April 1921
105. Letter to Hugh Bell 23 June 1921
106. Letter to Hugh Bell 30 June 1921
107. Letter to Hugh Bell 7 July 1921
108. Wallach p.331

109. Letter to Florence Bell 28 February 1924
110. "The Post Hole" Issue 9 2010-01-25 pp.16-21 p.17
111. Letter to Hugh Bell 22 January 1924
112. Letter to Hugh Bell 13 February 1924
113. "The Post Hole" Issue 9 2010-01-25 pp.16-21 p.18
114. Julia M. Asher-Greve, "Gertrude Bell: A Woman Larger than Life" pp.142-197 in *Breaking Ground: Pioneering Women: Archaeologists* (2004) Ann Arbor p.161

Conclusion

1. https://en.wikipedia.org/wiki/Great_Britain_women%27s_Olympic_football_team
2. https://www.2020dreams.org.uk/shop/publications/the-rise-of-the-girl-gangs/
3. https://www.bbc.co.uk/news/uk-england-london-45088435
4. https://peopleshistorynhs.org/
5. https://charitydigital.org.uk/topics/topics/shelter-nets-18000-from-online-lady-hale-spider-t-shirt-sales2-6196
6. https://www.independent.co.uk/news/uk/politics/lady-hale-boris-johnson-supreme-court-appointments-conservatives-a9261131.html
7. http://www.worldcoalition.org/Global-overview-of-women-facing-the-death-penalty.html
8. See *Balkan Insight* 29 April 2020
9. *Balkan Insight* 7 May 2020
10. https://transylvanianow.com/pm-orban-wont-pick-up-the-gauntlet-thrown-by-iohannis/
11. *See British Journal of Psychiatry* DOI: https://doi.org/10.1192/bjp.2018.175

Bibliography

Unless stated otherwise, all places of publication are London

Beasley, Maureen (2017), *Ruby A. Black: Eleanor Roosevelt, Puerto Rico, and Political Journalism in Washington,* Lexington Books USA

Bell, Lady Florence (1930), *Letters of Gertrude Bell,* Benn

Bell, Gertrude (1920), *Review of the Civil Administration of Mesopotamia,* HMSO

Brabazon, James (1988), *Dorothy L. Sayers,* Gollancz

Brown, James (1985), *Gardens of a Golden Afternoon,* Penguin

Catherwood, Christopher (2004), *Winston's Folly: How Winston Churchill's Created Modern Iraq,* Carroll & Graf

Christie, Agatha (1922), *The Secret Adversary,* available via Project Guthenburg

Christie, Agatha (1925), *The Road of Dreams,* Geoffrey Bles

Christie, Agatha (1993), *An Autobiography,* Harper Collins

Cornish, Paul & Saunders, Nicholas (eds) (2014), *Bodies in Conflict: Corporeality, Materiality and Transformation*, Routledge, New York

Cusak, Veronica (2004), *The Invisible Soldier: Captain W.A.P. Durie, His Life and Afterlife,* McLelland & Stewart, Canada

Dillon, Emile Joseph (1920), *Inside The Paris Peace Conference,* Project Gutenburg

Durie, Anna (1920), *Our Absent Heroes*

Falk, Quentin (2012), *The Musical Milkman Murder,* John Blake

Filson and Young (1923), *Notable British Trials*, Glasgow

Fry, Ruth (1926), *Quaker Adventure The Story of Nine Years Relief and Reconstruction*, Nisbet

Gelardi, Julia (2005), *Born to Rule: Granddaughters of Victoria; Queens of Europe,* Headline

Goc, Nicola (2016), *Women Infanticide and the Press 1822-1922,* Routledge

Graves, Dianne (1997), *Crown of Life: The World of John McCrae,* The History Press

Graves, Robert (1941), *The Long Weekend: A Social History of Great Britain 1918-1939,* Readers Union

Hardy, Anne and Conrad, Lawrence (2001), *Women and Modern Medicine,* Clio Medical

Hardy, Thomas (1994), *The Works of Thomas Hardy,* Wordsworth Poetry Library

Horn, Pamela (1995), *Women in the 1920s,* Allan Sutton, Stroud

Howell, Georgina (2007), *Daughter of the Desert: The Remarkable Life of Gertrude Bell,* Pan

Hutton, Isabel (1960), *Memories of a Doctor in War & Peace,* Heinemann

Jekyll, Francis (1934), *Gertrude Jekyll; a memoir,* Bookshop Round Table

Jekyll, Gertrude (1921), *Garden design on old-fashioned lines,* Black's Gardening Dictionary, A. C. Black

John, Angela V. (2009), *Evelyn Sharp Rebel Woman 1869-1955,* Manchester University Press

Kaushik, Roy and Saha, Sourish (2016), *Armed Forces and Insurgents in Modern Asia,* Routledge

Kent, Robin (1970), *Agony Aunt Advises,* W.H. Allen

Kenyon, Frederick (1918), *How the Cemeteries Abroad Will Be Designed,* HMSO

Leathard, Audrey (1980), *Fight for Family Planning,* Macmillan

Longworth, Philip (1967), *The Unending Vigil*

Lowndes, Marie Belloc- (1927), *What Really Happened,* Doubleday

Lutyens, Edwin (rep. 2009), *Cemeteries of the Great War,* Uitgeverij

Macdonald, Brian (2015), *Alice Diamond and the Forty Elephants: Britain's First Female Crime Syndicate,* Milo

Macmillan, Margaret (2004), *Peacemakers Six Months that Changed the World,* John Murray

Mandache Diana ed. (2004), *Queen Marie of Romania Last Chapters of My Life,* The History Press

Meyrick, Kate (1933), *Secrets of "the 43",* Parkgate Publications

Michael, Moina (1941), *The Miracle Flower: the Story of the Flanders Field Memorial Poppy,* Dorrance and Company, Philadelphia

Moore, Sarah (2008), *Ribbon Culture,* Palgrave Macmillan

Mulley, Clare (2019), *The Woman who Saved the Children,* One World

Newman, Vivien (2018), *Suffragism and the Great War,* Pen & Sword, Barnsley

BIBLIOGRAPHY

Newsham, Gail (1994 edition), *In a League of Their Own!* Wheatons, Chorley

Pakula, Hannah (1985), *The Last Romantic: Queen Marie of Romania,* Simon & Schuster

Pankhurst, Sylvia (1931), *The Suffragette Movement – An Intimate Account of Persons And Ideals,* Longmans Green and Company

Rennie, Jean (1977), *Every Other Sunday,* Coronet

Reynolds, Barbara (1995), *The Letters of Dorothy L Sayers 1899-1936 The Making of a Detective Novelist,* Sceptre

Rose, June (2007), *Marie Stopes and the Sexual Revolution,* Tempus

Saunders, Nicholas (2013), *The Poppy: A History of Conflict, Loss, Remembrance, and Redemption,* One World

Sayers, Dorothy L. (1974), *Busman's Honeymoon,* New English Library

Sharp, Evelyn (2008), *Unfinished Adventure: Selected Reminiscences from an Englishwoman's Life,* Faber & Faber

Sutherland, Halliday, *A Statement of Christian Doctrine against the Neo-Malthusians,* Kindle edition

Tate, Tim (2016), *Girls with Balls,* John Blake

Thompson, Laura (2018), *Rex v. Thompson,* Head of Zeus

Van Emden, Richard (2012), *The Quick and the Dead,* Bloomsbury

Wallach, Janet (2005), *Desert Queen,* Anchor Books

Weis, René (2001), *Criminal Justice,* Penguin

Wensley, Frederick (1931), *Detective Days,* Cassell and Co

Williams, Jean (2003), *A Contemporary History of Women's Sport, Part One: Sporting Women, 1850-1960,* Routledge

Wilson, Francesca (1945), *In the Margins of Chaos Recollections of Relief Work In and Between Three Wars,* Macmillan

Wyles, Lilian, (1952), *A Woman at Scotland Yard,* Faber & Faber

Yates, L. K. (1918), *The Woman's Part: A Record of Munitions Work,* George Doran, New York

Theses

Bourne, Judith (2014), *Helena Normanton and the Opening of the Bar to Women,* King's College, London

Brand, Pauline (2007), *Birth Control Nursing In The Marie Stopes Mothers' Clinics 1921-1931,* de Montfort University

Garratt, James (2018), *Tribute to the Fallen: The Evolution of Canadian Battlefield Burials during World War One,* University of Western Ontario

Melling, Althea (1999), *'Ladies' Football': Gender And The Socialisation Of Women Football Players In Lancashire C.1916 – 1960,* University of Central Lancashire

Roberts, Sian Lliwen (2010), *Place Life Histories and the Politics of Relief: Episodes in the Life of Francesca Wilson, Humanitarian, Educator, Activist,* University of Birmingham

Stow, Lee Karen (2007), *She Bought Poppies not Bandages: Moina Belle Michael's Appropriation of the Flanders Fields Poppy,* University of Lincoln

Articles

Ackershoek, Mary Anne, "'The Daughters of his Manhood' Christie and the Golden Age of Detective Fiction" in *Theory and Practice of Classic Detective Fiction,* ed Jerome H. Delamater and Ruth Prigozy, Contributions to the Study of Popular Culture, Hofstra University (1997)

Bălăucă, Roxana, "There is an hour of which I have never spoken" in *Philobiblon* – Vol. XVII (2012) – No. 1, pp.231-246

Baughan, Emily, "'Every Citizen of Empire Implored to Save the Children!' Empire, internationalism and the Save the Children Fund in inter-war Britain", *Historical Research*, Volume 86, Issue 231 (February, 2013), pp.116-137

Bogacz, Ted, "The Report of the War Office Committee of enquiry into 'Shell Shock'", *Journal of Contemporary History,* Vol 24, No 2 (April, 1989), pp.227-256

Budreau, Lisa, "Mourning and the Making of a Nation: The Gold Star Mothers Pilgrimages 1930-1933", *Stand To!* (September, 2004), pp.5-8

Crosby, Kevin, "Keeping Women off the Jury in England and Wales in the 1920s", *Legal Studies* (2017), pp.695-717

Douglas, James, "'The Ilford Murder' The Case For and Against a Reprieve", *Sunday Express* (1922)

Dunlop, Tessa, "Romania's Wartime Queen", *History Today* (November, 2018)

Edmondson, Charles and Levis, R. Barry, "Russian Famine Relief, and the Fate of the Orthodox Clergy, 1917-1923", *Journal of Church and State,* Vol. 40, No. 3 (summer, 1998), pp.619-637

Greve, Julia M. Asher, "Gertrude Bell: A Woman Larger than Life" in *Breaking Ground: Pioneering Women: Archaeologists* (2004), pp.142-197

Hall, Lesley, "'The Subject is Obscene: No Lady Would Dream of Alluding to It': Marie Stopes and her courtroom dramas', *Women's History Review,* 22:2 (2013), pp.253-266

Harsanyi, Doina Pasca, "Blue blood and ink: Romanian aristocratic women before and after World War 1", *Women's History Review,* 5:4, pp.497-511

Hecquet, Marceline, «Nous… qui avons laissé faire», *La Mère Éducatrice,* 6, n° 6 (June, 1923)

Mahood, Linda, "Eglantyne Jebb: remembering, representing and writing a rebel daughter", *Women's History Review,* 17:1, pp.1-20

Meier, William M., "Going on the Hoist: Women, Work, and Shoplifting in London, ca. 1890–1940", *Journal of British Studies,* Vol. 50, No. 2 (April, 2011), pp.410-433

Muckle, James, "Saving the Russian Children: Materials in the Archive of the Save The Children Fund Relating to Eastern Europe in 1920-23", *The Slavonic and East European Review,* Vol. 68, No. 3 (July, 1990), pp.507-511

Patnaik, P. V. Geetha Lakshmi, "'An Unsuitable Job for a Woman?': Woman as Writer and Protagonist in Detective Fiction", *IJELH International Journal of English Language & Literature,* Vol 4, Issue 4 (April, 2016), pp.135-138

Quinlan, Paul D., "The Importance of Marie in Romanian History", *Balkan Studies* (1991), pp.35-41

Wilks, Ann, "The 1922 Anglo-Iraq Treaty: A Moment of Crisis and the Role of Britain's Man on the Ground", *British Journal of Middle Eastern Studies,* 43:3, pp.342-359

Parliamentary Papers

Ministry of Reconstruction Report on Domestic Service Parliamentary Papers 1919 XXIX p.22

The Report of the War Office Committee of enquiry into "Shell Shock" HMSO1922

Websites accessed between 1 September 2019 and 10 July 2020

All contemporary British newspapers accessed via www.britishnewspaper archive.co.uk

All contemporary North American newspapers accessed via www.newspapers.com

All contemporary French newspapers accessed via gallica.bnf.fr

Contemporary monetary values calculated (using 2018 values) via inflation.iamkate.com

Oxford Dictionary of National Biography www.oxforddnb.com

Chapter 1

https://api.parliament.uk/historic-hansard/commons/1919/jun/02/restoration-of-pre-war-practices-no-3

https://www.britishpathe.com/video/women-footballers/query/womens+football

http://libraryblogs.is.ed.ac.uk/hcalibrarian/2017/07/28/why-football-banned-women/

https://www.oldpolicecellsmuseum.org.uk/content/learning/bad-girls/victorian-girl-gangs

https://www.crimeandinvestigation.co.uk/crime-files/london-gangs/key-figures

https://www.occrp.org/en/daily/11232-thousands-of-girls-caught-up-in-gangs-in-england

https://www.headliners.org/girl-gangs-in-south-london

Chapter 2

https://hansard.parliament.uk/Lords/1919-04-09/debates/35758c81-20bc-41cd-a52b-bbe4efe9791c/WarGraves

https://api.parliament.uk/historic-hansard/commons/1920/may/04/imperial-war-graves-commission

https://hansard.parliament.uk/commons/1920-08-10/debates/e7f77edc-1ed0-40ad-a983-176f5e25b926/WarGraves

https://shapingoursorrow.cwgc.org/anger/rallying-the-opposition

https://chaumierelesiris.com/tag/commonwealth-war-graves-commission/

https://www.parksandgardens.org/places/winchester-college-garden-of-remembrance

https://livesofthefirstworldwar.iwm.org.uk/story/65060

https://shapingoursorrow.cwgc.org/anger/anna-durie-a-mothers-defiance/

https://psychcentral.com/lib/the-5-stages-of-loss-and-grief/

https://yougov.co.uk/topics/politics/explore/not-for-profit/Royal_British_Legion

https://poppyladymadameguerin.wordpress.com

https://aboutflowersblog.com/buddy-poppy-the-story-of-a-little-red-flower/

https://samilhistory.com/2017/11/07/legions-and-poppies-and-their-south-african-root/

https://unc-lefolgoet.pagesperso-orange.fr/bleuet.html

BIBLIOGRAPHY

Chapter 3
http://theworldismycountry.info/posters/lift-the-hunger-blockade/
https://www.bbc.co.uk/news/science-environment-11040319
https://blogs.ucl.ac.uk/museums/2014/05/08/war-love-and-coal-new-exhibition-from-ucl-museum-studies-students
https://time.com/4065338/margaret-sanger-clinic-history/
http://ww1centenary.oucs.ox.ac.uk/body-and-mind/the-british-army%E2%80%99s-fight-against-venereal-disease-in-the-%E2%80%98heroic-age-of-prostitution%E2%80%99
https://www.catholicworldreport.com/2017/03/03/stopes-v-sutherland-the-legal-battle-between-a-eugenicist-and-a-catholic-doctor/
www.hallidaysutherland.com
http://mariestopes.org.uk/central-london
https://api.parliament.uk/historic-hansard/lords/1926/apr/28/welfare-centres
https://theconversation.com/how-the-catholic-church-came-to-oppose-birth-control-95694; https://catholicstraightanswers.com/what-is-the-churchs-teaching-on-contraception/

Chapter 4
https://first100years.org.uk/eliza-orme-2/
https://ials.blogs.sas.ac.uk/2019/12/17/women-at-the-bar-the-sex-disqualification-removal-act-1919-and-the-admission-of-women-to-the-legal-profession/
https://api.parliament.uk/historic-hansard/lords/1919/jul/22/sex-disqualification-removal-bill-hl
https://first100years.org.uk/ivy-williams/
https://castleassociates.org.uk/
https://www.irishtimes.com/culture/heritage/queen-of-the-nightclubs-1.1607995
https://en.wikipedia.org/wiki/William_Joynson-Hicks,_1st_Viscount_Brentford

Chapter 5
https://crimereads.com/the-original-ladies-of-crime/
www.mentalfloss.com
https://edithjessiethompson.co.uk/

https://www.deathpenaltyproject.org/wp-content/uploads/2017/12/DPP-50-Years-on-pp1-68-1.pdf
https://babel.hathitrust.org/cgi/pt?id=uc1.$b47213&view=1up&seq=484

Chapter 6
https://www.youtube.com/watch?v=sxfSXl_jPMMhttp://www.rebeccastarrbrown.com/2018/05/01/from-kent-to-bucharest-marie-of-edinburgh-queen-of-romania
http://www.tkinter.smig.net/QueenMarie/MammaRegina/index.htm
https://archive.org/details/reviewofciviladm00iraqrich/page/n2/mode/2up
https://www.globalpolicy.org/iraq-conflict-the-historical-background-/british-colonialism-and-repression-in-iraq/48076-the-queen-of-quagmire.html
https://api.parliament.uk/historic-hansard/commons/1921/jun/14/middle-eastern-services

Conclusion
https://en.wikipedia.org/wiki/Great_Britain_women%27s_Olympic_football_team
https://www.2020dreams.org.uk/shop/publications/the-rise-of-the-girl-gangs/
https://www.bbc.co.uk/news/uk-england-london-45088435
https://charitydigital.org.uk/topics/topics/shelter-nets-18000-from-online-lady-hale-spider-t-shirt-sales2-6196
https://www.independent.co.uk/news/uk/politics/lady-hale-boris-johnson-supreme-court-appointments-conservatives-a9261131.html
http://www.worldcoalition.org/Global-overview-of-women-facing-the-death-penalty.html
https://transylvanianow.com/pm-orban-wont-pick-up-the-gauntlet-thrown-by-iohannis/

Index

INDEX